ALAN C. TURNBULL,
ST. ALBERT, ALTA.

PCH'D: APR. 27, 2000,
FROM: GREENWOODS
        BOOKSHOPPE,
      HIGH ST.,
     EDMONTON, AB.
      #

SHANGHAI

SHAN

The Rise and Fall of a Decadent City

GHAI

STELLA DONG

William Morrow
An Imprint of HarperCollins*Publishers*

HarperCollins books may be purchased for educational, business, or
sales promotional use. For information please write: Special Markets
Department, HarperCollins Publishers Inc., 10 East 53rd Street, New
York, NY 10022.

FIRST EDITION

Designed by Renato Stanisic

Map by David Lindroth

Printed on acid-free paper

Library of Congress Cataloging-in-Publication Data

Dong, Stella.
    Shanghai: the rise and fall of a decadent city / by Stella Dong.
        p.   cm.
    Includes index.
    ISBN 0-688-15798-X
    1. Shanghai (China)—History.   2. Shanghai (China)—Social
conditions.   3. China—History—19th century.   4. China—
History—20th century.   I. Title.
DS796.S2D65   2000
951'.132033—dc21   99-41902
                          CIP

00   01   02   03   04   BP   10   9   8   7   6   5   4   3   2   1

To the memory of my father,
Hep Tai Dong

CONTENTS

ACKNOWLEDGMENTS

Many people who lived in or passed through pre-1949 Shanghai were kind enough to share their recollections of the city with me. Sadly, many have passed away since our conversations. Deepest gratitude to Alexander Buchman, Jack and Yuantseng Chen, William and Ruth Coltman, John Davies, Hugh Deane, Cecil Ezra, Emily Hahn, Lawrence Kadoorie, Irene Kuhn, Henry Lieberman, John Murray, John W. Powell, Hans Roenau, Maud Russell, Eric J. Schmidt, John S. Service, H. K. Shen, Helen Foster Snow, Henry Sperry, Walter Sullivan, Jerry Tannenbaun, Sam Tata, L. Z. Yuan, Victor J. Zirinsky, James D. White, and Zhou Wan Rong.

My appreciation also to the Shanghai Academy of Social Sciences, my host while I was in Shanghai. Its director, Wang Dehua, and staff, in particular Tien Kuopei, greatly facilitated my exploration of Shanghai's past by arranging for interviews with scholars and other specialists in Shanghai's culture and politics. Bai Yang, Du Xie, Ma Chengyuan, Sen Jie, Tang Zhenchang, Wu Kuofan, and Zhang Guangyin all were most generous with their time. In Hong Kong, Frank Ching, Karen Lam, and Bette Wei helped me locate other former residents of Shanghai. Pan Lee deserves special thanks for hospitality above and beyond the call of graciousness.

Much gratitude to the many people who have assisted me in the completion of this book in ways large and small: Debra Baker, Lorna Belkin, George Braziller, Susan Brownmiller, James Culp, Sharon Frost, Rebecca Goodhart, Robert Gottlieb, Ceri Hadda, Kathryn Harrison, Eric Head, William Hinton, Li Hong, Jin Bohung, Rebecca Karl, Allegra Kent, Larry Klepp, Jack Knowlton, Liang Heng, Lily Ling, Eleanor Lubin, Elmer Luke, Steve Mass, Erica Marcus, Lynn Pan, Marcy Posner, Helen Rosen, Jonathan Seliger, Arkady Selenow, Alex Smithline, Barrie Soloway, David Shipley, David Vigliano, Hueyun Wang-Mokotoff, Frances Wood, Ron Yakir, James Yeargin, Robert Youdelman, and Glenn Zeitzer.

I am indebted to Cynthia Gould Dunn and Kwan Lau: They not only were generous with their time but allowed me to use photographs from their respective private collections for this book. Hats off to Janet Byrne for her unflagging support of this project through its long gestation and for her kindness in volunteering to edit the manuscript's first version.

Without the resources of numerous libraries and archives in the United States and elsewhere I could not have written *Shanghai: The Rise and Fall of a Decadent City.* I wish to acknowledge the help of the librarians and staffs of the New York Public Library's research divisions, Columbia University's Butler and Starr East Asian libraries, and the Chinese Information and Culture Center in New York; the East Asian Library at the University of Washington in Seattle; the Hoover Institution in Palo Alto, California; the British Library, the library of the School of African and Oriental Studies in London, and the Public Record Office in London; and the Shanghai Municipal Archives in Shanghai.

Thanks to my editor at William Morrow, Henry Ferris, for his editorial acumen, and to his able assistant, Ann Treistman.

And very special thanks to Helen Chien, Kate Delano-Condax Decker, Djane Richardson, and Judith Yeargin.

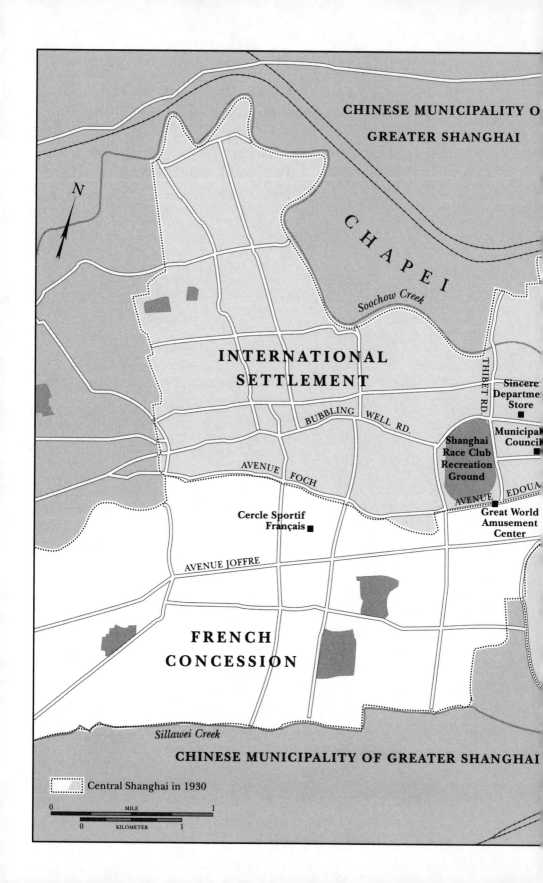

N

CHINESE MUNICIPALITY O
GREATER SHANGHAI

C H A P E I

Soochow Creek

INTERNATIONAL
SETTLEMENT

THIBET RD.

Sincere
Departme
Store

BUBBLING WELL RD.

Municipa
Counci

Shanghai
Race Club
Recreation
Ground

AVENUE FOCH

AVENUE EDOUA

AVENUE

Cercle Sportif
Français

Great World
Amusement
Center

AVENUE JOFFRE

FRENCH
CONCESSION

Sillawei Creek

CHINESE MUNICIPALITY OF GREATER SHANGHAI

Central Shanghai in 1930

0   MILE   1

0   KILOMETER   1

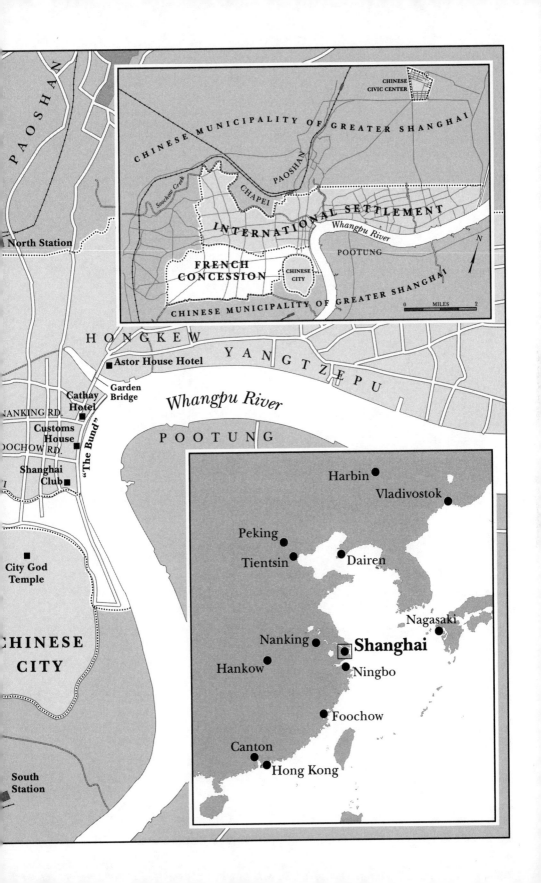

SHANGHAI

Put this fishing rod in the ground here
And hoist this piece of linen,
so that ships which pass here on their way
from the gold coast can see us.

Put up the bar room table there under the rubber tree:
That is the city, this is its center . . . this entire Mahagonny
exists only because everything is so evil,
because no peace reigns and no harmony and
because there is nothing upon which one can rely.

—SONG FROM BERTOLT BRECHT'S
THE RISE AND FALL OF MAHAGONNY

THE UGLY DAUGHTER RISES

In Shanghai's prime, no city in the Orient, or the world for that matter, could compare with it. At the peak of its spectacular career the

If God lets Shanghai endure, he owes an apology to Sodom and Gomorrah.
—SHANGHAI MISSIONARY

swamp-ridden metropolis surely ranked as the most pleasure-mad, rapacious, corrupt, strife-ridden, licentious, squalid, and decadent city in the world. It was the most pleasure-mad because nowhere else did the population pursue amusement, from feasting to whoring, dancing to powder-taking, with such abandoned zeal. It was rapacious because greed was its driving force; strife-ridden because calamity was always at the door; licentious because it catered to every depravity known to man; squalid because misery stared one brazenly in the face; and decadent because morality, as every Shanghai resident knew, was irrelevant. The missionaries might rail at Shanghai's wickedness and reformers condemn its iniquities, but there was never reason for the city to mend its errant ways, for as a popular Chinese saying aptly observed, "Shanghai is like the emperor's ugly daughter; she never has to worry about finding suitors."

Other great cities—Rome, Athens, or St. Petersburg, for instance—might flatter themselves that they had been conceived for virtuous, even heroic, purposes. Not so the ugly daughter who reveled in her bastard status. Half Oriental, half Occidental; half land, half water; neither a colony nor wholly belonging to China; inhabited by the citizens of every nation in the world but ruled by none, the emperor's ugly daughter was an anomaly among cities. The strange fruit of a forced union between East and West, this mongrel princess came into the world through a grasping premise—the right of one nation to foist a poisonous drug upon another.

Born in greed and humiliation, the ugly daughter grew up in the shadow of the Celestial Empire's defeat by outsiders in the Opium War. Nonetheless, within decades, she had become Asia's greatest metropolis, a brash sprawling juggernaut of a city that dominated the rest of the country with its power, sophistication, and, most of all, money.

The two characters making up the Chinese word *Shang-hai* together can be translated as "above the sea," a reference to the fact that the port stood on mudflats barely above sea level. Westerners, however, turned the word into a verb denoting a despicable act. To know its English meaning is to comprehend the modern city's ignoble essence. To quote one lexicon:

shanghai . . . [fr. *Shanghai,* China; fr. the formerly widespread use of unscrupulous means to procure sailors for voyages to the Orient] **1a:** to put aboard a ship by force often with the help of liquor or a drug . . . **b:** to put by force or a threat of force into or as if into a

place of detention . . . **2:** to put by trickery into an un-
desirable position . . .

It was a form of shanghaiing that created the modern city
of Shanghai. A flotilla of Her Majesty's gunboats invaded the
prosperous town of 250,000 "Celestials" in 1842, not departing
until they had received a ransom of three million silver dollars
from its wealthier residents. A few weeks later, the force of
"red-haired barbarians," as the Chinese referred to the British,
threatened to attack Nanking, the ancient Ming capital. In sor-
row and despair, the Tao-kuang emperor sued for peace, dis-
patching three imperial emissaries to Nanking. On August 29,
1842, aboard a British gunboat anchored outside the city, they
opened the door to a century of China's exploitation by outsiders by signing the Treaty of Nanking. The treaty's terms,
virtually dictated to the Chinese, were among the harshest ever
extracted of a defeated government. They called for, among
other things, the payment of an indemnity of 21 million silver
dollars, the cession of Hong Kong, a low tariff on foreign
goods, and the opening of five Chinese ports—among them
Shanghai—to foreign trade and residence.

Jealous of Britain's victory, other Western powers, led by
France and the United States, requested similar treaties with
Peking. Adopting the philosophy of "soothing the barbarian,"
the emperor complied. To ensure that none of its rivals would
obtain from the dynasty advantages it could not share in, Britain had cleverly insisted upon a "most favored nation" clause
in its agreements, requiring Peking to extend a concession won
by one nation to all others. One of the most important of these
subsequent privileges was that of extraterritorial jurisdiction.
A cornerstone of Western power in the treaty ports, extraterritoriality–"extrality," to use its treaty port abbreviation—
granted foreigners immunity from the laws of China. Under
this principle, subjects of the treaty powers could be tried for

crimes and misdeeds committed in China only by their own consuls or their nation's courts. Fittingly, the Treaty of Nanking and the subsequent edifice of agreements for which it provided the foundation, came to be known as the "unequal treaties."

Western gunboats and firepower were the instruments by which Britain defeated the five-thousand-year-old Flowery Kingdom, but opium paved the way. Opium, the addictive drug that Britain was so bent upon selling to the Chinese that it waged a war against them for the privilege, built modern Shanghai. Without the opium poppy, the most evil and profligate of flowers, the "Whore of Asia" would never have been created.

The drug that seduced the Chinese was brought by *fan kuei*, or "foreign devils" as the Chinese called foreigners. When the "barbarians from across the sea" first appeared, they hardly seemed capable of being the menace that would puncture the Celestial Empire's splendid isolation, let alone destroy a civilization its four million people considered the most glorious in the world. To the Chinese, the *fan kuei* were bizarre creatures. Everything about them, from their bushy whiskers to their unnaturally pale flesh, seemed outlandish, even grotesque. When they spoke, they made harsh, guttural sounds; their "legs and feet stretched out and bent with difficulty," reminding one scholar of "prancing Manchu ponies" and "water buffaloes"; and they dressed ridiculously. Another official also remarked on the devils from across the seas' resemblance to animals. They appeared to him to be "playing the parts of foxes, hares and other such animals on the stage." Even more striking, he commented, was the fact that foreigners "really do look like devils; and when people call them 'devils,' it is no mere empty term of abuse." Altogether, from the Chinese point of view, Europeans were no less than beasts given human form.

"The Chinese do habitually call, and consider, Europeans 'Barbarians,' meaning by that term, peoples in a rude, uncivilized state, morally and intellectually uncultivated," reported Thomas Taylor Meadows, the most outstanding of the first British interpreters in China. "Of the words signifying the European, their vocabulary, though rich in vituperative and abusive epithets, had nothing more contemptuous than that. Comparing themselves to all other peoples, there could be no nation as evolved as themselves in point of civilization; all but themselves were Barbarians, and accordingly met with a policy founded on a long experience and a just appreciation of their more or less barbarous characteristics." Meadows, who had traveled widely among the Chinese, noted that they "were always surprised, not to say astonished, to learn that we have surnames, and understand the family distinctions of father, brother, wife, sister, etc.; in short, that we live otherwise than as a herd of cattle." On the matter of the barbarians' preoccupation with profit, all could agree. An imperial adviser opined: "The whole country of England relies for its livelihood on the trade of its crowd of merchants. Superiors and inferiors compete against each other. There is none who does not look only for profit. If that country has some undertaking afoot, they turn around first to listen to the commands of the merchants."

"We possess all things. I set no value on objects strange or ingenious and have no use for your country's manufactures. Our ways bear no resemblance to yours." So the Chien Lung emperor had famously informed George III's envoy to the imperial court in his rejection of England's request for expanded commercial relations in 1793. Britain, seeking more markets for the products of its factories and rapidly growing colonial empire, wanted tea and silk from China but had nothing to offer in exchange—until the British East India Company, holder of a monopoly over the China and India trades, suggested opium. Having fallen heir to the Moghul empire's rich poppy fields, the Company planted even more of the poppy in Bengal and Malwa. Because the Ching government had long banned opium smoking and, by 1800, had issued an edict against its sale and importation as well, the Company could not openly flout Peking by bringing the drug directly to its destination. Instead, it sold opium wholesale to private merchants known as "country traders" who transported the contraband in their own specially built fast ships to smuggling depots outside Canton.

The illicit trade in the languor-inducing drug throve from the start. Initially, opium had been a luxury consumed by a privileged few—idle sons of the gentry, bored wives of wealthy merchants seeking diversion, and other members of the leisured class. Thanks to Britain's efforts, the habit had spread to ordinary Chinese: everyone from merchants and shopkeepers to common laborers and even nuns. By catering to vice, the Company and private traders not only had shifted the formerly lopsided China trade in their favor, but were making huge profits as well in the substance the Chinese had taken to calling "foreign mud."

Opium was without question the most valuable commercial crop of its time: compact and imperishable, with a safe market and a rising demand, it was such a spectacularly lucrative commodity that few China traders were able to resist carrying it. In addition, little stigma was attached to dealing in the drug. As a missionary bemoaned in 1839: "The most eminent merchants engaged freely in the traffic. . . . Throughout India and China, many of the most distinguished merchants—men who would be slow to partake in any other than what they regarded as . . . honourable pursuits—have been foremost in this traffic."

Among these upstanding men, the undisputed leaders of the drug traffickers were two Scotsmen, William Jardine and James Matheson. Their firm, Jardine, Matheson and Company, Jardine's for short, was destined to become the largest trading concern in Asia, an entity rivaling the East India Company itself with arms extending into every port in the Far East and a finger in every commercial endeavor, from shipping to manufacturing, mining to transportation. From Shanghai, its future headquarters, Jardine, Matheson would dominate all of

China's industry and commerce for almost 150 years. However, like so many fortunes in the East, that of the "Princely Hong" (a *hong* was a trading firm), as the company would later be known, was firmly based in foreign mud. Through sedulous cultivation of opium smuggling, Jardine and Matheson became the wealthiest traders in China, and through shrewd manipulation of their connections at home, the partners did more than any of their fellow merchants to open China to foreign inroads.

William Jardine, the elder of the partners, was a British East India Company surgeon turned opium trader whom his fellow traders nicknamed "Iron-Headed Old Rat" for the way he patiently withstood a series of blows at the gate to a Canton official's office when he once attempted to deliver a petition. Jardine encouraged his friends to invest in opium, describing it as "the safest and most gentleman-like speculation I am aware of." Nor did he ever appear perturbed by his critics' barbs, not even when, toward the end of his career, he bought himself a seat in Parliament, and Disraeli mocked him in his novel *Sybil* as "a dreadful man! A Scotchman, richer than Croesus, one Mr. Druggy, fresh from Canton, with a million in opium in each pocket, denouncing corruption and bellowing free-trade."

His partner, James Matheson, was the son of a baronet, but made his way to Calcutta to work in an uncle's counting house before becoming a buccaneering opium trader in Canton. It was Matheson who pioneered the risky—but highly profitable—practice of sending armed opium vessels up the coast to provinces not yet addicted to opium. The strategy worked: new customers emerged and sales soared. Soon not just Jardine, Matheson but the other China traders were sending armed ships up the coast—and bullying and bribing officials along the way. By the end of the 1830s, Jardine's was supplying more than one-third of all the opium smuggled into China.

One thing had become clear to the Ching emperor in Peking: wherever the foreign devil ventured, misery, corruption, and disorder followed. Complicit with the foreign traders was a vast illegal organization, the *yao-kao*, that had emerged to move the contraband into every part of the empire. Its members and those who assisted it included everyone from the customs officials who were bribed to look the other way when an opium shipment arrived to the porters who transported the drug down local creeks and overland to the dealers who ran opium shops and dens in every city and town. By the end of the thirties, Jardine's and its ilk had smuggled enough opium into China to supply the habits of twelve million smokers—one in ten Chinese.

A confrontation was inevitable. It was triggered by the steady drainage of silver from Peking's treasury as a result of China's opium imports. The threat of the government's bankruptcy on top of the social and political problems created by the illicit traffic prompted the emperor to dispatch, in 1839, an opium suppression commissioner to Canton. The official confined the foreign merchants to their quarters, confiscated their drug stocks, and destroyed them. The action provided Jardine's and the other British opium merchants a not unwelcome excuse to demand the concessions they had long sought from China.

In London, where he had arrived just before the opium seizure, Iron-Headed Old Rat organized a powerful lobby of Midlands industrialists, City bankers, and merchants to deluge the foreign office with petitions calling for force against China. At the same time, Jardine used his millions to buy a partnership in a banking house headed by a member of Foreign Secretary Henry Palmerston's inner circle, to be followed by a seat in Parliament. Within days of Palmerston's receiving the official report of the events in Canton, Iron-Headed Old Rat and the commodore of his opium fleet were ensconced in the foreign secretary's office, Jardine explaining the detailed maps of the China coast he had brought so that, as he wrote Matheson, "his Lordship might have a clear idea of the country with which we must cope. The extent of armament, number of troops necessary and number of shipping were all discussed." In Palmerston, who had advocated a vigorous policy toward Britain's trade interests abroad, the merchant found an ally. Soon afterward, Palmerston received a "paper of hints" from Jardine. It suggested a strategy for the military campaign: British ships would blockade China's coastline, then send a fleet up the Peiho River to Peking demanding that the authorities sign a treaty opening up the northern ports to trade—"say, Amoy, Foochow, Ningpo and Shanghai . . . if we can get it."

When Parliament passed its war resolution—by a slender five-vote margin—the expeditionary force of sixteen warships, four thousand troops, and 540 guns conformed to Iron-Headed Old Rat's suggestions. Nor did Jardine, Matheson's assistance to the British government end there. The firm leased out its best vessels, pilots, and translators to the service of the fleet, and even cashed the army quartermaster's bills in London. When the British plenipotentiary arrived in Hong Kong, James Matheson's house was the first he set foot in, and when the expeditionary force moved up the coast, the firm's opium ships—opium chests and Chinese sale placards on board—followed behind. Later, Palmerston thanked Jardine for his help, declaring that he was able to "give our affairs in China, those detailed instructions which have led to these satisfactory results mainly owing to the assisance and information which you, my dear Mr. Jardine, so handsomely afforded us."

It was said that the day, June 19, 1842, the long-nosed, hairy barbarians took Shanghai, even the dogs realized that evil spirits were upon them. If a canine chanced to cross a foreigner's path, it would "prick up its ears and skulk away with its tail between its legs," recorded a Shanghai man. "Not one dog in the whole city dared bark." Though in his own household he had a dog with a "quite dreadful" bark, when the foreigners came and "the dog saw what they were like, he skulked away to the safety of the stove and would not eat for the whole day."

℀

Foreign Shanghai, the city that Occidentals designed but Oriental sweat and labor built, sat on ground so porous that one American engineer described it as "not much more solid than dirty water." Yet, upon this questionable foundation, along the Bund (waterfront street), rose the tallest buildings in Asia. When the first British merchants arrived in 1843, they were given 140 acres of muddy foreshore north of the walled Chinese city of Shanghai to be the British Settlement. By driving deep into the ground piles upon which they laid the foundations of their houses, the British were able to keep their buildings from flooding at high tide. The work of pounding the piles into the earth was done by Chinese manual laborers—coolies—who worked in teams, throwing all their weight behind the spokes of massive circular pile drivers. As they worked, the men could be heard chanting in unison a slow and monotonous "Ah ho! Ah ho!" This sound, a "dirge-like chorus depressing to the spirits," as one newcomer described it, was the ever-present song of the Orient. Easing the coolies' toil, the "singing" began early in the morning and ended only after dusk.

For the Western "free trade adventurers" who had pitched tents on the northern banks of the muddy Whangpu, Shanghai presented a blank slate upon which they could impose their own ways of doing business. Instead of being crowded into a "foreign ghetto," as they were in Canton, declared one merchant, in Shanghai one might "take a health- (or fever-) giving walk every day of his life with no risk to his limbs or his feelings." The missionary no longer, as at Canton, "took his life in his hands when he ventured to explain the message to his Chinese brother." Moreover, the Shanghainese, as the Chinese residents were called, were amiable and peace-loving, in contrast to the "vicious and hostile" Cantonese. "The very beggars seem a kind of jolly crew," a British botanist, Robert Fortune, approvingly noted.

Equally welcome was the northern port's more temperate climate. Located in the center of China, Shanghai was spared both typhoons and the paralyzing heat of the south. Though it stood at nearly the same latitude as New Orleans and Cairo, the Yangtze port became tropical and uncomfortably hot only in the summer. In contrast to the south, Shanghai also had distinct seasons: the winters were so cold that furs were required and snowstorms not uncommon; spring was crisp, bright, and breezy; and the drizzly autumns reminded the English of London. But in summer, Shanghai turned into a steambath. The dampness hung so thick in the air that even the walls of the buildings appeared to sweat. Laborers stripped down to sandals and knee-length trousers, while tradesmen and shopkeepers moved outdoors, fanning their naked stomachs with paddle fans. Westerners, on the other hand, unaccustomed to the stickiness of summer, changed their clothes as often as three times a day and suffered from prickly heat, athlete's foot, ringworm, and other "distressing skin problems." Another hazard of residence in the Whangpu port was the necessity of boiling water and settling it with alum before it could be used for cooking or bathing, because parasites infected the local waterways. "We are all of us all too familiar with the peculiar faint smell which hangs about our 'clean clothes,' " pronounced another foreigner. "And if it is not extra bad, we say, 'Oh! Clean clothes in Shanghai always smell like that, and always look brown.' "

Nonetheless, almost from the moment it became a treaty port, Shanghai supplanted Canton as China's leading port. Its foreign population did not exceed one hundred until 1848, but well before then, all of the biggest British and American trading firms had moved their headquarters from Canton to the northern port. Behind the forest of masts in front of the foreign settlement's anchorage, the outlines of a European settlement—walled compounds surrounding white bungalow-style houses, brick warehouses, a club, a church, and even a racecourse—were readily discernible as well. For convenience and camaraderie, American merchants lived alongside their Anglo-Saxon cousins in the British Settlement. The French, however, anxious not to dilute their national prestige by too close an association with the other treaty powers, asked for their own settlement—the swath of land sandwiched between the British Settlement and the Chinese city's waterfront. The Americans had an unofficial settlement in Hongkew, the swampland on the opposite side of the British Settlement across the Soochow Creek, a waterway that intersected the Whangpu.

As rapidly as the foreign settlements had developed, no one could have imagined that the wilderness of marshes Shanghai's chief magistrate disparagingly referred to as the "barbarian enclosure" would mushroom into a sprawling metropolis, one so huge it would dwarf the original Shanghai.

Chinese Shanghai, a bustling commercial city, had existed as early as the tenth century, and before that it had been a fishing village called Hu Tu, after the *hu* (bamboo stakes) that fisherman sank into the mud to anchor their nets. By the seventeenth century, Shanghai had become a major port in China's coastal junk trade, situated as it was close to the midpoint of the coast and, more important, only fourteen miles from the mouth of the Yangtze, the great river that gave access to China's interior. Situated in the richest and most fertile part of China, an area known as the "land of fish and rice," Shanghai shared the same temperate climate and loamy soil as the legendary fabled delta cities of Soochow and Hangchow, but its chief claim to fame was as a trading emporium. In the sixteenth century, to protect it from the raids of Japanese pirates, the city surrounded itself with a circular wall three and a half miles in circumference.

By the eighteenth century, the city had outgrown its walls, spilling out from its eastern gate into the land between the wall and the Whangpu River. The introduction of cotton to the lower Yangtze delta brought more wealth to Shanghai. Its teahouses were always filled with merchants transacting business and its narrow, twisting lanes always busy with porters, water carriers, and itinerant tradesmen and vendors peddling everything from tongue scrapers to lottery tickets. Retired officials often made their homes in the city, building spacious houses with gardens behind white plaster walls. Near the city temple, lanes of shops purveying jade, silver, gold, ivory, porcelain, and finely carved wood furniture testified to the affluence of the town's inhabitants. And from the Chinese City's waterfront, the line of junk boats from as near as neighboring Ningpo and as far as Annam extended for a mile into the river.

The two Shanghais, European and Chinese, had so little to do with each other that they might have been separated by two hundred rather than two miles. Westerners scrupulously avoided the Chinese City, whose narrow precincts they considered "filthy" and "unsavory," while the only Chinese who ever had anything to do with the Westerners were servants or domestics. Yet, within the space of a decade, the relationship between the two enclaves was to change irrevocably as the confluence of a Chinese civil war and foreign military intervention in the port's defense transformed the British Settlement into an enormous municipality while the Chinese City shrank in importance to become a mere appendage to foreign Shanghai.

The process whereby "the part swallowed the whole," as the eminent statesman Tang Shao-yi put it, began with the greatest civil war China—or the world, for that matter—had yet seen. This was the Taiping Rebellion, a revolt against the Ching dynasty that convulsed China for ten years, devastating the richest parts of the country, bringing death and suffering to millions, and nearly toppling the emperor from his throne. Its leader was a failed scholar who believed himself God's second son, divinely appointed to lead a revolution against the Ching rulers. He called his movement the Taiping, "Heavenly Kingdom." Preaching a mix of Christianity and Chinese mysticism, the prophet drew to his cause the multitudes of Chinese whose lot had deteriorated as a result of Ching misrule and the Western intrusion; among them were peasants who had lost their lands because of higher taxes and boatmen and cotton workers whose livelihoods had been destroyed by changes wrought by the opening of the treaty ports. So many recruits flocked to the ranks of the Chinese messiah's cause that by 1851, he and his disciples led a Taiping army in a legendary fourteen-hundred-mile trek from southeastern China toward the coast, capturing towns and slaughtering as they went—but also gathering adherents. By the time the Heavenly Kingdom's army took Nanking, the great city at the foot of the Yangtze delta, its ranks had swollen to several hundred thousand. In March 1853 the Taipings invested Nanking, making it the capital of their rebel movement.

Shanghai, two hundred miles away, felt the ripples of the Taipings' arrival in Kiangsu province only six months later when a secret society captured the Chinese City, causing a mass exodus of its inhabitants into the suburbs and the British and French settlements. The society, the Small Swords, claimed affiliation with the Taipings, but actually belonged to the Triad, an anti-Ching brotherhood fast degenerating into a criminal organization. Imperial troops ousted the Small Swords from the walled city a year and a half later, but not before the settlements' merchants discovered that they could make huge profits in erecting cheap wood and brick tenements that could be rented out to the native refugees for several times their land's value. Shanghai's British consul, Rutherford Alcock, one of the few to disapprove of the land-jobbing tide, found himself powerless to halt it. To his remonstrations, one *taipan*—head, or "big manager," of a trading firm—responded with what might be considered the credo of the Westerner in China:

> It is my business to make a fortune with the least possible loss of time. In two or three years at farthest, I hope to realize a fortune, and get away; and what can it matter to me, if all Shanghai disappear afterwards, in fire or flood? You must not expect men in my situation to condemn themselves to years of prolonged exile in an unhealthy climate for the benefit of posterity. We are money-making, practical men. Our business is to make money, as much and as fast as we can— and for this end, all modes and means are good which the law permits.

But the profits made during the Chinese City's occupation were nothing compared with the fortunes to be made six years later, in 1860, when the Taipings erupted out of their Nanking stronghold to overrun the Kiangsu plains, seize the provincial capital of Soochow, and threaten Shanghai. From throughout the delta came a horde of panic-stricken Chinese, filling every street and even crowding the river and creek. Among the refugees, too, were many wealthy merchants and officials who could afford the most exorbitant rents. Speculators, smelling quick profits, bought every available empty lot and threw up row after row of two-story tenements, which were occupied almost before their bamboo scaffoldings had come down. In a matter of weeks, the settlements' sharp-nosed businessmen were raking in profits as high as 10,000 percent. Soon, everyone "save the unlucky naval, military and consular recipients of fixed salaries," remarked one historian, was scrambling for a piece of the mudflat port, leading to a rush so frantic that it was compared to "the early days of the Australian gold diggings."

As many as 300,000 newcomers swamped the port, causing Shanghai to grow faster than any other city in the world—faster than Chicago, San Francisco, or Melbourne, other boomtowns whose streets were being thrown up at the same time as the Whangpu port's. Land values soared to astronomic heights: an acre worth fifty pounds in 1850 jumped to twenty thousand pounds by 1862. "Whilst one class of speculators was investing hundreds of dollars of borrowed capital in the erection of new streets," said the same chronicler, "another class was greedily buying up every foot of land to be had."

The Western powers twice intervened to prevent Shanghai from being captured by the Taipings during the next two years—the first time in August 1860 when British and French soldiers posted at the Chinese City's gates and ramparts drove back a Taiping army, and the second time in the winter of 1862 when British and French troops helped imperial forces drive back an even larger rebel contingent. The treaty powers fought on the side of the Ching dynasty on these occasions because it served their interests. But had the Taipings been responsive to their overtures, they might have thrown their support to the rebel cause, for the Allies had been seeking further trading concessions from a resistant Ching court. Indeed, by a strange twist of fate, the same day British and French soldiers first held Shanghai for the Ching dynasty against its enemies, another Western force was breaking down the forts at Taku on its way to Peking to force the emperor "to feel the stick," in Palmerston's famous words. By sacking and burning to the ground the emperor's fabulous Summer Palace at the end of the conflict known as the Second Opium War, the Westerners obtained their desired concessions—and no longer had need of the Taipings.

Foreigners also played a role in the civil war by fighting for either side. Before the treaty powers had abandoned their neutrality, Shanghai's native businessmen were so concerned about defending Shanghai that they availed themselves of an offer from a Yankee adventurer, Frederick Townsend Ward, to form a European, Filipino, and Chinese mercenary force to augment the government's poorly prepared troops. The businessmen, who included the wealthy refugee gentry from Soochow, paid the contingent's prize money and expenses. Although far from always victorious in its engagements, the force won the emperor's approbation and the title "Ever Victorious Army." When Ward was killed, a British officer, Major Charles George "Chinese" Gordon, took over his command, with more tangible results.

In addition to Ward, hundreds of other Western mercenaries and desperadoes, hearing of the civil war in China, had made their way to Shanghai eager for lucrative excitement. Plenty was to be had. Many European soldiers of fortune worked for the Taipings, others hired themselves out as bodyguards or as heavily armed escorts to protect merchants' goods from plunder or piracy on the coast, and still others ran guns from Shanghai's foreign arms dealers to the imperial forces or the Taipings. In fact, the British Settlement's merchants did such a flourishing trade in weapons that guns ranked second only to opium in profitability. Some of the foreign community's biggest opium suppliers were also its biggest arms purveyors.

By the time the Taipings were routed out of Nanking, in 1864, the Chinese officials in charge of the campaign had learned the value of Western military technology. One of these, Li Hung-chang, a protégé of the redoubtable Tseng Kuo-fan, the imperial commissioner for suppressing the rebels, had raised a private army for Kiangsu's defense with the aid of funds contributed by Shanghai's refugee gentry; they had also paid for Western guns and ammunition as well as the army's training by British and French officers. In 1863 he urged the government to establish an arsenal in Shanghai; it became the forerunner of numerous modernization projects. It was also a first step toward Li's establishment of his power base in Shanghai. From this position, Li, the shrewdest and most dexterous of Chinese officials, would go on to become the Ching court's most influential—and richest—adviser.

As for Shanghai, rather than falling back under Chinese control as a result of its invasion by hordes of Chinese, it became even more a semicolonial city as its foreigners, to strengthen their control of the settlements, foisted a host of quasi-legal institutions upon corrupt or acquiescent local officials. By 1863, the Western community had created a foreign-controlled body, the Shanghai Municipal Council, to administer the affairs of the British and American settlements, which had been merged into a foreign municipality, the International Settlement. At the same time, the French Concession also declared itself a municipality, but one governed directly by the French through their consul. In addition, the two foreign enclaves had expanded to three times their original size, their boundaries pushing deep into the countryside. European Shanghai would grow further still, wrapping itself around the ancient Chinese City like the flesh around the seed of a particularly succulent piece of fruit.

Sinking her tentacles deep into the Whangpu's miasmic swamps, Shanghai, that tumultuous hybrid, had shot up like a hothouse flower to become the head of a new order. Where Peking's star was falling, that of the emperor's ugly daughter was rising. The port, now the sixth largest in the world, stood like a beacon on the Yangtze mudflats, luring adventurers to her shores with the promise of quick and easy riches. And heeding her siren song came the dreamers, schemers, and reprobates of the world.

GOLD IN THE YANGTZE MUD

Whether taipan, freebooter, mercenary, or younger son obliged to earn a living, there was hardly a foreigner in Shanghai who did not aspire to go home far richer than when he arrived. "The merchants here cannot resist the golden harvest which only awaits the gathering, but come out here for a few years and return wealthy men. The profits some of them make are enormous. They never seem to think of going home with less than one hundred thousand pounds and many are not content even with that." So wrote a young junior clerk, Edward Bowra, of his fellow Shanghailanders, as the Westerners called themselves. "Commerce was the beginning, the middle, and the end of our life in China—that is to say, that if there was no trade, not a single man, except missionaries, would have come there at all," confessed another British trader, Charles Dyce. Though Shanghai's foreigners included, as Bowra put it, "many of considerable social position at home," the wealth accumulated by even these men had been made through their own efforts. The port's rugged, free-for-all atmosphere was nothing if not democratic. Family connections counted for little next to ambition and enterprise—mingled perhaps with shrewdness and a certain amount of ruthlessness. "A man's career here is in his own hands," the fortuneless but hopeful Bowra wrote home, "and he makes or mars his fortunes unaided and unrestrained by those petty restrictions of class and caste and the jealous rivalries which are so rife in convention-ridden, sham-loving, Mammon-worshipping England. . . . Here are prizes waiting to be won. . . . All is for the quick eye, the stout heart, the strong will."

Such aspiring tycoons had an opportunity to realize their fondest hopes during the land boom caused by the flooding of refugees into the British Settlement. As a result of the frenzied land grabbing during that period, all of the Settlement's open spaces had disappeared: gone were the paddy fields, reedbeds, and garden patches of yore, and in their place came range after range of new streets, each jammed with Chinese houses. It was as a result of the ruthless tactics used by land-hungry foreigners that the remaining Chinese landowners in the area had been pushed out. Some merchants stepped over Settlement lines to claim rights to property in Chinese jurisdiction territory; others coerced native property owners into selling their land cheaply. "When an unscrupulous foreigner desired to possess himself of the land of a native," wrote one early foreign resident, J. W. Maclellan, he hired "a corrupt minor official, who bullied the proprietor into selling," and, after "one lot had been secured in this way, the right of pre-emption was exercised and more land acquired."

Chinese settled in the neighboring French Concession as well, but because the French had exclusive control over the enclave and discouraged foreigners from buying property purely for speculative purposes, land-jobbers could not gain a foothold in the concession. Moreover, while the French community was small—consisting of fewer than a dozen substantial French property owners and even fewer commercial enterprises—the concession's authorities hoped to preserve the most valuable parts of the enclave for French concerns. By 1862, for instance, the Messageries Maritimes, the French national shipping line, had decided to establish a branch in Shanghai. To emphasize their intention to keep the French Concession's administration exclusively in French hands, in May 1862, the French appointed their own Municipal Council and promulgated a municipal code similar to the International Settlement's. But, as the concession remained under the French consul's control, the French Municipal Council's decisions were subject to veto by that official—who himself took his orders from the French colonial government in Hanoi.

The real estate mania had pushed the Settlement's borders all the way to its outer limits at Defence Creek—an area once considered "far out in the country"—long before the Taiping Rebellion's end. Behind the Bund, a former mud towpath that was now a broad promenade, sprawled a jumble of streets filled with a busy and noisy population. The first wooden structures built during the Taiping Rebellion had given way to more solid-looking houses located along alleyways, *li*, running perpendicular to the main streets. The *li* and adjacent lanes were the scene of constant activity as peddlers and itinerant cooks roved about, the former crying their wares in high-pitched voices and the latter banging brass gongs to announce their presence. Open-fronted food and clothing stalls clogged the lane openings, while pedestrians were constantly being pushed up against the walls to make way for wheelbarrow runners, water carriers balancing shoulder poles with buckets hanging from either end, blind men tinkling brass gongs with wooden hammers, beancake peddlers, long-robed merchants, and frowzy mendicants nipping at their heels.

This development had occurred—as so much did in Shanghai—haphazardly and without planning. Roads followed the windings of creeks and cow paths. The streets at right angles to the Bund came to be named after Chinese cities—Soochow, Peking, Nanking, Kiukiang, Hankow, Foochow, Canton—while those paralleling the Bund bore the names of provinces: Szechwan, Kiangse, Honan, Shantung, and so on. The Settlement's main east-west thoroughfare, which led to the racecourse, was named Nanking Road and thronged even more than before with crowds of blue-gowned Chinese so that its foot traffic now spilled out onto the roadway, alongside traps, carriages, rickshas, and carts pulled by small, swift Mongolian ponies.

The young port was growing, and nothing, it seemed, could arrest the phenomenal pace of its development. As if the real estate boom had not made its displaced adventurers and desperadoes rich enough, yet another opportunity for speculation appeared with a sudden demand for Chinese cotton. The American Civil War had cut European manufacturers off from their main source of cotton. As a result, Chinese cotton, which was in plentiful supply in the lower Yangtze's moist fields, boomed. The fiber was also within easy reach of Shanghai. Recognizing another bonanza, the same businessmen who had made piles in real estate plunged their profits into cotton. By the end of 1861, more than three million pounds sterling had accumulated in the hands of cotton's "lucky buyers" and the fluffy white stuff had become Shanghai's number one export.

China's losses were always Shanghai's gains. Another boon to trade came with the Ching dynasty's defeat in the Second Opium War. The Treaty of Tientsin, ratified at the end of 1860, redounded to Shanghai's benefit by enabling Western traders to penetrate the Chinese interior. The treaty not only provided for the Yangtze's opening to foreign navigation but established four new treaty ports inland and, in addition, exempted foreign goods from China's domestic transit taxes. Also assisting the Western merchants' exploitation of China's rich hinterland was the advent of steam navigation along the waterways. Goods brought to an inland port by junk boat from one of the great river's tributaries could now be loaded onto steamships for transportation to Shanghai. Important new products such as pig bristles and wood oil from Szechwan and animal hides from the north were discovered for the export market. More important, the larger carrying capacity of steamships enabled merchants to ship larger quantities of goods along the river.

For Shanghai, the treaty's most important provision was the Ching government's acquiescence in a tariff on opium imports—in effect, legalization of the drug trade. The bulk of the narcotic imported into China came through Shanghai, and from there it was sent downriver into China's heartland. Despite defeat in the original Opium War, the Chinese government had not rescinded the ban on opium trafficking. On the other hand, it did nothing to hinder the trade either. As a result, the amount of opium sold through Woosung, the town outside Shanghai, more than quadrupled between 1843 and 1857. Legalization of the drug trade meant that the foreign traders no longer needed to store and sell their supplies of opium at Woosung. Instead, the drug could now be brought directly into the Settlement; it was stored in two old sailing hulks moored permanently along the Bund's riverfront. In addition, opium retail shops and smoking divans licensed by both foreign municipalities—and yielding substantial revenues to both—proliferated by the hundreds.

Commerce throve as never before. The Bund's southern extremity bustled with quick-trotting coolies loading and unloading merchandise along the greasy piers and brokers rushing about in sedan chairs, orders and the latest rates from London and New York in hand. In the first year alone of the Yangtze's opening to "free trade," Shanghai's customs revenues tripled. When duties were paid on incoming and outgoing goods, they were handed over not to Chinese, but to Western customs officers, who forwarded the receipts to Peking. This peculiar arrangement had come about in 1853 when, during the disorder of the Small Swords revolt, the British consul had begun collecting import duties for absent Chinese officials. The revenues he collected were so much larger than they had been under the previous peculation-prone administration that the British persuaded the court to allow Westerners to supervise the entire country's customs service.

Awash in easy money, Shanghai's Westerners celebrated their newly minted wealth giddily and with gusto. In hotel bars, saloons, and private dining rooms, whiskey and champagne flowed by the barrelful as the entire foreign community indulged itself in an orgy of extravagance. "Everybody made lots of money in those days, and it used to be the custom to 'shout' for a case of champagne at a time, to treat everyone within hailing distance," declared one habitué of Shanghai's saloons, William Mesny. Similarly, a British taipan, Sir Thomas Sutherland, recalled, "Those were the good old times, when every Englishman in China was youthful, the great firms princely, the hospitality unbounded, and the prospect of achieving fortune with ordinary industry and luck appeared to every young fellow as assured."

On the Bund, colossal white piles—the beginnings of what would be known as Shanghai's "million-dollar skyline"—were rising. Ornate Italianate and neoclassical buildings that looked as if they had been plucked straight off the boulevards of Europe would soon all but replace the old colonial-style bungalows. Of these paeans to taipan wealth, none expressed the merchant colony's ascent into wealth and respectability more than the four-story Shanghai Club, erected on the spot where an early American merchant's dry goods store had once stood. The most extravagant of the Bund's new edifices, the club had been bankrolled by Shanghai's most prominent taipans and was intended to be a men's club on par with the best in London and New York. Indeed, it more than fulfilled these requirements—no toff could find its blackstone foyer, gleaming mahogany-paneled bar, or wainscoted reading room beneath his standards—but at a cost that nearly bankrupted its sponsors. In keeping with its other excesses, the club had a fully equipped gas kitchen and a rooftop viewing pavilion. To pay off its debts, the club's shareholders turned over management of the establishment to the Municipal Council—whose councillors were, of course, all Shanghai Club members—which then rented out its twelve private rooms to paying guests until the establishment became solvent. In the meantime, all of foreign Shanghai's leading citizens regularly stopped at the club's first-floor bar in the evening for a game of billiards or cards or to quaff down a gin and bitters before dining upstairs.

As they did everywhere, the British re-created in Shanghai their familiar institutions and amusements. The Englishman's daily routine hardly varied from what it had been at home. "He builds himself a mansion in the handsomest style that his firm or himself can afford, and he furnishes it as a rule with home-made furniture, plates, glass, etc., all of the best quality," explained one Shanghailander, Walter Medhurst. "For his business through the day the Shanghae [sic] resident generally keeps a Norwich car, brougham or some other convenient kind of vehicle in which to traverse the settlement in all its parts. For evening exercise, if a subordinate, he goes to cricket or rackets, or bowls, or takes a gallop on a pet pony, or trots out his dog cart or phaeton. If a head of house or a married man, he drives out in some more pretentious vehicle with a pair of Cape or Australian horses." Groceries and delicacies for the foreign merchants' tables were hardly unfamiliar fare, for they were bought wholesale from Fortnum & Mason, Crosse & Blackwell, and other British establishments. "Wines of superior quality are, as a rule, placed on the table, all of course imported from England."

Food and the rituals surrounding its consumption assumed such a disproportionate role in the foreign colony's life that it was always possible to pick out a taipan by his florid complexion and wide girth. "Like the officers of the army and navy, the taipans have the unmistakable appearances peculiar to their breed, well-filled waistcoats, jowls inclined to be puffy and a ruddy roundness of face," remarked a visiting Englishman, Ronald Bodley. "I suppose it is the natural effect of meeting one another so often at the club bars." The menu at a typical dinner, as recounted by Settlement physician Edward Henderson, began with "rich soup and a glass of sherry." Then "they partake of one or two side dishes with champagne; then some beef, mutton, or fowls and bacon, with more champagne, or beer; then rice and curry and ham; afterwards game; then pudding, pastry, jelly, custard, or blancmange, and more champagne; then cheese and salad, then bread and butter, and a glass of port wine; then in many cases, oranges, figs, raisins, and walnuts are eaten with two or three glasses of claret or some other wine." Finally, said the exasperated doctor, "this AWFUL repast is finished at last, with a cup of strong coffee and cigars!"

Fun, frivolity, and an exuberant sociability had come to prevail in the Western colony. Balls took place throughout the year. Isabella Bird, the intrepid Victorian travel writer, marveled at the "phenomenal energy" with which the Whangpu settlements' residents amused themselves, "a fatigue even to contemplate." Of course, what made this immoderate pursuit of pleasure and leisure possible in the treaty port, as elsewhere in the colonial world, was an abundance of servants and the cheapness of food and spirits. Phalanxes of houseboys, cooks, laundresses, stable hands, amahs, gardeners, table boys, and porters relieved "Missy" (as all foreign women were referred to no matter what their age or marital status) from all domestic chores. At the office it was the same: native managers and clerks took charge of the day-to-day work, leaving the taipan and his assistants free to enjoy two- or three-hour lunches, or "tiffin," as the midday meal was called.

Every foreigner, no matter how poor, had a "boy," a manservant dressed in the ubiquitous long-sleeved blue gown and black cap and devoted to making his master's life as carefree as possible. Whether laying out the master's morning clothes, cleaning, or replenishing stock in the liquor cabinet, the servant performed his tasks so well that he usually became indispensable to his employers. Small families relied upon a head servant, the "number one boy," who supervised household affairs and hired all the necessary staff, from cooks to laundresses to children's amahs. The Chinese "boy," declared the authors of a guide for newcomers to China, "is patient and industrious and loyal to his employer. He will work long hours without complaining, seems never to require any time to sleep, eat or rest and no matter what storms may rage over the household, he is usually cheerful and smiling. Without being told he learns all the requirements of the household and the likes and dislikes of the master and the mistress. . . . No matter how much one may determine not to be, he rarely avoids being spoiled by the Chinese 'boy,' and when he returns to lands less well supplied with servants, will often long for the long-gowned boy of the China coast."

Philistines to the core, Shanghailanders rigorously ignored any serious pursuit outside of business. While their small circulating library languished for lack of patrons and funds, no expense was spared on food and liquor. Maintaining large messes and well-stocked wine cellars, the big hongs—large business establishments—vied with one another in lavishness. Spending eighty thousand pounds a year on entertainment alone, Jardine's employed a French chef and opened its dining room to the entire foreign community. Not to be outdone, the biggest American hong, Russell's, brought Negro cooks from Mississippi to prepare such Southern specialties as baked beans, hominy grits, and hotcakes with maple syrup. When Commodore Perry visited Shanghai in 1854 during his expedition to Japan he casually mentioned that his favorite mineral water was from Congress Springs in Saratoga Springs; a servant brought a bottle to his room the next day.

Shanghai at this time had so few European women that the ratio of men to women in the Western colony never sank below ten to one. It had yet to acquire the opulent bordellos specializing in recruits from San Francisco that it would later boast, nor had it yet become a happy hunting ground for unmarried Western women. Owing to the dearth of foreign females, many of the foreign bachelors—and not a few married men with wives back home—took a Chinese mistress. Mistresses were often disguised as "maids," but were always young and attractive. From these informal liaisons, children were often sired, the luckier of whom were well provided for and might grow up to marry a Westerner. Indeed, some of Shanghai's "best families" two generations later had Chinese blood from a grandmother who had been a merchant's concubine. When marriages across racial lines did take place, the unions were regarded with horror by both whites and Chinese. To ensure that such marriages occurred as seldom as possible, nearly all British assistants had contracts that did not permit them to marry until after they had served five years in China. It became customary for these bachelors to find brides in England during a "home leave," and to send for them at the end of the five-year moratorium on marriage. So widespread was the practice of cohabiting with a Chinese mistress that even Sir Robert Hart, the inspector general of the Imperial Maritime Customs Service, had fathered three children with a Chinese woman when he was stationed in Ningpo and Canton in the 1840s and 1850s. As he later acknowledged, the arrangement was "a common practice for an unmarried Englishman resident in China" at the time.

Such evidence of moral laxity, moreover, did little to ease a mutual antipathy that had come to exist between Western businessmen and missionaries. One of the earliest and most public clashes over the concubine issue occurred in the 1850s when the British vice-consul of Ningpo ran afoul of the Church of England's senior representative in China by taking as his mistress a pupil at a Protestant girls' missionary school in Ningpo. When he was transferred to Foochow, he took the girl with him, which so outraged the head of the school, an upright Englishwoman named Miss Aldersey, that she reported him to the Bishop of Victoria in Hong Kong. The outraged bishop denounced the vice-consul from his pulpit, forcing the errant diplomat to send the girl back to her home.

By the early 1880s, Shanghai sheltered, as one American, Percy Finch, put it, "the biggest evangelical army in Christendom, a force that included missionaries from every important Protestant denomination in the world. The American Protestant missions were the largest, the best-organized, and the most disapproving of the foreign colony's reprobate ways. While the Roman Catholics, particularly the Jesuits, who had established the Siccawei mission with its famous observatory outside Shanghai, were liberal in their outlook and more interested in scholarly pursuits than evangelism, the Protestant missionaries had come to China specifically to save souls.

To these earnest evangels, most of whom had small-town or rural backgrounds and fervently believed in their cause, Shanghai's mix of vice, intrigue, and materialism made it one of the unholiest cities imaginable. For them, the port well deserved to be called "the Sodom and Gomorrah of the Far East" as much for the avarice and godlessness of its foreigners as for the heathenism of its Chinese. The treaty port merchants, for their part, relegated missionaries to the bottom of their social ladder, put off by their abstemious ways and threadbare clothing as well as by their denunciation of the foreign community's chief diversions—drinking, dancing, and cardplaying. The more fundamentalist of the American missionaries so frowned upon these activities that, in one of the outposts, they forbade their children to attend a children's party being thrown by the American consul's wife, on the ground that "cocktails had at times been served in the Consul's house, and that it was hence no fit place for a child."

Missionaries excepted, Shanghai's foreign denizens exercised a general leniency toward all forms of moral impropriety. As one Shanghai resident, Edward Parker, expressed it, "It is true that the ways of mankind savour more of San Francisco or Alexandria than of London, especially so far as casual visitors are concerned; but after all Shanghai is tolerant rather than vicious, and the mixed population is so good-natured that any one but a murderer may rehabilitate himself or herself after a long period of industry, repentance, and quiet." Neatly encapsulating the creed that united all of Shanghai's foreigners, he added: "Hence . . . every one knows who every one is, and what every one does; the strait-laced are at liberty to tabu the easy-going if they choose; but Peruvians do not behave like Germans, nor Frenchmen like Yankees; and so it comes round that with twenty nationalities to please nearly everybody ends up by submitting to the inevitable, and, whilst living, letting."

The Anglo-Saxons also brought their favorite sports to the new locale. Shooting, hunting, racquetball, rowing, billiards, and bowling were all avidly, even excessively, pursued, as "shaking up the liver" was believed necessary to ward off disease and counteract the worst effects of Shanghai's moist and insalubrious climate. Among the young assistants who worked for the hongs, "griffins" as they were called, "manly games" were pursued with fanatical devotion. "In London, after business hours, we got rowing and cricket in the summer, and football in the winter," said Charles Dyce, a British trader. "What a contrast it was in Shanghai! Every kind of sport was available, and almost at our doors. We could rise early and go for a ride across country before breakfast, or we could take out the gun and kill a brace of pheasants."

While every sport had its devotees, none generated as much excitement as horse racing. The Settlement's pride was its racecourse, a twelve-acre plot paid for by residents' contributions. Racing held such an important place in Shanghai's social life that all banks and businesses closed after eleven o'clock in the morning for ten days during the twice-yearly racing meets to allow everyone to participate. For the socially ambitious, ownership of a winning pony was mandatory. At first, riders imported their horses from overseas, mainly Arabia and Australia, but soon the shaggy, hard-mouthed horses from the Mongolian steppes became the breed of choice. When races were not being run, the track's inside field was used as an all-purpose recreation area for everything from cricket matches to polo. Outside the track was a bridle path where taipans and junior assistants exchanged greetings while taking their ponies out for their morning runs.

As for the Chinese, they were baffled at the inordinate amounts of time and energy Westerners devoted to games of sport, chalking it up to another foreign devil eccentricity; that white men paid servants to do their cooking, cleaning, and laundering but spent a day swatting a ball back and forth in the sun seemed the height of absurdity to Chinese. "Belong foreign man custom," they would mutter upon these occasions. Indeed, it was not the Europeans' amusements that struck them as queer but everything else—their penchant for putting milk in their tea; the huge quantities of beef and mutton they consumed; the scandalous way they allowed their women to mix publicly with men.

Needless to say, Westerners similarly regarded most Chinese customs as bizarre, but their attitude toward the Chinese was necessarily colored by their position as conquerors. As such, they felt vindicated in their view of their hosts as morally and mentally inferior people. "To the resident, even for a few months, the Chinaman seems vulgar, selfish and by no means cleanly in person or mind," opined William McFarlane, an English columnist for the *Shanghai Mercury*. "His manners are out of a book; for every occasion he has a code of etiquette, firm and immutable, but in the ordinary amenities of life he is too often utterly wanting in natural politeness . . . the most flagrant breaches of what even a savage learns to respect are openly committed, even by individuals of high rank. That graceful polish and chivalrous attention to the feelings of others which the social usages of the West require . . . is in China utterly absent. . . . Their partiality for opium, especially in the form of smoking, is distinctly a national characteristic. Their immorality is marked; yet it is carried on under an outward show of propriety."

In the same vein, Elijah Bridgman, the first American missionary in China and the editor of the *China Repository*, condemned the natives of Shanghai for being "as insensible as the very rock to ordinary moral influence. Doubtless there are pearls and a few precious stones to be found; but in the mass as I have yet seen it, the common and baser qualities greatly predominate." With a condescending tone common to the missionary in China, he added, "One thing is certain—the minds of this people must be remolded and their manners reformed for as yet they are but half civilized."

Nothing revealed more about the nature of the relationship between Chinese and their disdainful "guests" than a mongrel language known as pidgin English, which, because the foreigners refused to learn Chinese, became the lingua franca of Shanghai. A makeshift language that mixed English, Chinese, Indian, and Portuguese words, pidgin ("business") English originated in Canton in the early days of the China trade. It consisted of several hundred words adapted to Chinese pronunciation and used with Chinese intonation and grammatical phrasing. A typical conversation between a taipan and his comprador, or Chinese manager, as supplied by China hand and American journalist Carl Crow, went as follows:

"Taipan: 'How fashion that chow-chow cargo he just now stop godown inside?'

Comprador: 'Lat cargo he no can walkee just now. Lat man Kong Tai he no got ploper sclew.'

Taipan: 'How come you talkee sclew no ploper? My have got sclew paper safe inside.'

Comprador: 'Aiyah! Lat sclew paper he no can do. Lat sclew man he have go Ningpo more far.' "

This conversation was perfectly intelligible to all Shanghai-landers. The taipan asked his comprador to explain why a shipment of mixed cargo (chow-chow) had not left the godown (warehouse). The answer was that the cargo could not move (walkee) because it did not have proper security (sclew) from its purchaser, Kong Tai. In reply to the taipan's assertion that he had the security in his safe, the comprador declared that that security was no longer good: the man who had guaranteed payment had defaulted and fled his creditors—that is, "Lat sclew man he have go Ningpo more far." "Ningpo more far" was a general expression for anywhere far enough outside of Shanghai to be not easily accessible.

Ironically, the language that was meant to lessen the distance between foreigners and Chinese instead increased it by reinforcing Westerners' view of the Chinese as ignorant and simpleminded people, since it never allowed for sophisticated discourse. This bastard jargon enabled the two races to transact business and communicate about daily affairs, but beyond that it was useless. Cultivated Chinese considered it demeaning to speak this inelegant polyglot gibberish, though Westerners indiscriminately addressed all Chinese in pidgin. A missionary woman attempted to explain to a mandarin that rain had leaked onto her organ through a hole in the roof: "Have got before time one piecee organ, belong makee sing song. Have puttee organ house inside. Roof topside have makee break. Lain come chop chop makee spoilum organ. Just now must catchee one more piecee." She repeated herself several times before an expression of understanding appeared on the mandarin's face. "Ah, I understand," he replied. "A rift in the lute, n'est-ce pas?" The mandarin, it turned out, had graduated from an American university and had lived in Paris for many years.

The patronizing attitude of many if not most Westerners and the resentment it engendered among the Chinese only widened the gap that separated the two groups. Since the newcomers made little effort to understand their hosts' culture, ignorance about Chinese ways abounded. The same insensitive approach to living among people of a different race had worked for white colonialists in India and Africa; there seemed no reason why it shouldn't work equally well on the banks of the Whangpu. Not only did the interlopers not bother to learn the language; they prided themselves on never "mixing with the natives," and those who did mix were regarded with suspicion and ridiculed. Taking a serious interest in anything Chinese was a dangerous signal that one was "going native," the gravest offense that a white man could commit, as nothing inspired more fear and dread among foreigners than the sight of one of their own adopting Chinese ways.

There were a few Westerners who took a scholarly interest in Chinese matters; they were regarded as eccentrics, and their odd behavior was tolerated. But sailors, army deserters, and others who actually lived among the Chinese—eating local food, wearing native clothes, and even marrying Chinese women—embarrassed other foreigners as having damaged the prestige of the white man. The unwritten code dictated that preserving the image of superiority was the sacred duty of every European in China. Any evidence that whites could happily adjust to Chinese customs was a source of deep embarrassment to the foreign community. To ensure that as few as possible of their number were tempted to go astray, the Shanghai residents maintained a special fund for shipping destitute foreigners back home.

In Shanghai, social intercourse between Chinese and Occidentals scarcely existed. The only Chinese whom foreigners came into contact with were servants and their compradors, and the latter, because they usually came from Canton, were almost foreigners themselves to the Shanghainese. In the world of the treaty ports, the comprador held a special place. The word means "buyer" in Portuguese; compradors handled the Chinese end of foreigners' business affairs. Suave, fast-talking power brokers wearing black caps and sporting two-inch fingernails, Shanghai's first compradors were almost exclusively southerners recruited from among merchants with whom the foreigners were familiar in Canton. The comprador was the foreigner's indispensable trading partner. Not speaking the language and having almost no contacts among the local merchants, Western businessmen relied heavily upon their compradors. So much responsibility devolved upon the comprador that the taipan was often as dependent upon the comprador to run his business as he was upon his "boy" to run his home. "Even in such lordly institutions as the British Banks on the Bund," sniffed Isabella Bird, the Victorian travel writer, "it seems impossible to transact even such a simple affair as cashing a cheque without calling in the aid of a sleek, supercilious-looking, richly-dressed Chinese, a shroff [bookkeeper or bill collector] or comprador, who looks as if he knew the business of the bank and were capable of running it."

Compradors hired their own Chinese staffs and "guaranteed" the honesty of each transaction with a security deposit to the taipan. They did not mind having to supply the hong with working capital, as their position gave them numerous opportunities to accumulate tremendous wealth of their own. Never a Confucian scholar, the comprador seldom had occasion to read the *Analects*, but what he lacked in elegance he more than made up for in quickness, initiative, and an unerring business sense. While gentry were inclined to disparage the comprador as an uneducated "head servant of servants" in a foreign establishment, he was looked up to with a respect bordering on awe by other Chinese because of the lucrative contracts and other favors he was able to dispense.

Chinese, too, had done well in the boom. They threw themselves into the spirit of extravagance with an exuberance that, if possible, exceeded that of the foreigners. The Shanghainese appetite for pleasure and, in particular, fascination with foreign novelties had not escaped Westerners. The Chinese, though "a hard-working and industrious people, are not behind other nations in their love of amusements," remarked China hand James Ball. "They enter with great zest and gusto into the enjoyment of them, most heartily assisting at shows and processions." Moreover, they made, he found, "unfailing provision for the relaxation of the tired workers and the delectation of the younger members of society," and holidays and religious festivals were "hailed with delight."

On Bubbling Well Road, a bucolic thoroughfare west of the old racecourse lined with magnificent willow and plane trees and bordered by creeks, the compradors ensconced themselves in European-style villas alongside the foreign taipans. In the style of the Chinese country gentry, they established huge households comprising extended families, concubines, and scores of servants in their Shanghai estates. The gabled Tudoresque mansion belonging to Sheng Kung Pao, the head of the imperial telegraph administration and Li Hung-chang's economic vizier, was said to be occupied by four hundred people, "family and retainers—a true Oriental family warren," in the words of Shanghai resident Charles Darwent. Winding far out into the suburbs, Bubbling Well Road was named after an ancient spring in the vicinity whose waters were said to have miraculous healing powers. Stretching on to Jenner Hogg's garden along Jessfield Road, which would soon become Jessfield Park, the road continued past the future grounds of St. John's University, a college founded by American missionaries and favored by the sons of Shanghai's elite.

Bubbling Well Road gave well-to-do Chinese women a rare opportunity to leave their homes. "Celestial beauties drive along this road, arrayed in splendid silks and satins, got up in the height of Chinese fashion," Darwent noted. The road struck Edward Parker as "one of the gayest sights in the world. . . .

On an afternoon, when landaus, broughams, cabs, jinrickshas, barrows, cavaliers, all go spanking along. The rich 'compradores' and 'shroffs' bring with them their whole harems, grandmothers, daughters, nurses, and womankind generally, decked out in the most gorgeous of silks and satins, glossy black hair, well greased and heavily laden with gold pins, flowers, jade, and kingfishers' feathers, fearful and wonderful paints and fards, bright red 'pants,' and invisible small feet. Everybody seems so happy that one forgets the dust, the noise, and even the danger; for the driving is too often both incompetent and reckless."

Bubbling Well Road led into Nanking Road. Both the city's most cosmopolitan street and the locale of the city's most prestigious native shops, Nanking Road was crowded at all times of the day and far into the night with so many people that the foot traffic spilled out from the pavements into the street— silk-clad gentlemen risked colliding with half-naked coolies balancing crates of fragrant sandalwood or silver dollars on either end of a bamboo poles; foreigners dapper in white pongee suits stepped gingerly past straw-sandaled water carriers; farm women carrying baskets full of quacking ducks on either arm stared wide-eyed at black-bearded Parsis in their flowing robes and curious, tall cylindrical hats; and barefoot street urchins darted gleefully beneath a silk-curtained palanquin borne on the shoulders of a quartet of chair bearers.

Nanking Road's most distinctive characteristic was its riot of red-and-gold signboards and banners, extending as far down the thoroughfare as the eye could see. Along its length were pagoda-roofed goldsmiths' and silversmiths' shops, porcelain and curio dealers, and silk emporiums whose shelves spilled over with rich satins and embroideries. Whereas in the Chinese City shopkeepers sat bare to the waist fanning their stomachs on sticky days in the summer, on Nanking Road the merchants and clerks wore long gray gowns and never rolled up their sleeves—a sign of ill-breeding—while serving customers. Here too were restaurants and teahouses, on whose second-story balconies could be seen Shanghai's *jeunesse dorée,* aristocratic young loungers. "Pale and silken clad, craning their necks to see," these scions of Shanghai's native elite with their "arched mouths, the coldness of their icy stare," and "the haughtiness of their gaze" reminded Alicia Little, an American writer known for spearheading Shanghai's first anti-foot-binding movement, of the decadent Romans during "the last days of the empire."

The hub of the Chinese entertainment district was Foochow Road, one street behind Nanking Road. Here, on narrow lanes that were always filled with crowds of pleasure-seekers and sedan chairs, were teahouses and native theaters. Practically a national institution, the Chinese theater was well attended by all classes of Chinese. Productions consisted chiefly of historical dramas with intricate and protracted plots. There was no scenery, simply a bare stage open to the audience, and no proscenium. On the other hand, the actors were heavily made up and wore elaborate costumes. Instead of spoken dialogue, they sang their parts in a high-pitched falsetto to the accompaniment of cymbals, gongs, three-stringed violins, and other Chinese instruments. Just as essential to the performance were swordplay, stylized dancing, whirling, leaping, and amazing acrobatic feats. Westerners found these productions incomprehensible, but nearly everyone else in the audience not only knew the play's plot and all its characters but could sing all of its arias, so familiar were these ancient dramas. For this reason—and because of the plays' usually protracted length—Chinese audiences always talked, laughed, drank tea, and nibbled on oranges and watermelon seeds during performances. "No attempt is made to keep silent during the performance," recorded one astonished visitor; "vendors of sweetmeats, peanuts and melon seeds cry their wares among the audience, and attendants distribute the steaming towels."

So avid were Chinese opera devotees that theaters opened

as early as seven in the morning and did not close until after midnight. They were at their most crowded, however, toward the end of the evening's program, when the best plays were performed and the most famous actors made their appearances. All actors were males; as on the Elizabethan stage, males performed female parts. The actors were so skillful in their female impersonations that, as one writer noted, "it is hard for a stranger to believe that they are, in fact, male actors."

Indeed, it was not by coincidence that being an actor was almost the same as being a male prostitute—and implied, at the very least, the availability of sexual favors to male patrons. This understanding began when the actors, as young boys sold to troupes by destitute parents, were trained to appear effeminate and even schooled in the "erotic arts." Actors who were unwilling to provide sexual services eventually found themselves forced to do so either to supplement their incomes or to advance their careers. So unusual was it for an actor to refuse the advances of a wealthy admirer that one such well-known performer felt compelled to record his feelings on the matter. "Our necks and legs touch and we fondle one another," he wrote. "Although we are both aroused, we have no sexual connection. He has often wondered at my restraint, but I have never changed my behavior."

Because they were considered male prostitutes, actors were relegated to the "mean" class, the lowest rung of the Confucian social ladder, which also included slaves and female prostitutes. Their children bore the stigma of their outcast status and were barred from sitting for civil service examinations, and thus from government office. Their patrons, on the other hand, were literati and high officials, for, far from being considered deviant, homosexuality—or at least bisexuality—had a long tradition among the Chinese aristocracy; emperors themselves had not only kept male lovers at court but promoted them to important positions.

Prior to appearing at the theater, many of the wealthier

members of the audience would have dined at a teahouse in the same district, entertained by one or more courtesans summoned from their residences, or perhaps attended a banquet with a favorite "flower"—courtesan—at their side. The custom of men gathering for food and conversation attended by professional hostesses was so common in Shanghai that one Westerner complained of its being "impossible for a party of officials, or men of letters, to meet on any social occasion without summoning a contingent of girls to keep them company." Nearly all of these hostesses were young—between the ages of fourteen and twenty—and had undergone tutelage in the art of entertaining and pleasing men.

As upper-class wives were expected to remain in the purdah of their houses (indeed, it was taboo even to eat at the same table as their husbands), these banquets were always all-male affairs except for courtesans and concubines. Alicia Little had the unusual opportunity of attending one such function, one at which "several natives of high rank" were present. "They came accompanied by their favorite concubines," she related. "And the ladies were carried in their palanquins right into the center of the dining room, where they got out, dressed in fresh and elegant costumes of light blue silk, and with their abundant black hair decked with natural flowers. They really looked very pretty. Their complexions, though far too much rouged, were delicate; and where the natural hue had been left unchanged, almost white.

"I regretted very much that I could not say a word they would understand," she continued. "They spoke [but] my host had . . . warned me to be very careful not to be too polite to them even in dumb show, for if their lords felt the very smallest spark of jealousy I should most likely see all the fair creatures take flight like a flock of frightened turtle doves." The dinner, which was served at a luxurious private restaurant, included several courses, but the ladies "put nothing into their dainty mouths but perfumed sweets or dried melon seeds" or such delicacies as pigeon hearts with ginger. Throughout the meal, much singing and instrumental music was to be heard—"oh so much a lot of it." When it was over, "the young women rose, and, still smiling, made their way out with difficulty on their poor deformed feet, clutching at the table, the chairs and the walls for support as they limped to their luxurious palanquins."

The lily-footed ladies at the dinner may have included one or two concubines—secondary wives—but most likely they were courtesans attached to the numerous courtesan houses and teahouses in the Foochow Road district. Like Japanese geishas, Chinese courtesans were trained to sing, play instruments, and provide refined feminine companionship to a well-to-do clientele. They were requested to entertain at banquets by messengers from the host carrying red "call tickets." Popular courtesans received as many as half a dozen tickets on a single evening and might spend only a short time at each "call." If a courtesan was especially famous, she would arrive on a sedan chair, accompanied by a retinue of musicians and servants, but otherwise she would be carried to her destination by a male servant. The practice, which arose after the International Settlement began taxing sedan chairs, was a common one in the streets around Nanking Road in the evenings, the girl riding on the servant's shoulders, "erect as a jade Pagoda."

Much like European courtesans, the elite of the "flower world" lived in luxurious circumstances and were free to pick and choose their lovers. They considered themselves artists more than prostitutes, as they had descended from a prestigious and exclusive group of women, *shu-yu*—"storytellers"—who entertained high officials and scholars in days gone by. Westerners in Shanghai called the courtesans "sing-song girls," an appellation which stuck. True, sing-song girls—unlike, supposedly, the *shu-yu*—engaged in sexual relations with their clients, but for a man to enjoy such privileges, he had to undertake a long and expensive courtship that included showering the courtesan with jewelry and other gifts and hosting numerous banquets at her establishment. The better courtesans' houses struck one Western visitor as "all alike, with their brilliant lighting and inner court, where the servants and the menials' brats play and a sly brute of a porter bellows out your name."

The first-class courtesan's rooms spared nothing in comfort and opulence. One habitué of the nocturnal district described them as being "like those of kings and noblemen." They were furnished with "silk curtains, night tables and wardrobes made of marble or fine hardwood, dressing mirrors, chandeliers, small round personal tables, flowers with glass covers, paintings made of coral and jade, Western clocks, fancy plates, silver water pipes, all flickering in the light of the red lamps, making one feel intoxicated." The most famous courtesans enjoyed near-celebrity status, their names appearing in the "mosquito" tabloid papers—so called because their gossip stung—alongside those of their current patrons. As much as an elite courtesan enjoyed a luxurious—and in many ways enviable—life, she knew that it was only a matter of time before her beauty would disappear and she would descend down the prostitute hierarchy to progressively less prestigious establishments or become a madam or procuress herself.

In the same alleyways of Foochow Road could be found teahouses—"sing-song houses," the foreigners called them—catering to lower-grade officials and ordinary merchants who could not gain entry to the first-class courtesans' houses. The females who lived and worked in these establishments had some of the training and skill of the courtesans, but their favors were available to whoever had enough money—and with no preliminaries. These second-tier houses were identified by strips of red paper, names such as "Temple of Supreme Happiness" and "Garden of Perfumed Flowers," and gaudily decorated doorways. Richly furnished in carved blackwood, the teahouses were barely occupied during the day, but at night, musicians began playing and the tables filled up with merchants and minor officials conversing and smoking long pipes. It was then that the house's sing-song girls appeared. "In and out among the square tables, filling the brilliantly lighted rooms, trail slowly little processions of young girls," related an American, Mary Gamewell. "Nearly all are pretty and very young. Clad in silk or satin, adorned with jewelry, their faces unnatural with paint and powder, they follow the lead of the woman in charge of each group. She stops often to draw attention ingratiatingly to her charges and expatiate on their good points." The chosen girl then sat down at the customer's table. Depending upon the grade of the sing-song house, the man could be allowed to spend the night in the girl's room upstairs right away or after one or two more visits. When every girl in the house had a client for the night, the house removed a red lantern that hung from a window above its doorway.

Streetwalkers, a new and distinctly urban phenomena, and outright brothels appeared in the period after the Taiping Rebellion. Called "wild chickens" or "pheasants" by the Chinese, streetwalkers worked in small groups under the supervision of an older woman who acted as their business agent. Young— but older than the average courtesan—and cheaply dressed, streetwalkers were conspicuous everywhere at night: standing in the glare of a streetlamp, seated on a bench, within the shadow of a doorway, or at the entrance to a lane. The pheasants did their best to attract customers, calling out to male passersby, often following them down the street, amah trotting close behind. If still unsuccessful, the girl might grab the man's arm, pleading with him to accompany her to her brothel. Country bumpkins and other newcomers to the city were favorite targets. When soliciting these prospects, the pheasants shed all maidenly inhibitions. "If a man is persuaded by them to enter a dark lane," recorded a Shanghainese, "a beehive of pheasants and madams will come forward and besiege him, and if he still is stubborn about it, they will use the kidnapping method. Country people are often manhandled by them to the point where they cry out for help." Fear of a beating by their madam should they fail to secure a customer for the night accounted for the pheasants' aggressiveness. In the late hours of the morning, a customer might find himself seized by the arm by a girl who would desperately plead, "Excuse me, please help me out!"

The streetwalkers' "rooms," dark, dingy cubicles separated from one another by curtained entranceways, were a far cry from the sumptuous quarters of the first-class courtesans. Yet it was possible for a female to sink even lower in Shanghai's prostitute hierarchy. Those women too old, ugly, or sick to walk the streets worked in the "flower and smoke rooms," barely furnished hovels with filthy quilts on the floor where customers were allowed to smoke opium and fondle the prostitutes. Lower still, there were "nail sheds," shacks in the poorest Chinese areas, patronized by coolies and laborers, who paid ten cents for quick sex. For foreign sailors, there was even a special group of prostitutes, the "saltwater sisters," down by the docks in Hongkew and around Frenchtown—as the French Concession was also known—who spoke pidgin and were exclusively Cantonese. The term "saltwater sisters" probably had its origins in the fact that the Cantonese prostitutes had traditionally served a seagoing population and also in their having been boat dwellers, operating from luxurious "flower boats"—floating brothels that took customers from vessels moored along the river.

A mere handful of brothels had existed in the Chinese city in 1842, but only two decades after Shanghai became a treaty port, it was well on its way to becoming the brothel capital of the world. Henry Parkes, the British consul, complained as early as 1864 that of a total of ten thousand Chinese houses in the International Settlement and French Concession, 688 were brothels, while houses for opium and gambling—two activities that went hand in hand with prostitution—were "beyond counting." Almost seventy years later, in 1930, when the port's population had swollen to three million, an international survey found that Shanghai had surpassed any other metropolis in the proportion of women practicing prostitution "as a specialty": in Berlin, one person in 580 was a prostitute; in Paris, one in 481; in Chicago, one in 430; in Tokyo, one in 250; and in Shanghai, one in 130.

An imbalance in the proportion of men to women explained in part why prostitution thrived in the port. But a far more important factor in its entrenchment in China's largest city was a two-thousand-year-old tradition of regarding women as both inherently inferior and expendable. An ancient maxim decreed, "Eight *lohan* [saintly] daughters are not equal to a boy with a limp." Of so little account was a daughter to the average Chinese father that when he was asked how many children he had, he would almost always exclude the girls in his reply. On the other hand, one Westerner wrote, if he happened to have only a daughter, his response would be along the lines of "only one girl," said in "such a tone of voice as to call forth the sympathy of his listener for his unfortunate position."

The whole weight of tradition favored the absolute submission of females. As a result, a woman's worth in the society amounted to little more than her value as an economic commodity—human "merchandise" that could be sold or bartered. The sale of women took many forms, and though it primarily affected females from poor families, not even upper-class women were exempt. Most commonly, an impoverished family might sell a daughter as an "adopted daughter-in-law" to the family of the girl's future husband in exchange for a sum of money. This arrangement both gave the girl's parents one less mouth to feed and saved them the cost of a dowry, but gave the girl's future in-laws the benefit of her free labor as a servant for years before the actual marriage. Yet another way for a family to dispose of a daughter was to sell her into domestic service, an arrangement usually made through a middleman who paid the parents a sum for the "sale." A third way was for her to be "pawned" to an employer or agent—that is, she would be sold into servitude with the possibility of eventually being "redeemed." Nor was the trade in females limited to unmarried girls—widows were sold into servitude by their in-laws, and even married women were sold by their husbands.

It was through outright sale or pawning that many females entered the world of prostitution. However, few parents know-ingly sold their daughters to a procurer or madam. Instead, labor contractors often promised parents that their daughter would be placed in domestic service in Shanghai, but she was likely to be sold in turn to a madam or brothel keeper. Once the girl had been taken to Shanghai, it was impossible for her family to discover her true occupation—or for the girl to re-turn to her village. Just as tragic were girls kidnapped from the countryside and brought to Shanghai by criminal gangs who specialized in selling girls into prostitution. Daughters of well-to-do families and especially attractive girls were preferred, as the former gave the abductors the opportunity of seeking a ransom from the victim's family while the latter could be sold for a better-than-average sum to a brothel.

A madam or brothel operator expected to recoup the cost of buying a girl at her first sexual encounter with a customer: for the privilege of deflowering a virgin, Chinese men were willing to pay large sums. At a courtesan house, extensive ne-gotiations between the madam and client, much feasting, and rituals and ceremonies similar to those for a wedding would precede the girl's defloration. Because so much could be com-manded for an evening with a virgin, brothel owners were known to dupe customers by presenting an experienced pros-titute as a virgin. This could be done, according to one ac-count, "dozens of times" with a single prostitute, and "chicken blood was used to supply the desired evidence of virginity." So much pride did men take in having had the chance to enjoy a virgin for a night that they invented phrases to describe the event: in general, such liaisons were known as "combing the hair," but when the deflowering was of a girl of thirteen, it was called "trying the flower"; if she was fourteen, "cultivating the flower"; if she was fifteen, "gathering the flower."

Once a girl was in a brothel keeper's or madam's hands, she had few opportunities of escaping, as she was never allowed outside her brothel without an amah or male servant. "It was not uncommon to see a little slave girl break away from her amah on the street," said Gamewell of the streetwalkers. "If she was caught, her body would rack for days from the keeper's cuffs and lashes." Another Shanghailander sympathetic to their plight commented: "You could see them, all along Nanking Road: young, poorly dressed Chinese girls, strolling hand in hand with their elderly amahs. They were not a happy-looking lot, and one could not help thinking that some of them might have found ways and means of going back to the village, if it had not been for those nasty amahs." But even if a girl succeeded in escaping, her alternatives were few. As respectable women were expected to seclude themselves from society, the only jobs available to females offered little in pay or prestige. These included work as a food or trinkets peddler, a clothes mender, a domestic, a laundress, a servant in a gambling house, teahouse, or brothel, or a worker in an orphanage or asylum. It was this dearth of options for women trapped into a life of "selling the skin and the smile" that led many to take their own lives. The annals of the brothels and sing-song houses are full of stories of women who took poison, hanged themselves from rafters with silken cords, or flung themselves into the Whangpu.

A refuge and rehabilitation home was opened for prostitutes at the turn of the century—the Door of Hope. Sponsored first by female missionaries, then by the Municipal Council and philanthropic organizations, the Door of Hope gave sanctuary to any runaway from a brothel who managed to cross its threshold. (The Municipal Council also passed a law making it a crime for anyone to stop a woman seeking its refuge.) Typical of those who found their way to the institution was one girl wearing a "little silken coat torn and hanging by one shoulder" whom Gamewell witnessed running past her, pale and exhausted, one evening near the Door of Hope's entrance. Only "ten paces" behind the girl were "a stout madam hobbling along on little feet" and "two burly men in blue peasant clothes lumbering along beside her." The crowd parted. "A few heads turned around out of curiosity, but none out of sympathy. The pursuers swept by. Suddenly the girl turned under a bright street light and began to pound with both fists against a kind of matchboard doorway." The door opened and the girl was admitted, leaving the madam to "shake her fist at the sign above the doorway through which her victim had escaped." After a runaway was taken in, she told her story to a magistrate at the International Settlement's Mixed Court, then was sent to the Door of Hope's residential home outside Shanghai ("far from the crowded, dangerous district with which the girls had grown too familiar," said another writer), where she learned to read and write and was taught handicraft skills. Many became Christians and married Chinese Christians in arranged matches.

Westerners also patronized Chinese brothels. With so many unattached males—Chinese as well as European—both living in and passing through Shanghai, it was not surprising that prostitution became as entrenched as it did. Or, as one nineteenth-century expert on commercial vice, Parisian physician Alexandre Parent-Duchatelet, pithily observed, "Prostitutes are as inevitable in an agglomeration of men as are sewers, cesspits and garbage dumps." Most of the brothels catering to foreigners were found in Hongkew, the former American Settlement. Because of its inconvenient location, only American missionaries and merchants looking for cheap land for their warehouses located themselves in the district. On the other hand, taverns, bordellos, and boardinghouses catering to Shanghai's large transient population found Hongkew ideal for their purposes. As Shanghai's popularity as a seaport increased, so did Hongkew's dives, which attracted a rollicking, high-spirited population of drunken seamen, beachcombers, and other rough men. The district's makeshift establishments were often little more than mud huts with bamboo roofs and supports. It was for this reason, in fact, that the tawdry strip came to be christened Bamboo Town.

As liquor was cheap and readily available—not only gin and whiskey but the even more potent local brews—brawling broke out nightly. And because of the large "floating population" who frequented Hongkew's brothels, the district was also a hotbed of venereal disease. At any one point, as many as two thousand soldiers and seamen might be in port. In 1859 it was estimated that nearly half of all British troops stationed in Shanghai had a venereal disease, a fair number of these cases no doubt contracted while sampling Bamboo Town's sordid delights. So unsavory was the district that it earned international notoriety when a scandalized Duke of Somerset told the House of Commons that never had he encountered a more "haphazard collection of tatterdemalion cosmopolitanism" than that which he found assembled along the American Settlement's seamy fringes. He proceeded to denounce Shanghai as "a sink of iniquity."

Westerners made little effort to control the spread of prostitution—both foreign landlords and the Municipal Council derived sizable revenues from brothels—until foreign physicians raised fears of Shanghai's becoming a "pesthouse of social disease." Between 1865 and 1870, for example, 20 percent of those visiting the Settlement's main foreign hospital came with a venereal complaint. Captains of merchant ships calling on the Whangpu port were unanimous, according to Settlement health officer and physician Edward Henderson, as to "the unusual prevalence of venereal disease [in Shanghai] . . . dreading its effects upon their men." And among the Settlement's constables—those responsible for keeping peace and order in the Settlement—sickness due to venereal disease so seriously depleted the force that the Municipal Council publicly enjoined any constable from "frequenting a brothel except in the execution of his duty." Finally, a French physician, Paul-Edouard Galle, was so alarmed by the high incidence of syphilis among his patients that he deemed the problem one of "epidemic proportions."

Ironically, venereal diseases had been introduced to China by Europeans. The first Chinese prostitutes infected with venereal diseases were the Cantonese girls who served foreigners in the south of China. Chinese physicians referred to syphilitic lesions as "Canton sores" and regarded syphilis as a Western import. When the first epidemics of syphilis broke out in the South in the early seventeenth century, infected prostitutes were forbidden to serve Chinese customers and reserved for the exclusive use of foreigners.

In an effort to curb venereal diseases' inroads among the foreign population, the Municipal Council opened a hospital to inspect all prostitutes working at brothels patronized by foreign sailors. Women who were found to be infected—or who failed to appear for their weekly examinations—were to be barred from working. Only prostitutes at brothels serving foreigners were required to visit the hospital, as it was judged impossible as well as 'impolitic' to extend the measures to all prostitutes. The plan provoked criticism from the start, and from both foreign and native quarters. Some foreign residents objected to the expense of the hospital, while others opposed it on moral grounds. Could any right-minded Christian ask God's blessing "on a scheme countenancing and protecting fornication, in fact making provision for the flesh to fulfill the lusts thereof?" demanded one outraged citizen. The hospital was short-lived, closing after failing to convince the public of its value. Prostitutes themselves resented having to appear for their inspections, especially since they were required to pay for their validation tickets, upon which their photographs were affixed. Soon, however, they realized that they could use their cards and photographs to advertise their services. (The tickets, after all, certified to the fact that they were disease-free.)

If Shanghai's taipans preferred to ignore the unsavory aspects of prostitution, the same could not be said of the missionary community. Deploring prostitution's baneful effects upon not only the girls it ensnared but its customers and public mores in general, missionaries launched intense drives to ban or regulate prostitution in the port throughout the nineteenth and twentieth centuries. Nor was their crusading limited to vice. In alliance with women reformers, missionaries led a movement to end foot-binding. The custom of binding the feet of young girls so tightly that the appendages turned into hideously mutilated stumps that fit into the tiny embroidered satin shoes that were the mark of female refinement had been slavishly followed by all but the poorest classes of Chinese women since the tenth century when, as one story tells it, a pretty concubine of a Tang-dynasty emperor decided to enhance her luster by bending the toes of her feet down like the "new moon" and walking like a "waving lily." Chinese men considered a woman tottering on her crippled feet to be the height of eroticism, so much so that no girl could expect to find a husband above the coolie class without bound feet.

In fact, foot-binding was the ultimate expression of Chinese women's subordination to men—their literal crippling by society. It is a testament to the leaders of the anti-foot-binding drive that within a brief thirty years, the thousand-year-old practice had largely ceased in the most populous parts of China. As a result of the influence of missionaries and Western reformers, Chinese women grasped the possibilities for radically transforming their position in society. In Shanghai especially, a new type of Chinese female would be born. But that metamorphosis would have to wait until the next century.

If the growth of prostitution is a benchmark for the growth of individual wealth in Shanghai, then the growing use of opium is an even clearer benchmark of that wealth. Opium dens, too, licensed by both the International Settlement and the Municipal Council, and yielding substantial revenues to both, proliferated by the hundreds. Rich men took their opium while lying on silken cushions, a servant at the ready to fill their gold-encrusted pipes, while clerks and coolies went to squalid opium dens, most of which were in the same Foochow Road area as the brothels and gambling dens. They were easily identified by the acrid smell of burning opium, which permeated the alleyways. At night, customers found their way to the establishments by the dull glow of red lanterns hung above their doorways. The light of one such den on the corner of Foochow and Yunnan Roads so intrigued one missionary, John Burke, a tall preacher whose Moore Memorial Church was just around the corner from the den, that he decided to pay a call on the den's keeper. Just inside the entrance of a dimly lit room, "with a haze of smoke hovering about," Burke made out a desk piled with pipes, thimble cups for measuring opium, and a jar of the narcotic itself, "thick and dark like hard molasses." To one side was a charcoal stove with an iron pot of opium slowly boiling over it. (Wholesale opium came in balls six or eight inches in diameter, which had to be broken up and mixed with water and cooked before they could be prepared for smoking.)

To a smiling "Wanchee look see?" from the amiable den keeper, Burke stepped farther into the room, making out "a low wooden platform, a foot high and about six feet wide, built out from the walls of the room." The platforms were divided into partitions and covered with mats. On that particular night, business was booming, and a pair of men occupied each available section, the men "lying on their sides with a kerosene lamp between them." As the customers had just begun inhaling from their pipes, the missionary (who spoke the Shanghai dialect) conversed with a man who was rolling and patting a pellet of opium between his fingers, readying it to be dropped inside a bowl and heated for inhalation through his bamboo pipe.

"How long have you been smoking opium?" the missionary inquired.

"About two years," the man replied.

"What is your business?"

"I am a clerk in a food store."

"How much do you make?"

"Twenty dollars a month."

"And how much do you spend for opium in a month?"

"Perhaps ten dollars."

"Have you a family?"

"Yes, a wife and four children."

"Is it not hard to support them properly and yet spend ten dollars for opium?"

"Very hard."

"Then why do you use opium?"

"The foreign smoke is very comforting. After three smokes I can go home and sleep in great luxury."

After watching the customer sucking the opium fumes into his mouth two or three times, then lying down on his pallet, a smile of contentment on his face, the missionary was invited by the den keeper to partake of a pipe, but he politely declined. As he walked out past the red lantern ("the evil glow of hell itself"), the preacher thought sadly that the man was wasting his "time and money" on the narcotic, but blamed the existence of his habit upon the weak Chinese government and the foreigners who brought the narcotic into the country.

Some thirteen million pounds of opium, far more than in any other period, were being imported into China throughout the 1870s. More than half of it entered through Shanghai. The opium habit, far from abating, had become entrenched among the Chinese—and nowhere more than in the Whangpu port. Over the next three and a half decades before the Chinese government once again declared opium illegal in 1917, the drug's importers continued to make large profits in the opium business, the number of chests they sent into China declining after 1880 only because of the growth of a native opium crop. By this time, Chinese growers in the southern and southwestern provinces were producing a poppy crop that Chinese smokers found agreeable, and the advent of steam navigation of the Yangtze made the domestically grown drug accessible to a larger market. Authorities in Peking still opposed both opium cultivation and smoking, but in 1890, they made an about-face in their official policy by revoking the prohibition on opium cultivation. They took this action in desperation, hoping that the cheaper native opium would drive the British importers out of business altogether so that the government could reverse itself and stamp out the vice once and for all. The officials were overoptimistic. The plan not only failed, but spread the opium habit even further.

Another change in the opium trade was the withdrawal of Jardine, Matheson from the narcotics importation business. With the advent of steamships and legalization of the opium trade, the firm had lost the advantage that its fleet of speedy clippers had given it in the freebooting days. In addition, subsequent heads of the firm sought, as one historian put it, to "distance themselves from the opium trade. Peddling drugs was hardly a suitable occupation for the lairds of extensive estates in Dumfriesshire." Taking advantage of the boom times during the post-Taiping period, throughout the 1860s, the firm diversified into other, more respectable lines of business, such as textiles, real estate, insurance, and shipping.

William Jardine had barely lived long enough to see his firm shift its headquarters to Shanghai. He died in England in 1843 of a long and painful illness at age fifty-seven. The drug merchant's death had lent credence to a superstition held by seamen along the China coast that those who prospered through the opium trade would pay for their ill-gotten riches in some terrible way. On the other hand, James Matheson, Jardine's partner, defied the soothsayers. Returning to England shortly before the end of the Opium War, Matheson won election to Jardine's old seat in Parliament, bought an island off the Scottish coast, built a magnificent castle there, and lived to the ripe old age of ninety-one. Control of Jardine, Matheson fell to a partnership of nephews and other relatives of the two founders. Ironically, the nephew who inherited all of Matheson's estate, Donald Matheson, distinguished himself as a fervent opponent of the opium business: at age eighteen, after twelve years in the Jardine, Matheson China offices, he found himself so repelled by the drug business that he resigned and devoted himself to charitable works; thirty years later he was elected chairman of the executive committee of the Society for the Suppression of the Opium Trade in honor of his generous contributions to anti-opium causes.

Jardine, Matheson's move was prompted in part by competition from Chinese poppy growers, and also the cornering of the market for supplies of Indian, Persian, and Turkish opium by Shanghai's Parsi- and Jewish-owned firms. As a result, by the early 1870s, the drug trade had devolved almost completely to a handful of Sephardic Jewish and Parsi firms. Of these drug merchants, whom one Shanghailander described as "quite inoffensive [for] their raison d'être was chiefly the opium trade," the most important were the two companies founded by members of the Sassoon family, David Sassoon and Company and E. D. Sassoon. Indeed, far from being "inoffensive," the Sassoons occupied a social position that many an Englishman envied, for in England, where one branch of the family had established itself, the family enjoyed London mansions, huge country estates, titles, and the close friendship of the Prince of Wales himself.

The quintessential Oriental merchant dynasty, the Sassoons traded in everything from hides to nankeen, pearls to tea, but the foundations of the family's wealth lay in opium and cotton. The Sassoon empire stretched from London to Bombay, and from there all the way to Yokohama and up and down the China coast. "Silver and gold, silks, gums and spices, opium and cotton, wool and whatever moves over sea or land feels the hand or bears the marks of Sassoon and Company," wrote family chronicler Sidney Jackson. The Midas touch ran in the Sassoon family: for centuries, the Sassoons had been enormously successful merchant traders in Baghdad, so much so that successive generations of Sassoon patriarchs had served the caliphs as chief banker; given the honorific title "Nasi" (Prince of Captivity), the clan's head customarily rode through Baghdad's streets arrayed in robes of gold as the "crowds bowed their heads until he and his retinue had passed."

By the end of the eighteenth century, Baghdad's prosperity—and with it, the Sassoons'—had begun to decline, while anti-Semitism, from which Baghdad had traditionally been free, was on the rise. The Sassoons found themselves at the mercy of Turkish racketeers. In 1829 the founder of the family's modern dynasty, David Sassoon, fled Baghdad and set up shop in Bombay. In only a few years as a merchant trader, he had become as powerful as India's most established Parsi traders. David Sassoon and his five sons traded principally in opium and cotton, but they were always ready to diversify into nankeen or pearls or tea. They were among the first to set up branches in Canton and Shanghai when the treaty ports opened to trade. Famously secretive, cautious, and reliable, the Sassoons invested heavily in real estate for offices and warehouses—not to mention residences for themselves—wherever they settled. Scrupulously observant, they closed all of their offices, whether in London or Hong Kong, on Jewish holidays and taught their cooks wherever they went to prepare kosher food. They intermarried with other Baghdad Jewish families and occasionally with prominent European Ashkenazic families like the Rothschilds and Guinzbourgs.

The Sassoons arrived in China only a few steps behind their British competitors, legend has it, because of David Sassoon's habit of picking up his own mail at the post office in Bombay. Noticing that his chief British competitor was receiving large amounts of mail from China, Sassoon made a few inquiries, then learned of the soon-to-be-opened treaty ports. A few years after sending representatives to open up offices in Canton and Shanghai, David Sassoon sent his second son, the bearded and bespectacled Elias, to China to oversee the China branches. Deciding that Shanghai and Hong Kong offered by far the best prospects for opium and textiles, Elias spent six years in Hong Kong before establishing Shanghai as headquarters for the company's China trade in 1850. Following his father's advice, Elias bought up warehouses and wharves and also bought real estate and made investments of his own. By the end of the 1850s, the firm had a branch in Yokohama in addition to its China offices and interests in every important port in the Middle and Near East. So entrenched a commercial presence was Sassoon and Company in the East that few skippers left port in any of the places where the company had offices without first calling on the branch manager to see what cargoes the firm had for their holds.

The secret to David Sassoon's success, according to his great rival, the Parsi baronet Sir Jamsetjee Jejeebhoy, was the use he made of his sons. The patriarch believed in keeping a tight family grip over his enterprise, and luckily for him, he had no shortage of sons and grandsons. At the same time, he knew how to give his sons enough freedom that they would be encouraged to remain loyal to the family business. For instance, he paid them generously and allowed each to invest on his own so that they could amass independent fortunes. Indeed, a son was required to prove his ability to accumulate large amounts of capital on his own before he could be admitted to the firm as a partner. Rarely was an outsider allowed into the family's inner circle. The fact that the Sassoons hired exclusively Iraqi Jews and were reluctant to promote them accounted for the preponderance of former Baghdad Jews among the great trading names in Shanghai and Hong Kong. Such families as the Ezras, Kadoories, Abrahams, Shamoons, and Solomons, all of whom made enormous fortunes in Shanghai, got their start with a forebear who worked in a Sassoon's godown, counting opium chests and cotton bales. After working for a time as a clerk or warehouseman for the Sassoons, particularly in the treaty ports, employees with a nose for business often struck out on their own.

Of these, none rose higher than Silas Hardoon, a nonrelative and another Baghdadian. Long before he died in 1931, Hardoon had not only surpassed his former employers in wealth but become the richest foreigner in the Far East, with an estate valued at 150 million dollars at its height. In addition to being the richest private figure in Shanghai, Hardoon would become one of its most controversial inhabitants, so much so that "he was never seen in public without an armed Irish bodyguard." He amassed his wealth largely through real estate speculation but also through shrewd trading in cotton and opium. He started out while a teenager as a night watchman for Sassoon's in Bombay, and his nimble wits, head for figures, and ability to make himself useful to his employers so won their confidence that in 1867, when Elias departed from the family firm to start his own business, E. D. Sassoon, Hardoon immediately replaced him as manager of the Shanghai branch. Elias's decision to strike off on his own came after David Sassoon's death, and though the split in the family provided fuel for local gossip, there was enough business to go around, and both Sassoon firms prospered. Hardoon served Sassoon and Company for ten years before being lured away by Elias to take up the same position at E. D. Sassoon.

The shrewd Hardoon was able to build up his funds without risking capital of his own by persuading his employers to invest in ventures and then, if they showed promise, buying into them himself. Among the most profitable of these were properties in the Chinese parts of Shanghai that Hardoon bought cheaply but resold at astonishing prices to factory, tenement, and office building developers in the post–World

War I building boom. Hardoon left E. D. Sasson in 1920 to make even more fantastic sums in large-scale real estate speculations and public utilities. As one of Shanghai's richest foreigners, Hardoon sat simultaneously on the councils of both the International Settlement and the French Concession. Perhaps because he had started out penniless, Hardoon had a miserly streak: he wrapped himself up in his overcoat in his office on cold days rather than install heating. All his life, even as a millionaire, Hardoon personally collected rent from all his tenants, climbing the stairs of the poorest tenement to "badger poor Chinese tenants who were a day behind in their payments," said one who knew him. "If on one of these calls he found the head of the family absent he would wait in the odorous kitchen for hours." He had started out in the real estate business, and it was while collecting rent that he met his Eurasian wife, Lo Chia-ling. A beauty as well as a devout Buddhist (and, according to the local gossip, a former "flower seller," that is, prostitute, in the Chinese City), Lo so inspired Hardoon that he installed her in a twenty-six-acre estate which he called Ai-li Park—everyone else called it Hardoon Park—to the west of Nanking Road. The estate, the biggest in Shanghai, had three separate residences and what were said to be the most breathtaking gardens and pavilions in Shanghai. Though he had established a synagogue and attended services there regularly, Hardoon was also a student of Buddhism. Under his wife's influence, he established a school for monks on his estate and financed the printing of the entire eight thousand rolls of the Buddhist canon. The Hardoons also adopted some dozen orphans of various nationalities, employing private tutors to teach them to read and write English, Hebrew and Chinese.

Devoted subjects of the British Empire, David Sassoon and his sons were prominent among the Bombay citizenry who turned out at the city's Esplanade in 1837 on the occasion of the celebration of Queen Victoria's ascension to the throne. The patriarch, noted Sidney Jackson, wore a Baghdadi costume of "richly embroidered turban and flowing robes, dark in colour ... of fine material, with a broad sash at the waist" augmented by a "striped pillbox, gay with tassel." David Sassoon's sons were fluent in English and Hebrew, the two languages in which the firm's checks were stamped. Along with their Talmudic studies, they also received a thorough grounding in English history. With the exception of Elias, David Sassoon's sons were unabashed Anglophiles who aspired to all the good things that entree into London's *beau monde* had to offer. One by one, they settled in England, acquiring London town houses, vast country houses, and estates in Scotland. Doors opened to them because they had style and just enough exoticism to make them interesting. Knighthoods and baronetcies came their way as well.

Except for Elias, the Sassoons preferred London and Bombay to Shanghai. After Elias's death in 1864, his son Jacob expanded the family property holdings in Shanghai and erected on the Bund a building, Sassoon House, that was as much a monument to his family's prestige as a company headquarters. Not until five decades later would a Sassoon—in this case, Jacob's son Victor Elice—again make Shanghai his full-time residence, but when he did he would raise the Sassoon name to its full height.

In Shanghai, the two Sassoon firms were distinguished from one another as Old Sassoons (David Sassoon and Company) and New Sassoons (E. D. Sassoon). By the turn of the century, foreign opium was brought into Shanghai largely through the two Sassoon companies and two other Sephardic Jewish firms, S. J. David and Edward J. Ezra. But the profits from the opium trade were hardly confined to these companies. Even as late as 1914, when the amount of foreign opium entering Shanghai had been drastically cut, the *North China Herald* declared, "Practically every foreign bank and every big Chinese piece goods, yarn or metal dealer is involved [in the opium trade]. Thus, the whole trade of the International Settlement is interconnected with this business." The two Sassoon companies, like the other opium importers, ceased shipping the drug into China only because of an international campaign by anti-opium crusaders which pressured Britain to agree in 1907 to require its nationals to phase out their imports of opium to China by 1917. Before winding up their opium operations, the Sassoons and their fellow British-Indian drug importers had managed to realize a huge windfall from their remaining stocks by selling them for several million dollars in a corrupt deal to the Peking government. The phaseout period also gave the opium importers ample time to branch into other areas. Indeed, the enormous profits made by these firms at this time became the basis of some of Shanghai's most spectacular real estate fortunes in the next decade.

A business as appalling as either the opium or the flesh trade, and one which Shanghai gave its name to, was the entrapment or forcible abduction of men, in most cases Chinese laborers, into the slave trade. Shanghai as a treaty port was barely out of its infancy, but it had already established itself as the city par excellence of exploitation: in the city that would become China's greatest metropolis, cunning, guile, and the utter absence of scruples triumphed over all. Lack of economic opportunities in China had increasingly forced Chinese to migrate temporarily to other parts of the world—anywhere from Southeast Asia and the East Indies to the United States and Latin America—in order to better their lot. To pay for the expense of their passage overseas, many Chinese became legal "indentures"—they signed up with emigration brokers who transported them to Hawaii, Cuba, Peru, or elsewhere with the understanding that after serving a fixed period of time with an employer they would be freed and paid whatever wages they had earned in excess of the charge for their passage; there was also the "credit-ticket" system, whereby migrants borrowed their passage money from the brokers who, in return, obligated them to pay back the sum along with interest upon beginning work in the New World. In the wake of the African slave trade's near eradication, planters, mine operators, construction companies, and other employers in the Americas and Australia sought a new source of cheap labor, for which they were willing to pay between four hundred and a thousand dollars per head.

To exploit this need, Westerners in China pioneered the Eastern equivalent of the African slave trade. Borrowing their practices directly from the now outlawed business, the foreigners who masterminded the business, which they jokingly referred to as the "pig trade" to distinguish it from the "poison" or opium trade, in which the same firms (some of them the biggest and most established in China) and individuals had a hand, hired smooth-talking native recruiters ("crimps") to entice unsuspecting villagers and young men into signing away their freedom by promising riches abroad and deceiving them about the true nature of their contracts. Where trickery failed, the coolie brokers turned to outright force: able-bodied men, usually but not always laborers, were kidnapped from their homes or from the street in broad daylight and kept prisoner in "barracoons" until they could be spirited aboard ships.

The British, French, and American shipping firms whose holds carried the crimps' victims never asked whether the men had boarded of their own free will: the more bodies the ships could fit into the lower section, the higher their profits. As many coolies had voluntarily signed contracts to go abroad, authorities had difficulty distinguishing between the voluntary and the involuntary emigrants. To crimps, shipping agents, and shippers alike, as historian Lynn Pan points out, "Coolies were commodities, barely human beings." Within the holds, conditions were so abominable that a large number of the hold passengers died, some of suicide, before reaching their destination. In the 1850s, 15 to 45 percent of the emigrants traveling on ships bound for the Americas died en route. Nor did the men's suffering end there. The emigrants, especially those sent to the Caribbean and Latin America, could expect long years of "indenturement"—a period which could be extended at an employer's whim—on sugar plantations, on construction projects, and in mines. They were forced to work as many as twenty-one hours a day and routinely whipped by overseers chosen for their cruelty. Just as on the transportation boats, many men died or killed themselves—usually by hanging or drowning—rather than endure their hellish lives.

In China, anger over the scandalous traffic had long been brewing. It reached a boiling point in 1859 when riots broke out in Canton and Amoy among Chinese frustrated at both the Ching government's inability to halt the trade and the foreign governments who protected its operators through their extra-territorial status. Chinese were also inspired to take action by Ching troops' repulsion of a British attack upon the Taku forts during the first phase of the Second Opium War in June. Emboldened by that victory, laborers and their supporters gathered on the French Bund in September to prevent the sailing of a French ship upon which captive coolies were held. Presented with the crowd's demand that he release his prisoners, the ship's captain refused. In response, the now seething crowd rampaged through the concession, destroying much property, including two Roman Catholic churches. Only after the local militia was called in to assist the French was the violence quelled. Because of this, the protest leaders accused Shanghai's officials of siding with the French against their own people. The protest was Shanghai's first—but certainly not its last—demonstration of resentment of Westerners and their privileges.

Just as the foreign merchants felt there was no limit to their success, they were struck, at the end of 1864, by the city's first depression. First came a bottoming-out of the commercial markets because of the hectic overspeculation in tea and cotton of the previous two years; this was followed in December by a panic in the real estate market as, contrary to all expectation, hundreds of thousands of Chinese left the settlements to return to their homes after the Taipings had been routed from Soochow. Those who owned or had invested in the building of tenements in the Settlement were dumbfounded at this exodus as entire streets, then neighborhoods, emptied of tenants. Builders who had spent a fortune on construction materials bought at inflated prices saw their projects stopped midway through completion, and all along the waterfront stood idle wharves and empty warehouses, many of them built during the boom in the full expectation that trade would continue to spiral. Investors watched with dismay as their fortunes plummeted to barely enough to buy passage home.

After the collapse, various foreign firms, including the once princely house of Dent's, went under, and six of the Settlement's eleven banks suspended payments. Equally devastated was the Municipal Council, which had overspent in anticipation of revenues from now departed residents. "The Council have got into a sad mess in their money matters," said the British consul, Harry Parkes. "Their money, while they had a large frightened Chinese population of refugees willing to pay heavily for their protection, came in readily enough and was as readily spent, and now with a falling revenue they find themselves 90,000 taels in debt." But Shanghai had been built upon speculation: the pattern of a boom followed by bust was to be repeated every two or three decades, as, gamblers by nature, the port's residents were only too easily tempted by the prospect of quick riches.

When economic stability returned, an important new factor had come into play, one which would cement Shanghai's standing as the head of a new order: the shifting of native capital from the countryside into the city. Many of the wealthy gentry and merchant families that had sought refuge in the treaty port during the Taiping Rebellion had remained in Shanghai and begun investing in its trade and commerce, often as partners with foreigners. Native investment in foreign enterprise had begun in the 1840s with the arrival of Cantonese compradors, but the refugees from the rich cities of the delta were wealthier and commanded more prestige than the Cantonese. The Chinese from northern Kiangsu were officials and landowners—members of the gentry class—while those from Ningpo, the former medieval port of entry for foreign traders, were merchant bankers and entrepreneurs who had long played an important role in the delta's trade. In fact, the process of the Chinese elite's joining forces with the port's Westerners had begun as early as 1861, when a group of refugee gentry had financed the raising of an independent army under Li Hung-chang's command that was outfitted with foreign weapons and trained by British officers. It worked together with the Allied forces in clearing the Taipings out of eastern Kiangsu.

In the rebellion's aftermath, these landowners, officials, and wealthy merchants discovered that Shanghai offered them not just physical safety but opportunities for enhancing their wealth. Attracted by the high profits of businesses in the Western settlements, Kiangsu's gentry and Chekiang's merchants joined the Cantonese compradors in investing in myriad foreign enterprises from warehouses to shipbuilding concerns. So much native capital went into these companies that of the five new foreign insurance firms established in Shanghai and Hong Kong between 1864 and 1871, only one had no Chinese shareholders or directors. Substantial Chinese capital also flowed into the Hong Kong and Shanghai Bank, a prestigious institution founded by a group of prominent taipans in 1865 to finance the China trade. The most outstanding of the early undertakings mixing native with foreign capital was Russell and Company's floating of a steamship line, the Shanghai Steam Navigation Company, in 1862, with a capital of one million pounds sterling, of which one-third had been supplied by Chinese investors.

The migration of native wealth into Shanghai was to have a profound effect upon the port's development. Between its Western businessmen and native elite was to spring a highly profitable, though never easy, marriage of convenience. Within this partnership, too, lay the seeds of China's industrialization and modernization. In Shanghai, more than anywhere else in China, progressive-minded Chinese recognized the need for China to adopt modern enterprises and technology; they sought not only to counter the growing domination of the country's economic life by foreigners, but, more urgently, to ensure the nation's survival.

Foremost among those officials advocating a program of modernization were Tseng Kuo-fan and Li Hung-chang. Their experiences with the Western forces during the Taiping Rebellion had convinced them that China could become strong and self-sufficient only by revamping its military forces along Western lines and by developing modern industries. In 1865, using funds from the Shanghai *likin* tax, Tseng and Li opened the first Chinese arms and munitions factory, the Kiangnan Arsenal, in Shanghai as the initial venture in a national "Self-Strengthening" campaign. The man they chose to buy the arsenal's machinery in the United States was another missionary-educated Cantonese, thirty-three-year-old Yung Wing, who had the distinction of being the first Chinese to graduate from Yale. A lifelong advocate of Westernization, Yung was so proud of his American education that when he was offered a job as comprador to Dent's, he declined, explaining that "frankly and plainly . . . the compradorship, though lucrative, is associated with all that is menial" and that to become "the head servant of servants in an English establishment" would disgrace his alma mater. Despite the Civil War's having cut production of industrial machinery, Yung was able to persuade a Massachusetts manufacturer to fill the Chinese government's order. From the moment that it opened in 1865, the Kiangnan Arsenal rapidly expanded. In only three years' time, it became a huge facility, including not just a munitions factory but a shipyard and translation bureau and training school staffed by Western advisers. Visiting the arsenal shortly after its machinery had been installed, Tseng Kuo-fan "stood and watched" the equipment's "automatic movement with unabashed delight," said Yung Wing, "for this was the first time he had seen machinery and how it worked."

In 1872 Li Hung-chang started the first Chinese-owned steamship line, the China Merchants Steam Navigation Company, by persuading the government to offer start-up loans and act as patron. In his search for backers, Li shrewdly went to the element of the business community that had both the financial capacity and the willingness to invest in modern industry—Shanghai's compradors. Among the powerful circle of Cantonese compradors in particular, Li found enough sponsors that he was able to launch China Merchants within a year. Headquartered in Shanghai, China Merchants rapidly expanded to twelve ships in four years, and nearly tripled its fleet to thirty in 1877 after buying the Shanghai Steam Navigation Company from bankrupt Russell's. By this time too, it had branches in Tientsin, Hong Kong, Hankow, and Canton. It did the bulk of its business carrying ordinary freight and passengers, though it also had lucrative contracts with the government to transship tribute grain up the Yangtze to Peking.

Much of the company's success was due to the skillful management of Tong King-sing, whom Li persuaded to leave Jardine, Matheson to become China Merchant's manager. A Cantonese who "spoke English like a Briton," according to one chronicler, Tong had been exposed to Western ways from an early age and was, in many ways, typical of the treaty port compradors. Educated at a Protestant missionary school in Hong Kong, where, by his own account, he received a "thorough Anglo-Chinese education," Tong went on to become an interpreter for the Hong Kong police court and the Shanghai customs service before joining Jardine's as a salesman in the newly opened interior ports along the Yangtze. Recognizing his capabilities, Jardine's quickly promoted him, offering him the prestigious post of chief comprador in 1863. By the time he joined China Merchants ten years later, Tong was among the richest men in Shanghai, having built a fortune from investing in pawnshops, native banks, shipping, insurance, and even a newspaper. At first, Tong had invested only in traditional Chinese concerns, but even before joining China Merchants, he had realized that profits were greater in modern enterprise and had increasingly shifted his attention toward the steamship business; after 1869, he bought shares in and served as a director of two British steamship companies and invested in ships managed by other foreign firms, including Jardine's. Tong disdained the backwardness of the scholar class and, commented one historian, "never let slip an opportunity to ridicule officials and their habits." All the same, his supposed disdain for the gentry class was not so great that it prevented him from following the practice among wealthy merchants of buying himself an official's title and position.

There were others like Tong. Hsu Jun, Dent's former comprador and the principal shareholder of China Merchants, had gone into business for himself as a successful dealer in tea, silk, and produce and the owner of native banks. But alongside these traditional businesses, he became Shanghai's first native real estate magnate by buying up 455 acres of land in and around the city, upon which he built over two thousand houses yielding a yearly rental of seven thousand Chinese dollars. In so doing, Hsu pioneered an area of enterprise—real estate management—that had previously not existed, for only in Shanghai could it be said, as one proverb had it, that "ten feet of ground are more valuable than a cubic inch of gold." Setting the trend for other well-to-do Chinese, Hsu Jun built a Western-style villa on Bubbling Well Road shortly after it was opened. The mansion, complete with gables and polished marble floors, was so enormous that visitors complained of getting lost in it. And though he too had bought himself a mandarin's title and button, rather than give his sons a traditional scholar's education he sent them to England to study technological matters. In addition to China Merchants, Hsu also invested in the Kaiping Coal Mines, another government-sponsored venture.

Their openness to new ideas made compradors among the most progressive-minded of the Chinese. Not uncommonly, they could be found among the most vocal advocates of social and political change. The best-known comprador of this type was Cheng Kuan-ying, a comprador for the British firm of Butterfield and Swire who wrote a persuasive work, *Warnings to the Prosperous Age,* deploring China's backwardness and calling for Western-style reforms, among them the establishment of a constitutional monarchy. Known as the "scholar-comprador," Cheng had aspired to join the literati, but after failing the first level of the provincial examinations in his native Kwangtung, he entered trade as an apprentice at a small British hong in Shanghai where his uncle was comprador. Learning to read and speak English from his uncle and missionaries, Cheng turned his scholar's curiosity to Western literature and science. He published his first version of *Warnings to the Prosperous Age* when he was just twenty, continuing to revise it until its last and most influential version in 1893. In 1882, at Li Hung-chang's behest, Cheng resigned from Butterfield and Swire to manage another of Li's industrial endeavors, the Shanghai Cotton Cloth Mill. Throughout the 1870s and 1880s, he invested in China Merchants and other of Li's projects, and afterward he devoted himself to social criticism and the propagation of Western-style reforms.

By the end of the century, the industrial projects launched by the champions of Self-Strengthening ranged from paper mills and shipyards to an imperial telegraph service (whose first line was between Shanghai and Hong Kong). But despite the support it attracted from treaty ports' compradors, the movement was doomed from the start. One problem was the central government's reluctance to foster—indeed, even its opposition to—a genuine reform program. T'zu-hsi, the narrow-minded, capricious, and avaricious dowager empress who had dominated the Manchu court since the death of the Hsien-feng emperor in 1860, refused to recognize the need for change. Instead, she sided with the conservative forces in Peking while appeasing the "Westernizers" by giving them limited authority to initiate modernization projects. Without Peking's commitment, the dynasty's modernization program amounted to no more than a handful of uncoordinated experiments launched by a few regional viceroys.

An even more serious shortcoming was the government's failure to encourage private enterprise. Indeed, seeing the profits in industrial enterprise, T'zu-hsi and her courtiers were so eager to monopolize them for themselves that they actively discouraged competition by frustrating all private entrepreneurs. A case in point was that of a comprador named Peng who tried to set up three different textile mills with foreign backing, but had to shut down each in turn as a result of interference from local officials. Such shortsightedness was a far cry from Japan, where a rapidly modernizing Meiji government was stimulating private enterprise by subsidizing fledgling industrialists—the genesis of such giant firms as Mitsui, Mitsubishi, and Sumitomo.

A final impediment to Self-Strengthening's success lay in corruption and the government officials' proclivity for collecting "squeeze"—bribes and payoffs. Corruption and nepotism had long been endemic among Ching officials. But with the new sources of revenue made available by government-sponsored industrial projects, the pickings were even more tempting. Few officials could resist skimming profits into their own pockets. Among these, none was more the master of soliciting graft and transferring public monies into his private purse than Li Hung-chang, the "Great Modernizer" himself. Over four decades as T'zu-hsi's trusted servant, viceroy of Chihli (the metropolitan province), and patron of the bulk of industrial concerns, Li had acquired such a large fortune that by the end of his life, his wealth ranked second only to the empress dowager's. From the statesman, his associates and underlings also mastered the arts of peculation and commanding squeeze. So many were discovered reaching into the public till that a common saying was "Every dog that barks for Li is fat." The draining of government resources into the hands of corrupt officials was not the only, but certainly an important, cause of China's failure to modernize.

Ironically, it was Japan, China's former tribute-bearer, that exposed the failure of Self-Strengthening. In 1894 the newly aggressive and expansionist Island Kingdom goaded its venerable neighbor into war over Korea. China, which deployed Li Hung-chang's much-vaunted Peiyang army and navy in the war, was expected to win handily. Instead, nearly half the Chinese fleet was lost in the war's opening battle off the Yalu River in August and almost all the remainder destroyed in the final battle at Weihaiwei seven months later. The subsequent Treaty of Shimonoseki, "negotiated" between a disgraced Li Hung-chang and the Japanese prime minister Hirobumi Ito, called for, among other things, payment of an indemnity of 200 million taels, the opening of seven Chinese ports to Japanese trade, and the cession of Formosa and the Pescadores to Japan. The defeat, infinitely more shaming to the Chinese than the Opium War (in which the disadvantage of unfamiliarity with Western fighting techniques could be claimed), intensified the debate between reformers and traditionalists in Peking. It also persuaded the Ching dynasty to modernize the country's structure and take the first timid steps toward institutional reform.

As was often the case, China's loss was Shanghai's gain. It was as a result of the Treaty of Shimonoseki that Shanghai would enter its next and most spectacular economic phase, as the industrial metropolis of China, for another of the treaty's clauses was that Japan be given the right to open factories in the treaty ports. Though Japan did not immediately avail itself of this privilege, other treaty powers did.

Attracted by Shanghai's proximity to the main cotton-growing areas as well as by the availability of coal, cheap electricity, and a huge labor pool, British, American, German, and Russian firms rushed to set up cotton mills, silk filatures, and other light industries and manufacturing enterprises on Shanghai's periphery. More important, the government's opposition to native capitalism had dissolved once foreigners had been allowed to open factories.

It was members of the gentry who took the lead in launching privately owned modern enterprises. The Ching dynasty's disgraceful performance in the war had demonstrated all too clearly to the scholars and officials who considered themselves China's protectors and moral guardians the utter ineffectiveness of the previous thirty years' policy of limited modernization. Despite the foreignness of modern machinery and industrial management to their Confucian upbringing, they nonetheless believed that China needed Western factories and industrial might to survive.

To compete with Shanghai's foreign-backed factories, Chinese industrialists faced great difficulties: not only were Western factories better capitalized, but their products enjoyed the same low treaty tariff extended to Western imports. Still, with the cry "National Salvation Through Industrialization" on their lips, a handful of forward-looking members of the literati were able to raise funds to start their own factories in areas ignored by the Westerners, such as flour-milling and food-processing. Gradually, by the end of the century, as the numbers of native as well as foreign-owned factories multiplied, huge red-brick buildings spewing black smoke covered the marshes and rice paddies of Hongkew—or Yangtzepoo, as the area became known—and the poplar trees that had once lined the Yangtzepoo Road disappeared to make way for miles of wharves and clanging dockyards.

CITY OF TRANSFORMATIONS

To adherents of the old order, Shanghai was heresy incarnate. There all the old rules had been turned on their head. And those whom the old order had despised—merchants, soldiers, prostitutes, and entertainers—had risen to the top. Worse still, the inhabitants of the Whangpu metropolis had turned their backs on Confucianism, indiscriminately embracing all that was new—that is, foreign. In Shanghai, tradition had given way to the West's insidious influence, causing Tseng Kuo-fan, the champion of Chinese resistance to the Taipings, to lament, said his youngest daughter, the "dissolute and empty ways of the cities" and to warn that "troubles lay ahead."

That exemplar of Confucian virtue, had he lived another fifty years, might with slight changes have been the character Mr. Wu in the great novel *Midnight* by Mao Tun. Mr. Wu, an aged scholar and patriarch of a former gentry family, comes to Shanghai to stay with his industrialist son. Seated in a "monster of a motorcar" as it roars down down the main thoroughfares toward his son's villa, the white-bearded scholar clutches his well-thumbed copy of the *Supreme Scriptures* to his chest. As his son speaks of labor troubles and violence, cigarette in hand and bodyguard at his side, the old gentleman nervously peers out the window.

> Good Heavens! the towering skyscrapers, their countless lighted windows gleaming like the eyes of devils, seemed to be rushing down on him like an avalanche at one moment and vanishing at the next. The smooth road stretched before him and street lamps flashed past on either side, springing up and vanishing in endless succession. A snakelike stream of black monsters, each with a pair of blinding lights for eyes, their horns blaring, bore down upon him, nearer and nearer! He closed his eyes tight in terror, trembling all over.

Throughout his descent into this "sinners' paradise," Mr. Wu silently repeats the same lines: "Of all the vices, sexual indulgence is the cardinal. Of all the virtues filial piety is the supreme." Looking toward his daughter-in-law, he is dismayed to see her dressed in a "sheath of close-fitting light blue chiffon, her full, firm breasts jutting out prominently, her snowy forearms bared." The old gentleman, his "heart constricting with disgust," turns away, only to see his youngest son, Ah-hsuan, gaping awestruck at a thinly dressed sing-song girl perched forward in her ricksha; the girl, "half-naked" to the shuddering old gentleman's eyes, reveals long expanses of bare legs and thighs underneath a nearly transparent voile dress. Mr. Wu collapses upon arriving at his son's gated mansion; his heart gives out as he damns Shanghai's immorality.

Mr. Wu's sense of Shanghai as embodying all that was objectionable about China's encounter with the West was shared not just by fellow old guardists but by the rest of the country. For the Chinese, an overwhelmingly rural, traditional people, the metropolis on the Whangpu was decadent, dangerous, and full of snares for the unwary: it turned young men into gamblers, opium smokers, and gigolos; young women became the slaves of its brothels. A twentieth-century poet exhorted the young men and women "wandering in the city," "You must know that there is abundant evil in the city, whereas there is abundant happiness in the country: there is darkness in the city, brightness in the countryside; the city is meant for devils, the countryside for humans; the city air is filthy, country air fresh. Why don't you don't you pack your bags, pay your hotel bills and return to your native soil?"

In the jaundiced view of the Chinese outside the city—and doubtless of many within—Shanghai was a place of sordid pleasures and exploitation. "A furnace for the making of men" is how Chiang Kai-shek referred to Shanghai long after the future leader of the Nationalist government had ceased to frequent the city's brothel quarter or the teahouses favored by the underworld secret societies. In this respect, the Whangpu port's denigrators looked upon it in much the same way that Midwesterners might look upon New York or Chicago—as an exciting but predatory place.

However high the Whangpu port might rank on the list of the world's most corrupt and decadent spots, its reputation did nothing to prevent it from becoming the destination of so many Chinese that its population doubled in the fifteen years between 1895 and 1910 and nearly tripled in the next twenty, to three million. So well traversed were the footpaths, canals, rail routes, and riverways that led to this Asian mecca that by 1885, only one out of every ten Chinese living in Shanghai could claim to be a native son or daughter.

Just as foreigners of dozens of nationalities had found their way to the City of Mudflats, so its Chinese residents hailed from every part of the country. First had come the Cantonese, accompanying the foreign traders north; then the Ningponese, whose merchants and bankers brought their entrepreneurial prowess to Shanghai commerce and industry; then gentry from Hangchow, Soochow, Wusih, and the other wealthy cities of southern Kiangsu, who joined forces with the Ningponese to dominate the Chinese business world; and finally, and most numerous of all, wave after wave of peasants from northern Kiangsu, Shantung, Anhwei, Hupeh, and other provinces who provided the great port with an enormous and always replenishable labor force. Jostling on its narrow alleyways were immigrants from every province in the country: it was impossible to mistake the short, quick-talking Cantonese for the burly Manchurians, and just as easy to distinguish a raw-boned Shantung laborer from an oval-faced, milky-complexioned man from Hangchow or Wusih. As these outlanders in search of economic opportunity filled up the city, it seemed that the term "Shanghainese" would lose all meaning.

But in the same way that New York took in Texans, Californians, and New Englanders alike while still producing a recognizable New York type, so Shanghai absorbed the natives of all China's provinces but still gave birth to a distinct type—in fact, perhaps the most easily identified of all the regional types. First, Shanghainese were not easily intimidated. They carried themselves with a certain prideful air. Part arrogance and part vanity, their attitude revealed, above all, an unassailable confidence. Capability and adaptability were also the marks of the true Shanghainese. Still, while they were capable of hard work, a Shanghainese was not above taking the easy way out. True sons and daughters of Shanghai were nothing if not opportunistic. Shrewd, cunning, and instinctively manipulative, they were quick to recognize an advantage and seize upon it. Unlike the upright and straightforward Pekingese, the Shanghainese never hesitated to use trickery, deceit, or flattery to obtain their ends. Smooth-tongued and skilled at invective, they were also capable of insincerity.

Shanghainese had an inbred flair for the theatrical, participating in as well as watching spectacles. For this reason, as one amused American, Julian Schuman, observed, "street brawls were an accepted part of the city's life, had their own rhythm and ceremony, and never failed to attract an enchanted audience." These featured "a great deal of shouted bluster and insult, some of it fairly ingenious. But rarely was a blow struck. The conventional windup was an appeal to the galley for adjudication, which was willingly rendered and usually abided by." While observing a Chinese opera performance in a Shanghai theater, another Westerner, Ernest Peters, noted that the city's inhabitants "act so much in ordinary life, indulge in so many gestures and have such a keen sense of the drama in their everyday affairs, that the further exaggeration of their style of acting passes almost unnoticed by one accustomed to the former."

Along with their love of a spectacle, the Shanghainese put great stock in their personal appearance. Shanghainese men and women felt it beneath their dignity to appear in society looking less than perfectly groomed and fashionable. The rich considered it their duty to dress as ostentatiously as possible at all times. (And if a few Pekingese sniped at their parvenu vulgarity, all the better to proclaim their wealth.) For the sake of cutting a good figure, Shanghainese would rather do without luxuries, even necessities, than lower their standards. Or, as the Cantonese—who put food above all else—were wont to say: "A man from Shanghai would rather put oil on his head than on his food."

For all their snobbery and devotion to materialism, the Shanghainese were China's most progressive people. In contrast to Peking, which deliberately pickled itself in the past, Shanghai had schools and universities teaching Western learning, a thriving urban press, and a politically informed citizenry. And where bureaucrats and men shackled to the weight of tradition dominated the capital, Shanghai was full of innovators, iconoclasts, and self-made men. Exposure to foreign influences had given them a worldliness and a receptivity to new ideas that their country cousins lacked.

Paradoxically, nowhere was the sting of China's domination by outsiders felt more strongly than in Shanghai. All the "frictions and irritations growing out of China's modern contacts with the West" could be found there, noted one perceptive Westerner, along with "every condition caused by the impact of western political thought and material evolution on that old nation . . . in its best and worst forms." From the well-to-do merchant denied admission to the Public Garden or the ricksha coolie whom the International Settlement's Sikh police routinely seized and beat for the smallest traffic infraction, hardly a Shanghainese could be found who had not smarted from being reduced to second-class citizenship in his own country. Most galling of all to Shanghai's Chinese was the fact that while they constituted 95 percent of the foreign enclaves' population, owned 90 percent of their property, and paid at least the same proportion of their taxes, they were not entitled to the franchise. In the past, the Shanghainese had not been concerned about their exclusion from the governments of the foreign municipalities. But by the last decade of the nineteenth century, they were no longer willing to tolerate infringements of their rights.

In the deeply conservative north of China, in 1900, outrage among the distressed peasantry at the presence of foreigners in the country exploded in the misguided attempt to turn back the clock known as the Boxer Rebellion. When the Boxers, determined to rid China of all Westerners, laid siege to Peking's foreign legations, the dowager empress T'zu-hsi lent them her clandestine support. The move backfired disastrously, precipitating the arrival of a treaty powers allied force, which sacked all of Peking's palaces and private residences—including T'zu-hsi's own—and stripped them of everything of value. In their "peace" settlement, the Western powers demanded the execution of T'zu-hsi's most reactionary advisers, the suspension of the civil service examinations in forty-five cities (to punish the pro-Boxer gentry), and, most crippling of all, an indemnity of 450 million taels. This amount, in addition to the payment of exorbitant interest rates to the foreign bankers who rushed to offer loans to the Ching government, was to keep the country on the brink of bankruptcy for the next four decades.

After the Boxer debacle, a group of radical students and scholars dedicated to the destruction of the Ching monarchy descended upon Shanghai. Recognizing that the Confucian system was doomed to extinction, these disaffected sons of the literati had pointedly turned their backs on the old ways. Long before the Ching government had officially abolished civil service examinations, the only route to positions of responsibility for centuries, these students and intellectuals had sought to carve out new roles for themselves. Many had studied abroad in Japan's Western-style schools, and a small but growing number had been to universities in England, Europe, and America. Outside China they had tasted, for the first time in their lives, the forbidden fruit of freedom of political expression. At the same time, they had been exposed to a dizzying array of political philosophies—everything from Henry George socialism to Jeffersonian democracy to Kropotkinism—and returning to China, they were eager to put theory into action. Notions of liberty, equality, and the rights of man were unknown to the mass of Chinese, but in Shanghai, they were avidly absorbed by students, scholars, and other thoughtful Chinese who now looked to the West for inspiration and answers to China's ills.

In the "open and untrammeled" metropolis, as the philosopher and reformer Kang Yu-wei described Shanghai, the members of this educated elite fashioned new careers for themselves as teachers, journalists, and political activists. The delta port, of all places in China, offered this intellectual vanguard opportunities to pursue these fields. As the base of the "new learning" movement, Shanghai had dozens of modern schools, many of them founded by missionaries, others by associations of progressive or even radical-minded scholars. More important, by the end of the Boxer Rebellion, the city was also home to China's first modern press and publishing industry. It boasted several Chinese-owned dailies, scores of magazines and journals, and a large Chinese-owned publishing company, the Commercial Press. The rise of this vigorous and newly grown press was directly related to the urgency felt by the intelligentsia to rouse the public to the threat posed to the nation's existence by the jockeying of the treaty powers for "spheres of interest" in China in the aftermath of the Sino-Japanese War. The literati responded to the danger of the empire's dismemberment in the way they knew best—with words. Armed with the modern printing press—an innovation unavailable to them outside the cities—they waged their war of words with spirit and ferocity.

By locating themselves within the International Settlement, these Chinese-owned publications supposedly made themselves immune to prosecution by the Chinese government. But this was not always true. The most notorious example of Ching authorities reaching into the concessions to punish opponents occurred in 1904 over a young writer, Tsou Jung, who had published a stinging indictment of the Manchus, *Revolutionary Army*. Had the work been less widely circulated or the writing less powerful, its author might have been ignored, but the book-length manifesto, which taunted the Chinese for their compliance to outsiders and called on them to assert themselves against the Manchu "barbarians," had caught the temper of the times and sold out immediately. Embarrassed by the tract's popularity, officials in Peking pressured the International Settlement's Mixed Court—the court the Municipal Council had set up for hearing cases involving Chinese—to try Tsou Jung for sedition. In the Mixed Court, cases were tried by a Chinese magistrate with a foreign—usually British—judge standing by for consultation, but in all but the most minor cases, the foreign "assessor" actually determined the verdict. At his trial's end, Tsou Jung was sentenced to two years in the Mixed Court jail—a humiliation rather than a triumph for the Ching government, as the ordinary punishment by a Chinese magistrate would have been decapitation. If foreign Shanghai defended the Chinese press's right to free speech, it did so mainly to protect its autonomy from Chinese authority.

Ironically, critics of anti-imperialism were able to assail both foreign encroachment and the failings of the Ching government from Shanghai's settlements only because of the relative safety that foreign control assured them. Protected by Western jurisdiction, these Shanghai opponents of the Ching regime promoted their cause through articles attacking the Manchus in a newspaper, the *Su Pao* (*Kiangsu Tribune*), written by the dissidents at Shanghai's unorthodox "new-style" schools that also attracted revolutionary conspirators from throughout the lower Yangtze provinces. The members of this budding revolutionary movement had no common program and disagreed about tactics, but were united by a common hatred of the Ching dynasty and a desire to save China from India's and Africa's fate.

Wealthy men sympathized with the radicals' cause: when funds were solicited by anti-Manchu organizations at well-attended rallies at Chang Su Ho's Gardens, a park off Jessfield Road ordinarily favored by swains courting blushing young maids, collection boxes always came back filled with large donations; these included, on one occasion, a diamond ring worth a thousand dollars. Gentry and merchants supported the revolutionary movement because they too chafed at their country's subservience to foreigners and had come to favor the overthrow of the Ching dynasty and its replacement by a Western-style representative government.

Buoying the spirits of Chinese everywhere in 1905 was Japan's resounding defeat of Russia in the Russo-Japanese War: heartening proof that an Asian nation could vanquish a Western power. In that pivotal year, Shanghai was even more the center of a rising tide of nationalism as its citizens joined together to boycott American goods in protest of the American government's refusal to lift its Exclusion Act. That measure, enacted by Congress in 1882 in response to a wave of anti-Chinese xenophobia, drastically limited the number of Chinese laborers allowed to enter the United States. Cases of Chinese citizens detained and mistreated by American immigration authorities were given wide publicity in the Shanghai press, rousing popular indignation. The Shanghainese, revealing for the first time their formidable array of guilds and associations and their ability to mobilize their membership for political protest, called for a boycott of American goods and services: throughout the summer of 1905, merchants refused to sell American goods, stevedores refused to unload American ships, shopkeepers refused to serve American customers, and servants refused to work for American families.

Businessmen, with their formation of the Chinese General Chamber of Commerce in 1902, were emerging as a political force to be reckoned with. In fact, it was at a special meeting of the Chamber of Commerce that the idea of staging a boycott was suggested. One of the most persuasive voices heard at the meeting was that of Yu Hsia-ching, the eminent comprador of the Netherlands Bank, who had leaped to fame seven years earlier, in 1898, by organizing his Ningponese compatriots in the first antiforeign boycott and general strike in Shanghai to stop French Concession authorities from destroying the Ningpo Guild's sacred burial ground. Yu would go on to become a director of the General Chamber of Commerce as well as one of Shanghai's most skillful power brokers, his success deriving in part from his ability to appeal to Shanghai's various constituencies—its foreigners, with whom he had ties as a comprador to some of their most prestigious firms; its Chinese merchants, with whom he had intimate dealings; and its workers, whom he could appeal to on the basis of his own origins as one of Shanghai's many "barefoot immigrants."

With the precedent of the 1898 boycott behind them, the Chamber of Commerce, supported by nearly every guild, workers' association, and radical society in Shanghai, launched the anti-American boycott in June 1905. From Shanghai, the action spread to Canton, Hankow, Tientsin, and twenty other cities on the coast and inland, so that American trade was stymied in all of China's commercial centers. In August, the American minister to China pressured the Ching court to issue an edict outlawing the boycott, but the ban was weakly enforced; the protest continued for another month, ending only in late September when cotton merchants could no longer sustain their losses. Westerners were astonished at the boycott's strength and duration: "The Chinese have awakened to a consciousness of nationality," wrote the London *Times*'s George Morrison. "Outrages on Cantonese who have emigrated to the Pacific coast are no longer resented only by the people of Kwangtung. They make all Chinese indignant."

In Shanghai, showing the degree to which a new, more militant spirit had been aroused among the general populace, a huge crowd of several thousand ordinary citizens—workers, merchants, shopkeepers—gathered on Nanking Road in early December 1905. They demanded Chinese representation on the Municipal Council. The absence of a native voice on the body—not to mention the restriction of the franchise to white property owners—had long rankled the Shanghainese. The demonstration had been meant to be peaceful, but somehow it erupted into a full-scale riot as the crowd began pelting the International Settlement's British and Sikh policemen with rocks and stampeded the police headquarters, Louza Station, which they set on fire. The station was reduced to near rubble, and the Town Hall, where the Municipal Council met, barely escaped the same fate.

Shaken by the violence, the Municipal Council broke precedent to meet for the first time with representatives of the Chinese community, led by Yu Hsia-ching. The rare spectacle of Shanghai's taipans—dour, poker-faced men, stiff in their white collars and cravats—sitting at a conference table across from their pigtailed, flowing-robed counterparts was about all that the demonstrators received for their pains. To Yu's proposal that the Municipal Council formally adopt a "Chinese advisory committee," the taipans politely assented, then apologized when the foreign taxpayers voted the measure down soon afterward.

Bitterly disappointed, these Chinese businessmen and gentry turned their energies instead to organizing a municipal council for the Chinese-controlled parts of Shanghai. To these leaders of Shanghai's bourgeoisie denied a voice on the International Settlement's Municipal Council, the establishment of the Chinese City Council provided a taste of modern self-government. It also whetted their appetite for self-government on a larger scale.

That opportunity came in 1911, on October 10, the tenth day of the tenth month, when the accidental discovery of an antigovernment plot by the officers in the Wuchang garrison sparked an all-out revolt in Wuchang and the neighboring cities Hankow and Hanyang. Changsha, in Hunan, revolted on October 22, followed by the entire province of Yunnan on October 31. In Shanghai, after more than a decade of demonstrations and political agitation, the public was primed for its part in the revolt. Crowds milled around newspaper offices, eagerly awaiting the latest reports of developments inland; in every teahouse, market, and street-corner stall, the talk was of nothing but revolution. Republican sentiments pervaded the entire populace, so much so that the largest moderate newspaper, the *Eastern Times*, was afraid to publish anything sympathetic to the Manchus for fear of inviting a mob attack.

Swiftly, mobilization for the revolution got under way as the leading Chinese merchants pledged money and their Merchants' Volunteers for use as the nucleus of an insurrectionary force to the representative of the organization loosely responsible for the coup in Wuchang, the Revolutionary Alliance. In Shanghai, where the alliance had established a central China bureau only three months earlier, its leader was Chen Chi-mei, a thirty-four-year-old Chekiangese who had studied police and military methods in Tokyo. Drawn to revolutionary politics, like many young men of the time, he had abandoned his work as an accountant for a Shanghai silk dealer to help organize the anti-American boycott in Shanghai. In Japan, he joined the Revolutionary Alliance, an umbrella group for the numerous anti-Manchu societies.

The alliance was headed by a mustached Cantonese with a broad face, piercing eyes, and a great sympathy for the poor and downtrodden, a man who reveled in "action at all costs and whatever the risks." This was Sun Yat-sen, a visionary who lacked practical political skills but nonetheless became the hallowed "Father of the Republic" upon his death. The son of poor Kwangtung peasants, Sun had been educated at missionary schools in Hawaii and Hong Kong. After studying medicine in Hong Kong and Macao but finding only limited opportunities to practice medicine in the south, he discovered his true calling as a revolutionary in 1894. Over the next fifteen years, he staged one failed revolt after another through his Revive China Society, the first of several such anti-Manchu organizations. Declared an outlaw by the Ching government, he fled to Japan, which became his on-and-off-again base as he traveled the world, raising funds and educating himself about Western government and political theory.

The exiled revolutionary had first come to world attention in 1898, when Chinese agents kidnapped him in London and were planning to ship him back to China. The press got wind of his difficulties (through a note smuggled out by a servant) and forced embarrassed Ching diplomats to free their by then famous captive. Sun was in the United States at the time of the Wuchang outbreak, but his associates moved quickly to make the most of their opportunity: in their enthusiasm to see Shanghai delivered to the revolution, everyone from the jewelers' and paper makers' trade guilds to groups of actors and entertainers clamored for a role in the insurrection.

By far the most valuable of these offers came from an unexpected source—Shanghai's secret societies, which placed three thousand gangsters at Chen Chi-mei's disposal in the form of an auxiliary force. Most of the potential resistance in Shanghai was neutralized as Chen adroitly negotiated with the leaders of the Ching troops in Shanghai and Woosung to lay down their arms. Only the commander of the guard at the Kiangnan Arsenal, a nephew of Li Hung-chang and a die-hard Ching loyalist, refused to listen to Chen's arguments—or to take a bribe.

The Shanghai rising was set for November 3. Nearly all the shops in the Chinese areas had closed and their shutters were locked tight. Early that morning, a fire broke out next door to the police station in Chapei. The police chief, mistaking it for a sign that the rising had begun, fled into the Settlement, to be followed over the course of the morning by other important Ching officials. A public announcement of Shanghai's independence from the dynasty by Li Ping-shu, the Chinese City Council's president, was followed at four o'clock by an unsuccessful attempt by Li Ping-shu and Chen Chi-mei to raid the Kiangnan Arsenal. Chen then decided to enter the arsenal to persuade its occupants to surrender. Possessed of great self-assurance and a liking for danger, the revolutionary believed that his presence alone would win the men over. Instead, he was taken prisoner, tied up, and threatened with execution by the arsenal's commander. But the next day, another assault by the city's impromptu revolutionary army—the Merchant Volunteers and the auxiliary corps of secret society members—forced the three-man guard to surrender. The commander fled downriver in a steamer, and Chen emerged unharmed.

White flags hung from every window and rooftop the next morning as the city's euphoric citizens celebrated Shanghai's entrance into the revolutionary fold. "Everybody was excited, waiting for some radical changes that would favorably affect their lives," a Chinese correspondent recorded in his diary. The jubilation even extended into the International Settlement, where Nanking Road was strung end to end with white cloth. Newsboys selling extras announcing the arsenal's fall cried out from every street corner, and the police in the Chinese areas now wore white armbands bearing the words *kwang fu*, meaning "restoration of the Han people." Chen Chi-mei, elected military governor of Shanghai, immediately named Li Ping-shu minister of civil affairs. Other wealthy merchants—men who could be relied upon to loosen their purse strings for the new government—were also given ministerial posts.

It was the backing of these respectable, moderate-minded businessmen that had convinced the foreign consuls not to interfere with the uprising. While Li Ping-shu and the minister of finance, Shen Man-yun, a director of the Chinese City Council and manager of the Hsin-cheng bank, had already provided the funds required for the uprising, Yu Hsia-ching personally gave Kiangsu's governor one million taels to pay his troops once the province declared its independence from Peking. Once Kiangsu—and above all Shanghai, with its big moneymen and supplies of arms and ammunition—had joined the revolution, Chekiang, Fukien, Kwangtung, and Szechwan followed in rapid succession. Within six weeks of the Wuchang outbreak, Ching authority in two-thirds of the country had collapsed like a house of cards.

So no one could mistake that a new order had dawned, Shanghai's new government announced that all men were to cut off their queues—a minor revolution in itself. Though disconcerting to many, the order was duly followed—lest resisters be seized and have their queues forcibly shorn off. Police in the Chinese areas roamed the streets with large scissors or knives in hand, slashing off the pigtail of anyone foolish or ignorant enough to appear in public with his badge of Manchu submission intact. "Many a poor innocent farmer, who had never heard of revolution, found himself rudely nabbed and clipped as he came into market," related a missionary; "men tried winding up their queues and hiding them under their hats, but the shearers always took off hats the first thing." On the other hand, the streets were full of young boys rushing home from the barbershops, eager to show off "our new style of hairdressing, which used up a generous amount of vaseline to paste the short hair down," as one then eleven-year-old writer recalled, and carrying in their hands "a small package containing our pigtails, which we brought to our mothers to keep."

Equally symbolic of the rupture with the past was the demolition of the brick wall that had girded the Chinese City since the sixteenth century. Their fervent nationalism notwithstanding, progressive Chinese were embarrassed by the contrast between the cramped and fetid native quarter and the foreign enclaves' wide thoroughfares and granite and marble palaces. "When strangers first come to Shanghai, wander about the Settlement, and see how clean and broad the streets are . . . how close the houses are, like prongs on a comb or the scales on a fish," declared one *Shen Pao* editorialist, "they cannot help asking in delight: 'Who had the power to do this?' We tell them: 'The Westerners.' " It was foreigners, said the same writer, who had managed to turn "a miserable and rustic area" into "a market to which men of all nations hasten like rivers to the sea, and to which merchants come with no regard for distance. If the Chinese area is compared to the Settlement, the difference is no less than that between the sky above and the sea below."

Hopes were high among Shanghai's progressive-minded citizenry that Chinese Shanghai too could one day claim an administration as efficient and a population as prosperous as those of the foreign enclaves. More than that, they looked forward to seeing China assume a place alongside the other world powers now that it had cast off its feudal monarchy.

Still, it would take more than the bloodless changing of the guard that occurred in 1911 to bring China into the modern world. The so-called revolution fizzled almost as quickly as it had begun. Sun Yat-sen, who had returned to China, was elected the provisional republic's president; but the new government needed money, and foreign banks would make loans to China only with a military "strongman" at its head. Sun bowed out to Yuan Shi-kai, a portly general with a walrus mustache and a fondness for overdecorated uniforms, who had built up the powerful Peiyang army and alone commanded its officers' loyalty. But the sly old general was no believer in democracy. He sabotaged the effort to establish a parliamentary government by arranging for his henchmen to assassinate the man most likely to be its prime minister—Sung Chiao-jen, the candidate of the republicans' newly formed Kuomintang ("Keep the Nation Together") party. (The murder took place at the Shanghai North Railway Station as the unfortunate politician was celebrating his party's victory and was about to board the train to Peking to take up his new duties.) Then Yuan dissolved the fledgling parliament. Clearly, the beady-eyed autocrat had betrayed the revolution. Opposition to Yuan came in the form of an attempt to rekindle the flame of revolution in a poorly organized revolt known as the Second Revolution. It failed miserably, forcing its instigators, Sun Yat-sen's band of revolutionaries, to flee along with their leader to Japan.

From this refuge, Sun and his confederates sought to reconstitute their tattered cause. One of those who had followed Sun into exile was Chen Chi-mei, the "hero" of the Shanghai revolution and the city's former military governor. He had been ousted from his position by one of Yuan Shi-kai's naval commanders, Admiral Cheng Ju-cheng, after the briefest of skirmishes between the admiral's navy and Chen's poorly equipped force. But the city's Chinese, especially its wealthy businessmen, were not sorry to see him go. For all his revolutionary credentials, Chen Chi-mei was ruthless and unscrupulous, standing out, said one commentator, as "more manipulative, more of an organizer and less of an idealist" than most of those in radical circles. As military governor, Chen had surrounded himself with gangsters and corrupt cronies from his native town of Huchow, in Chekiang, and had filled city offices with them. Chen had formed his contacts with the Shanghai underworld during an earlier period in Shanghai working for a pawnbroker and silk dealer; he was said to have joined one of the criminal secret societies at that time. To head the police, he appointed an infamous gangster chief, Van Kah Der, who kidnapped rich merchants and bankers for funds to fill Chen's chronically depleted war chest. Chen's "reign of terror" also included the assassination of political opponents or critics, the most notorious being the murder of Chekiang's military governor, Tao Cheng-chang, head of the Restoration Society and one of Chen's longtime rivals for control of the lower Yangtze's revolutionary movement.

This murder was accomplished by Chen's most dedicated lieutenant, a twenty-four-year-old fellow Chekiangese named Chiang Kai-shek. The future Nationalist strongman, then a callow and wolfish-looking junior officer in Chen's revolutionary army, had slipped into a room at a hospital in the French Concession where Tao was recuperating from an illness. He was said to have exchanged sharp words with Tao, lost his temper, then killed the bedridden man with a single shot. Chiang, the son of petty merchants in a village not far from Ningpo, had been a scholarship student at a military school in Japan when he met Chen, then already a member of Sun Yat-sen's inner circle. Chen, nine years older than his fellow provincial, took the younger man under his wing. When Chen was sent to Shanghai to organize the revolution, his protégé accompanied him. The inordinately ambitious, if unpolished, Chekiangese became not just Chen's right-hand aide but his bosom companion. It was Chen who was said to have introduced his protégé to Shanghai's brothels and sing-song houses. Bitter at the revolutionaries' setbacks, Chen Chi-mei—often accompanied by his young confederate—would slip in and out of Shanghai from Japan to foment one plot after another aimed at undermining Yuan's government. On one of these visits, he arranged for the assassination of Admiral Cheng Ju-cheng, his replacement as Shanghai military governor: the admiral was shot by a marksman as he emerged from his car after it was halted by a bomb thrown by a confederate. The tactics that Chen favored were ruthless and unimaginative, but such were the methods of revolutionaries—or those who called themselves revolutionaries—of the day. Given this limited repertoire and his failure to command popular support, it is not surprising that Chen failed to undermine Yuan Shi-kai's authority in Shanghai or elsewhere.

Hubris, not the Kuomintang's thwarted conspirators, brought down Yuan Shi-kai. The militarist's great ambition was to restore the monarchy with himself as emperor of a new dynasty. A mob of his supporters—"citizens' representatives," they called themselves—gathered in Peking at the end of 1915 to call for the president to head a new "Glorious Constitution" dynasty. Yuan's announcement that he would "yield" to this public demand precipitated the collapse of not just his monarchical dreams but his government as well: one by one, his regional commanders declared their independence of his authority. An enraged and humiliated Yuan renounced his imperial aspirations in March 1916. Three months later, he was dead. The cause, declared his doctors, was "uremia of the blood brought on by nervous prostration."

Just before his death, however, Yuan had the satisfaction of eliminating at least one long-standing thorn in his side. His agents in Shanghai assassinated Chen Chi-mei, using the ruse of needing his signature on loan papers to enter his closely guarded hideaway in the French Concession, then shooting him. One of the assassins was caught and executed, but the others escaped punishment. Chen was given an elaborate funeral, complete with professional mourners carrying flowers, paper figures, and a photograph of the great man himself at the front of an elaborate procession that wound its way through the streets of Shanghai before delivering him to the train station in Chapei, where his coffin was sent to his native Huchow for burial. At the funeral, Chiang Kai-shek, haggard-looking and dressed in white calico mourning robes, cried, "Alas! From now on, where can be found a man who knows me so well and loves me so deeply as you did?"

Still, Chiang was not bereft of friends. The Chekiang bravo was taken up by another patron, and a rich one at that. This was Chang Ching-chang, or "Curio Chang," as Westerners called him, a crippled millionaire banker who had made a fortune selling Chinese curios to foreigners in Europe and was also a major shareholder in a large bean curd establishment in Paris. He had contributed heavily to the Revolutionary Alliance, giving Sun Yat-sen a check for $250,000 upon their first meeting, and later contributing $1 million more to the cause. When Chen Chi-mei was Shanghai's military governor, Chang Ching-chang had raised funds for him as his vice-minister of finance. A "kingmaker by instinct," Chang Ching-chang had taken the measure of the striving Chekiangese and decided he could make something of him.

The republican cause's deep-pocketed benefactor was also intimately connected with the leaders of Shanghai's most powerful secret society, the Green Gang. Through his new patron, Chiang Kai-shek met Huang Jin-rong, the bald, pit-faced patriarch of criminals in the French Concession whom the French had appointed their chief of police, and his protégé, Tu Yueh-sen, a sinewy wharfside tough destined to outdo his teacher to become the real master of Shanghai.

CAPITALISTS, WARLORDS, AND THIEVES

During World War I and in its aftermath, Shanghai burst with Chinese millionaire industrialists as Western businessmen left for the war front and the diminished supply of European goods boosted the demand for Chinese exports to new heights. The rich grew richer, while those with money to invest found themselves accumulating fat profits in textiles, flour milling, cement factories, tanneries, and other light industries. Industry had dramatically changed Shanghai's landscape. Directly across from the International Settlement loomed the stark wastelands of Pootung, most of this dreary industrial district discreetly obscured from the view of Bundside strollers by the Whangpu's curve. In Pootung were the factories and godowns of the big foreign firms—Jardine, Matheson; British-American Tobacco; Standard Oil—and the docks of Nippon Yusha Kaisha, Robert Dollar, and the China Merchants Steam Navigation Company.

On the Soochow Creek's north side, west of Hongkew, had sprouted the Chinese industrial area, Chapei. As native capitalism had burgeoned, so had the city's Chinese population. Chapei, the largest of the Chinese municipality's three districts—the others were Pootung, the Chinese walled city; and Nantao, the jumble of streets around the old quarter—was home to the bulk of Shanghai's working classes as well as headquarters for the larger native businesses, guilds, and chambers of commerce. Attracted by Shanghai's booming economy, so many immigrants—peasants and merchants alike—had made their way to the Whangpu metropolis that its population approached three million by the mid-1920s. Slightly more than half of this population lived in the Chinese municipality, the largest number in Chapei.

Together Yangtzepoo and Chapei comprised Shanghai's biggest industrial districts. Along Yangtzepoo's riverfront, busy machine yards resounded with the clanging of iron against metal, and at every change of shift, shrill whistles sent crowds of blue-gowned workers surging in and out of windowless redbrick and cement factories. All along the river, on either side, were cotton mills, silk filatures, and chemical and engineering works. China's largest shipyard and Shanghai's arsenal, the vast Kiangnan Dock and Engineering Works, occupied an imposing installation on the Whangpu's southern edge near Pootung, but traveling farther toward the river's easternmost end, one encountered perhaps the most awesome sight of all, the gigantic main plant and generator of the Shanghai Power Company, which supplied nearly all of Shanghai's electricity.

The new money flooding Shanghai could be seen everywhere. Modern banks founded by native financiers sprang up by the score to handle the increased capital flowing into Shanghai, and on the Bund, the Bank of China took its rightful place alongside its European counterparts in the vacated premises of the German Club. On the streets, enormous billboards advertised the Great Wall brand of cigarettes manufactured by the Nanyang Brothers Tobacco Company, the first Chinese-owned cigarette company, while young men wearing fedoras and Western-style leather shoes and pants below their cotton robes listened to the newest Chinese opera sensation blasting from a phonograph outside a Chinese theater and small hucksters yelling "Cheap sale! Cheap sale!" passed out flyers to tourists in front of a photographic supplies store.

Fast coming down were the old-fashioned tile-roofed Chinese buildings on Nanking Road, to be replaced by ten-, fifteen-, even twenty-story concrete towers anchored into Shanghai's ever-shifting subsoil by cement rafts. Overseas Chinese entrepreneurs, catering to the expensive appetites of the city's new rich, opened the city's first big department stores, which further defined Shanghai as the most stylish and up-to-date place in China, and more than that, transformed shopping from a search for necessities into a diversion in itself. Going to Nanking Road expressed the outsized getting-and-spending energy of the Shanghainese and their infinite ability to be transfixed by the next novelty, be it flocked wallpaper, French cloche hats, or toy electric trains. The two largest department stores, Sincere's and Wing On, Shanghai's Macy's and Gimbles, occupied modern reinforced-concrete buildings topped by spires diagonally opposite from each other on Nanking Road.

Filling these emporiums' shelves and display cases were goods from around the world—American cosmetics, French truffles, Scotch whiskies, German cameras, American fountain pens, Japanese toys, English leather wallets and shaving kits—alongside a bewildering array of Chinese products. But more than providing merchandise, the department stores catered to the Chinese appetite for entertainment by offering diversions galore—you could eat and drink at any one of several restaurants, play Ping-Pong, take in a Shaoshing opera or a movie, go up to the rooftop garden for a spectacular view of the city, or even check into an in-store hotel for the night. The amusement center at Wing On, an entire two floors and a rooftop of theaters, restaurants, cabarets, and game rooms, was so extravagant that one visitor declared, "To call Wing On's a department store is like calling Barnum and Bailey's an elephant show."

Inside a Nanking Road emporium, or perhaps stepping out of a shiny black motorcar, a chauffeur or husky bodyguard at her side, a woman might be seen, the daughter or concubine of one of Shanghai's nouveau riche businessmen—a comprador, banker, or industrialist. Always "expensively dressed, neatly made up, very, very pretty," as one China hand, Ernest Hauser, described the type, this lady might be wearing "a tight, ankle-length dress of light green silk, slit above the knee, with short sleeves and with a stiff little collar around her porcelain neck." Her hair was "in a permanent wave," and she was "slim and tender and aristocratic, and she made you think of Li Po, in a Chinese department store. But you would see more of them, later, at the tea dance at the Astor."

Or perhaps at the Majestic Hotel on Bubbling Well Road, which along with the Astor House Hotel hosted afternoon tea dances that became the first places where "polite" foreign and Chinese society met. At both venues, more whiskey than tea was served. These "teas" dragged on late into the evening, with drunken guests occasionally falling into the magnificent fountain that occupied the center of its clover-shaped Winter Garden ballroom. The Majestic also had a Summer Garden ballroom that bordered on a large garden designed by a celebrated Japanese landscape artist. "It was here that I first heard Vincent Youmans's 'Tea for Two,' and the combination of that melody, the moonlight, the perfume of jasmine, not to mention the Shangri-la illusion of the courtyard, made me feel that I had really entered the Celestial Kingdom," recalled Wallis Warfield Simpson of her time as a footloose soon-to-be divorcée. "No doubt about it, life in Shanghai was good, very good, and, in fact, almost too good for a woman" remarked the future Duchess of Windsor of the foreign colony's giddy social whirl.

A distinctly modern Shanghai style, one that was brash, flashy, and unapologetically luxury-loving, was emerging in the midst of this prosperity. Parties, when rich Chinese threw them, were on a lavish scale. "People vied with one another in entertaining," said one-time Shanghailander Emily Hahn. "Those were the days when families would celebrate birthdays with enormous feasts that lasted several days, importing famous actors by the troupe and having their private plays performed for the benefit of their relations." For any banquet, it was not enough to have the food prepared by the household's cooks. Instead, chefs from a half-dozen of the most famous restaurants in Shanghai would be invited to compete with one another by preparing dishes to be served at each of the tables.

"From the teeming activity of wharves, warehouses and factories to the Capuan villas of the Bubbling Well," marveled J. O. P. Bland, a journalist who had once been the Shanghai correspondent for the London *Times* and also served as secretary for the Shanghai Municipal Council. "The evidence of Shanghai's wealth, increasing and prolific, abounds on every side." Moreover, said Bland, "The ease with which money has been made, by both merchants and mandarins, is reflected in the monstrous cost of living and in a degree of luxury in some respects unequaled either in New York or Buenos Aires. I have seen something of the stupendous wealth of both these cities during and since the war. I have walked their streets and dwelt in their hotels, wondering, like a poor relation, at the princeliness of their pomp and vanities, the lavishness of their resplendent lives. But in the matter of mellow creature comforts of savoury fleshpots deftly served, no Croesus of America, North or South, can ever hope to attain to the comfortable heights and depths that Shanghai takes for granted. And neither Fifth Avenue nor the Calle Florida is in the habit of treating the dollar with quite the same splendid insouciance as Shanghai's Nanking Road."

The rich Chinese enjoyed luxury at a level unknown to or considered excessive even by the foreign taipans. They lived in the western district or the French Concession in villas set in the midst of acres of landscaped gardens shielded from view by high brick walls. The only hint of the opulence that lay within would be a pair of great iron gates set between chiseled stone gateposts and ornamented with large brass pendant knockers. Occasionally one saw a limousine purring outside the gate while retainers inside unbolted and pulled open the gates. Inside, up a graveled driveway and past bamboo pavilions and artificial rockeries, would be a many-winged house in the style of an English manor. As the household almost always consisted of not just a wife and immediate children but concubines and their offspring, relatives, and in-laws, a veritable army of servants lived and worked on the grounds—cooks, gardeners, amahs, houseboys, and coolies of all kinds.

The houses themselves had all the comforts of East and West. Their rooms were spacious and airy, heated by fireplaces in the winter and cooled by electric fans in the summer. Scroll paintings hanging from the walls and marble-inlaid mahogany furniture gave the impression, erroneous or not, that the family had illustrious antecedents, while European couches and wing-back chairs added comfort and fashionability. In addition to the conventional Chinese pavilions and rockeries, swimming pools, tennis courts, indoor gymnasiums, and even stables could be found on many tycoons' estates. Following the example of their British counterparts some well-to-do Chinese had taken up riding and attending the popular biannual meets in Kiangwan at the International Race Club, which a group of influential Chinese had established in 1911 when the Shanghai Race Club refused to admit Chinese. By the end of World War I, however, the Shanghai Race Club had opened its doors to all nationalities—largely because Chinese patronage of the race meets accounted for the lion's share of revenues.

Though alike in their wealth and desire to preserve it, these Chinese magnates were otherwise a mixed group. Some were descended from illustrious officials or had married into their families. Their Confucian upbringing notwithstanding, these highborn gentlemen, or their forebears, had the prescience to recognize that the preservation of their family wealth lay in industrial enterprise or banking. Because the Yangtze delta had always been home to some of China's most prestigious and cultivated families, many of Shanghai's leading businessmen hailed from the Kiangnan gentry. Among these, for instance, was the Pei family, owner of one of Soochow's legendary gardens. In the modern generation, Pei Tsuyee was a prominent Shanghai banker and one of the first Chinese members of the Settlement's Municipal Council; his son, the architect I. M. Pei, came to be even better known. Similarly, other of Shanghai's captains of industry had inherited their positions from fathers who had made their own fortunes. This was especially true of the compradorships of the biggest trading firms and banks; a single family's association with a firm like Jardine, Matheson or the Hong Kong and Shanghai Bank was jealously guarded, and the eldest son was groomed to replace the father as the firm's number one comprador. Still other tycoons had started out in modest, even poverty-stricken, circumstances, working hard and investing shrewdly. The most famous of these were the Jung brothers of Wuxi, Jung Te-sheng and Jung Tsing-ching, who, starting out as apprentices in Chinese money shops, rose to become China's biggest cotton and flour industrialists. Known as the "Rockefellers of China," the Jung brothers ran their sprawling empire from Shanghai.

Overseas Chinese businessmen who had made their fortunes abroad and begun investing in modern enterprises in Hong Kong and the treaty ports during the World War I boom composed yet another group of Shanghai tycoons. Almost all

Cantonese, the overseas Chinese were the most adaptable of all Shanghai's capitalists: they were quick to exploit new ideas to their advantage and shifted easily from one area of modern enterprise to another. Shanghai's most visible family of overseas Chinese magnates was the Kuo family, owner of the Wing On department store as well as of vast real estate holdings and banks, textile mills, and insurance companies, among other concerns. The founders of the Kuo fortune, again two brothers, had emigrated to Australia to work as grocers after a flood had destroyed their livelihood as farmers in their native Kwangtung and raised enough capital through their extended family to open their department store chain before branching out into real estate and cotton milling. (They owned four cotton mills in Shanghai.)

Like other Westernized Chinese, the Kuos played tennis, lived in Tudoresque villas fronted by sweeping English-style lawns, and commanded standing tables at the Majestic Hotel's Sunday tea dances. Typical of their Western orientation was their usage of their English instead of Chinese names: Kuo Le and Kuo Hsuan, for example, were better known, especially among foreigners, as James and Phillip, respectively; a younger brother, Kuo Hsun (who managed the Shanghai cotton mills), anglicized his name even further from the Cantonese Kwok Sun to William Gockson. By bringing Western commercial flair to Nanking Road, Chinese entrepreneurs like the Kuos set the tone for Shanghai's emerging middle class. As became department store magnates, they never appeared in anything that was less than impeccably tailored. The Kuo women were among the first in Shanghai to marcel their hair and wear the new knee-skimming flapper-style dresses, and their progeny became leading members of Shanghai's young "fast set."

Their wealth and prestige notwithstanding, none of these families would rise to as high a place as that to be occupied by the clan sired by one Charles Jones Soong, a Western-educated preacher turned businessman, whose offspring would dominate China so thoroughly as to be likened to an imperial dynasty. The unlikely patriarch of this latter-day "Soong dynasty" was born not Charles Jones Soong but Sung Chiao-shun, the son of a family of poor Hainan Island traders. As a teenager, Chiao-shun was sent to work in an uncle's tea shop in Boston. Despising his job, he ran away from the shop by stowing away on a Coast Guard cutter, where he was discovered, but, as luck would have it, he was taken under the wing of a devoutly religious captain. In Wilmington, North Carolina, while visiting friends of the captain, Chiao-shun, or Charlie as he would henceforth be known, declared, eyes shining and a "happy expression on his face," that he had found the Lord at a revival meeting. Within days he had not only become a baptized Christian—taking the name Charles Jones Soon—but been adopted as the ward of a Durham philanthropist and industrialist who agreed to finance the new convert's education so that he could return to China as a missionary. At both Trinity College in Durham and Vanderbilt University's theology school, the Chinese youth was popular for his good nature, directness, and sly sense of humor. ("I'd radder be soon den too late," he joked upon being introduced to strangers.)

When the time came to leave his benefactors, he did so with a heavy heart, for he had become attached to American ways and left many friends behind. Indeed, in Shanghai, where Charlie found himself in 1886, he might as well have been a foreigner, for his short, square build and unfamiliarity with Mandarin immediately marked him as a southern Chinese: when he "stalked out onto the platform" of a school at Woosung where the Methodists assigned him to teach, the boys burst into giggles, accustomed as they were to grave and slender scholars. On the other hand, Westerners—especially Young J. Allen, who allowed only Confucian-trained scholars into his inner circle—considered the Chinese preacher yet another "Chinaman."

Banished to the town of Kwinsan outside Soochow, the Chinese preacher expressed his exasperation to a fellow missionary—the tall American William Burke—upon overhearing a villager remarking about the two: "Two foreign devils! A giant and a dwarf!" At this, Charlie turned to Burke, exclaiming in indignation, "Do you see, Bill? The foreigners treat me like a Chinese and here you witness a Chinese saying I'm a foreigner." Nor did he find his work among "parishioners" redeeming. Chinese of all classes shunned Christianity as foreign barbarism; converts usually came from the poorest and most desperate class of Chinese, who sought food or other material reward from attaching themselves to the foreign missions—for which reason they were derided as "rice Christians."

Six years as an underpaid proselytizer for an unwelcome religion was more than enough to convince Charlie to give up missionary work for the business world. All around him, he saw men far less familiar with Western ways than he embarking upon careers in industry. With his American contacts, Charlie Soong—he had also added a "g" to his name so that it would conform to Chinese pronunciation—established himself as a Bible printer, comprador for a flour mill, and agent for imported machinery. Before long, he had become a prosperous Chinese burgher, a member in high standing of Shanghai's bourgeoisie. A further boost to the ex-preacher's social status came with his marriage to Ni Kwei-tseng, a missionary-educated Methodist whose forebears were one of Shanghai's oldest Christian gentry families and who had been available as a marriage partner for Charlie chiefly because her unbound "big feet" had dismayed suitors of her own class. The marriage would produce six children, four of whom, Charlie's three daughters and his eldest son, would be the basis of the future "Soong dynasty."

Critical to the elevation of Charlie's progeny and the creation of one of the most extraordinary ruling cliques in modern history was Charlie's meeting with Sun Yat-sen in the early

1890s. Charlie met the future president of the Chinese Republic during one of Sun's first visits to Shanghai, around 1890. He felt such an instant affinity to the outlawed revolutionary—who, like himself, was an overseas-educated Chinese who had converted to Christianity but who firmly subscribed to Western progressive ideals—that he immediately joined the intense "Little Doctor's" nascent anti-Manchu society. As its treasurer and fund-raiser, Charlie became an important figure in Shanghai's revolutionary underground: by day his presses turned out Bibles, but by night they spewed out anti-Ching broadsides to be distributed at the Chang Su Ho's Garden rallies not far from his printing shop on Shantung Road. Whenever the peripatetic Sun managed to slip into Shanghai, he stayed with Charlie's family in their large half-foreign, half-Chinese house in the suburbs of Hongkew, where Sun's conspiratorial society convened under cover of night. Throughout the next eighteen years, Charlie devoted himself to his good friend's cause: he was at Sun's side when Sun was elected the republic's provisional president, and also at this much earlier time, when Sun—outmaneuvered by Yuan Shi-kai—fled to Japan in 1912.

Much impressed by the self-reliant women he had met in the American South, Charlie wanted his own daughters to be equally independent: his eldest daughter, Ai-ling, became the first Chinese girl in Shanghai to own a bicycle, which she rode all the way over the fields of Yangtzepoo, over the Garden Bridge, and into the International Settlement's traffic, scandalizing the neighbors. The Soong girls attended the posh McTyeire School on Yunnan Road, which educated most of the daughters of Shanghai's Chinese elite. But rather than marrying his daughters off to the sons of other wealthy families, Charlie departed from tradition by insisting that they continue on to college—and not just any colleges, but American ones.

Fourteen-year-old Ai-ling became the first Chinese female to enroll in an American college when Charlie sent her to the

Wesleyan College for Women in Macon, Georgia, in 1904. Four years later, Ching-ling and Mei-ling, fifteen and ten respectively, joined their older sister. Though she was too young to attend college, Mei-ling had insisted upon accompanying Ching-ling to the United States. The Soongs' high-spirited youngest daughter did not like to be excluded from anything, and when upset she suffered a strange skin disorder. At home, Mei-ling had grown accustomed to having her whims indulged, and at Wesleyan she was similarly accommodated by having a special three-girl preparatory class created for her that included the college president's own daughter. Ching-ling, on the other hand, was known for her studiousness and patriotic fervor. When Charlie sent her the new flag of the Chinese Republic in 1911, the normally shy student astonished her classmates by ripping the Ching dynasty's dragon banner off her dormitory wall, stamping on it, then shouting, "Down with the dragon! Up with the flag of the Republic!"

Ai-ling went back to Shanghai in 1910. At first, she helped her father raise funds for the revolution. Then, upon Sun Yat-sen's triumphant return to China a year later, she became his English-language secretary. But when the Second Revolution failed, all of the Soongs were forced to join Sun in exile, having become publicly identified with him. They settled temporarily in Yokohama. One day, Ai-ling met H. H. Kung, the stout, bespectacled scion of a wealthy family of bankers from Shansi that claimed direct descent from Confucius; he was recently widowed, his first wife having died just before he left for Japan. In a matter of months, Ai-ling had become Kung's wife. Ching-ling, who had graduated from Wesleyan a year earlier and had joined the family just before they went into exile, took over Ai-ling's position as Sun's secretary.

When Ching-ling, a demure twenty-one-year-old who favored lacy gloves and picture hats, renewed her acquaintance with the now world-famous Sun, she carried, as she wrote a friend, "a box of California fruit to Dr. Sun from his admirers here" as well as a "private letter [of which] . . . I am the proud bearer." The entrance of this young, radiant, and ardently revolutionary female into the exiled revolutionary's life flattered him and revived his sagging spirits. "Modernization made flesh" is how one of Sun's biographers described Ching-ling's impact upon the tired fugitive. For Ching-ling, twenty-two years younger than Sun, the attachment to her "idol" was far more idealistic than romantic. She later told Edgar Snow: "I didn't fall in love. . . . I wanted to help save China and Dr. Sun was the one to do it, so I wanted to help him. On my way home from Wesleyan College I went to see him, in exile in Tokyo, and volunteered my services. He soon sent me word in Shanghai that he needed me in Japan. My parents would never consent and tried to lock me up. I climbed out of the window and escaped with the help of my amah." Once in Tokyo, Ching-ling found that Sun had hastily arranged for a marriage ceremony and even gone to the trouble of divorcing his first wife so that "scandal would not harm the revolution." Charlie followed Ching-ling to Tokyo, "bitterly attacked" Sun for betraying his trust, and attempted to annul the marriage, but failed. "When he failed he broke all relations with Dr. Sun and disowned me."

The friendship was irreparably broken—and the first link in the legendary Soong dynasty forged. Charlie would die four years later in 1918 of stomach cancer. He would witness neither the deification of Sun Yat-sen into a Nationalist icon nor the marriage of Mei-ling to Chiang Kai-shek just months after his slaughter of the Communists in Shanghai had elicited a stinging denunciation of him as the "betrayer of the revolution" by Ching-ling, who would thenceforth become her brother-in-law's most vocal opponent. While Ching-ling would cast her lot with the Communists and left-wing causes, her siblings would cast theirs with Chiang Kai-shek. Chiang's Nationalist government would bring corruption and nepotism far worse than that of the last days of the Manchus, and his wife and her family would siphon off Nanking's wealth into American bank accounts.

Of the Soong daughters whose marriages had collectively given the clan its power, a popular adage said: "One loves power. One loves fame. And one loves China." The adage referred, in order, to Ai-ling, Mei-ling, and Ching-ling. Ai-ling, while appearing to be an old-fashioned, retiring Chinese wife and mother, managed to become the single richest woman in China by, among other manipulations, speculating on the financial markets with the benefit of state secrets provided to her husband, H. H. Kung, who alternated with his brother-in-law T. V. Soong as Chiang's finance minister. A classic behind-the-scenes power broker, Ai-ling conceived of and arranged the "grand alliance," as writer Harold Isaacs described it, between the youngest sister, Mei-ling, and Chiang Kai-shek to link the fortunes of the Soongs and Kungs to the man well on his way to becoming China's new strongman. Of Ai-ling, another American, George Sokolsky, declared, "Not only do the other members of the family recognize her intellectual superiority, but even friends of the family come to her for advice, especially when a situation is ticklish or unpleasant and requires an astute mind and gentle handling. She goes to the heart of a problem, is quick and certain. It pays to be her friend." Those who offended Ai-ling, on the other hand, he noted, "find themselves unrelentingly wiped off the slate, victims of a social ostracism as potent as it is debilitating."

In H. H. Kung, Ai-ling had found the ideal partner—a husband with a prestigious name and an inordinately large fortune who bent to her will. The amiable but avaricious Kung shared with his wife an obsessive interest in acquiring money. He had the "shrewd rural-exchange merchant's eye out for quick profits in personal side deals," said Edgar Snow, but no understanding of modern banking, so that when he occasionally stood in for his talented brother-in-law T. V. Soong as Chiang's finance minister, he would create utter chaos. Aside from the fact that the two men belonged to the same family and found profit in serving Chiang Kai-shek, they had nothing in common. Whereas Kung was an old-style Chinese, Soong was the model of the American-educated businessman—impatient, efficient, and aggressive. The stocky Harvard-trained financier sought to reorganize the Chinese government's finances along modern lines but always found himself frustrated by his conservative brothers-in-law. He would frequently clash with "the General-issimo," as Chiang preferred to be called, but could always be coaxed back to one ministerial post or other, as he, like his oldest and youngest sisters, found power—and money—intox-icating. Through his control of the Central Bank of China (which some simply called "the Soong Bank") and his public offices, Soong accumulated such a large fortune that he was rumored, at one point, to be the world's richest man.

For Mei-ling, Charlie Soong's willful and pampered youngest daughter, the desire to outshine Ching-ling played no small role in her decision to marry Chiang Kai-shek, an otherwise unlikely match. When Mei-ling returned to China in 1917, she was far from the svelte and smooth "Madamissimo" she would be twenty years later when she charmed millions of dollars of Lend-Lease aid out of the American Congress. She was slightly plump and had not shed her American collegiate ways. Yet she was clever and vivacious and had a degree in English literature from Wellesley, all of which drew her immediately into "the best circles of Shanghai society." She was much sought after as a guest at the teas and dinner parties thrown by the likes of Mrs. Edwin Cunningham, the wife of the American consul, who always liked to include the wives or daughters of important Chinese among those she invited to the consul's villa for luncheon followed by mah-jongg in her boudoir. With the group of well-connected, Westernized Chinese with whom she associated, Mei-ling planned fashion shows, played tennis, and attended the gala race meets at the Kiangwan International Race Club. At the same time, as was expected of the daughter of one of Shanghai's most prominent Christian families, she engaged in church and YWCA work and even sat on the Municipal Council's Child Labor Commission.

Yet what Mei-ling really craved was luxury and excitement. Unhappy with her parents' modest home in the French Concession, Mei-ling had begged Charlie to buy a larger house— a palatial mansion on Seymour Road with formal gardens and a tennis court—but he had refused. "Don't send your children abroad," Charlie Soong said half jestingly to a friend. "Nothing's good enough for them when they come back. 'Father, why can't we have a bigger house? Father, why don't we have a modern bathroom?' Take my advice; keep your children at home!" When Charlie died a year after her return to Shanghai, Mei-ling promptly bought a villa she had had her eye on and moved her mother and brothers into it. Mei-ling always had an enormous flower arrangement in the sitting room and changed it herself daily. Visitors to the Soongs' "pretentious" residence, as one foreigner put it, were apt to find Mei-ling in semiforeign tennis togs or riding breeches (this pioneering a new path for Shanghainese women). Later, when she was the Generalissimo's wife, her expenses became legendary. She had, as journalist John Gunther observed, "numerous fur coats, fine wraps, and carefully fitted print dresses" along with "toeless shoes with spiked heels," and she "carried smart handbags, and decorated her ears with diamond clips," all of which betrayed "an expensive state of mind."

The opulent environs of Shanghai's magnates were a far cry from the muddy, grease-splattered docks along the Chinese Bund below the French Concession, where the czar of Shanghai's underworld, the illiterate but infinitely imaginative Tu Yueh-sen, got his start. As Shanghai's invisible master, Tu inspired such fear among its residents that a stream of important foreigners would cross a crowded dance floor to pay their respects—their "endless bowing and scraping" reminded one newspaperman, John Pal, of "Roman Catholics gesticulating at the altar." The son of a struggling rice shop owner in Pootung, Tu had lost both parents by the time he was nine. An uncle, a carpenter, took care of him for the next five years, during which time Tu consorted with the local delinquents and became addicted to gambling. He supported his habit by, among other means, stealing from his guardian. For this he was eventually thrown out of his uncle's house. Thus, at fourteen, already an experienced gambler and thief, Tu made his way across the Whangpu to seek his fortune in the big city—and never looked back. For a time, he worked as a fruit hawker in the warren of streets around the Little East Gate, but he lost his job because of a penchant for slinging fruit at hapless passersby and then graduated to small-time robbery, extortion, and opium dealing.

The future underworld lord had an appropriately sinister appearance. His face was pitted and mottled, like a "large-celled honeycomb," his mouth was small and twisted, and his ears were large and protuberant, for which reason he was nicknamed Big-Eared Tu. Shoulderless and wiry, Tu had a simian grace when young, but addiction to opium eventually enervated him so that his walk was more a shuffle, his long bony arms swinging like loose appendages. Strangers stiffened at the sight of the satrap's two-inch-long opium-stained nails and were startled by the emptiness of Tu's eyes: one visitor likened them to the eyes of a taxidermist's bird, while yet another described them as "so dark . . . they seemed to have no pupils, blurred and dull—dead, impenetrable."

Tu's transformation from sinewy dockside hood into the great metropolis's vice and crime king began with his joining the Green Gang, an ancient secret society that was fast becoming Shanghai's most important underworld organization, and his introduction to a character almost as menacing as Tu himself. This was Huang Jin-rong, the head of criminals in the French Concession and, simultaneously, the man whom the concession's colonial government had appointed chief of Chinese detectives. Behind his back, he was called Pockmarked Huang, because a childhood case of smallpox had left his face deeply pitted. A short, thick-waisted man with a nearly bald head and fishlike eyes set wide apart on a fleshy face, Huang looked every bit the thug that he was. Huang's father had been a Soochow police constable who had retired to Shanghai and opened a teahouse. At his father's teahouse, a favorite hangout of local gangsters, Huang had become friendly with two neighborhood hustlers, with whom he organized the loafers and ne'er-do-wells from the neighborhood into their own gang of robbers and extortion artists.

When Pockmarked Huang was twenty-four, his father used his connections to arrange for his son to enter the French Concession police force. Huang's advancement was quick. He was aggressive and fearless, but he also had the help of his petty gangsters and their followers in solving a number of difficult crimes. Before long, Huang had brought his lieutenants into the Sûreté's police force. He advanced to inspector and, a few years later, to the head of the "Frenchtown" Chinese detective squad itself. Huang brought all of the concession's criminals under his patronage by demanding a cut of their proceeds: the hooligans who made themselves at home in teahouses and refused to leave until paid to "protect" the establishment; the vagabonds and cripples who loitered outside shops until paid to leave; the thieves who lifted cargo from ships' holds and warehouses; even the pickpockets who roved the tramways, all acknowledged the pit-faced detective's suzerainty over their activities. Huang's control of crime in the concession was such that a watch stolen anywhere in its precincts could be restored to its rightful owner within twenty-four hours merely by his passing a few well-placed words to one of his mobster followers.

All of the police chief's underlings belonged to the Green Gang, by now Shanghai's biggest criminal society. An offshoot of the Triad or Red Gang, it had appealed to the same kind of men who enlisted in the Triad—peasants and out-of-work laborers—but by the end of the century it had degenerated into a frankly criminal organization specializing in drug smuggling, extortion rackets, and bribery. Since the advent of industrialization in 1895, Shanghai's exploding population swarmed with a huge and growing underclass, which provided ready recruits for the criminal organization. As with the Triad, membership in the Green Gang involved taking secret oaths and vows of unswerving loyalty to the society. Members recognized one another and assessed one another's rank and status in the organization by special signals—anything from the way in which a cigarette was removed from its packet to the direction in which a pair of chopsticks were turned, or a particular way of proffering money in payment. Betrayal of secrets or disloyalty to the organization was always met with swift and unequivocal punishment in the form of a severed ear, a broken limb, kneecapping, or death—usually violent as well as painful—itself.

Like gangsters everywhere, members of Shanghai's criminal fraternity could be easily spotted: muscular men who had a loose-limbed way of moving—as if they had spent a lifetime looking over their shoulders to see who, if anyone, was following them. Ordinary hoodlums or thugs dressed in the short coat and trousers of the working classes but could be recognized by furtive looks behind caps pulled low over their brows. The more senior members of the underworld wore long gowns and habitually left the top button of their gowns undone and rolled their sleeves up enough to show their knuckles—something no gentleman would do. Instead of caps, they wore fedoras, and beneath their gowns they often concealed knives or guns.

The Green Gang had established its ascendance over the

Triad by infiltrating the police of both settlements, which allowed its leaders to participate in—if not control outright as in Pockmarked Huang's case—the regulation of its various rackets.

Pockmarked Huang shifted between his roles as mob boss and police chief with the tacit consent of Frenchtown's authorities; so long as the most important crimes were solved, that is, those affecting French and other European interests, the French happily overlooked his other life as the concession's "capo of crime." To a lesser degree, the same understanding operated across the way in the International Settlement, where Sheng Shing-shan, the leader of Shanghai's biggest Green Gang society, the Big Eight Mob (so named because it amalgamated eight smaller gangs), headed the Chinese detective squad. Sheng's successor would be another Green Gang boss, the genial, obese, beer-guzzling Loh Li-kwei, whose long tenure would be ended only by his assassination for collaborating with the Japanese in 1938. Sheng and Loh saw to it that every Chinese detective they hired had either a Green Gang connection or a criminal record—and usually both. As one reporter explained the police chief's dual role, foreigners "figured crime was there to stay. So they decided to let the pot merely simmer, leaving it to Loh Li-kwei to see that it never boiled over." It was this thoroughly corrupt and cynical arrangement that would give Shanghai its reputation as a "fabulous gangster city . . . the biggest and wildest free-for-all, unparalleled by any other metropolis," a place so unabashedly amoral as to make "the Chicago of Al Capone appear a staid, almost pious, provincial town," as the writer Han Suyin put it. The comparison to Prohibition-era Chicago would be echoed by others—in Shanghai, "racketeering flourishes with a velvety smoothness that makes Chicago gangsters seem like noisy playboys," Edgar Snow wrote in the thirties.

To ensure that the bribes that came their way were regular and substantial, Frenchtown's officials relied upon Pockmarked Huang. For Huang, his position with the French police had the benefit of enabling him to stamp out any criminal activity not controlled by the Green Gang, and thus to consolidate his own power. So highly did the mobster–detective chief's French employers value him that they relied on his expertise to resolve cases outside of Shanghai (his biggest feat was the rescue of a French bishop kidnapped by bandits while traveling in Shantung) and even decorated him.

From the payments and bribes that came his way, Huang acquired a sizable fortune, which he invested in a string of theaters, amusement centers, gambling houses, opium dens, restaurants, and other establishments. One of these, the Cornucopia Teahouse on Rue Consulat, became his headquarters. Every morning after ten o'clock, he could be found seated at his table, where, dressed in brocaded finery and sipping a cup of tea, he heard petitioners' cases and the whispers of informants and accepted fat bags of coins and envelopes from coveys of hangers-on and "well-wishers."

There Tu Yueh-sen first presented himself to Pockmarked Huang, offering tips as a police informant. Eventually he joined the boss's swarming household of servants, bodyguards, and assorted retainers as an errand runner. Huang lived with his formidable wife, Miss Kwei, in one of several row houses that he owned on a lane off Avenue Edouard VII. A small, steely-eyed former brothel keeper from Soochow sometimes known as Sister Hoodlum, Miss Kwei advised Huang on all matters, personal and financial—and he listened. Recognizing Tu's talents, Miss Kwei used him as an enforcer and loan collector in her own various illicit enterprises, for she was as astute a business manager as her husband; in fact, she controlled the entire night soil business in Shanghai, a highly lucrative monopoly, as she collected profits from both those who gathered night soil (human manure) from the city's households and the farmers who bought it to use on their fields. At Miss Kwei's prodding, Huang allowed Tu to run a few tables in one of his gambling houses, and Tu soon graduated to managing one of Huang's bigger Frenchtown opium dens. Tu handled both assignments with such aplomb that he was put in charge of all of the Green Gang's opium dens in the concession, and he became Huang's expert on the stealing—and protection—of opium shipments on the waterfront.

By now, opium was by far the most lucrative of all the Frenchtown boss's illicit lines. The sticky poppy—or rather, the possibilities for cornering its supply and distribution—would catapult Tu from junior lieutenancy in Pockmarked Huang's organization to a position of unquestioned power over all of Shanghai. Tu glimpsed the opening of a golden door to stupendous opportunities in 1918, when Peking outlawed opium trafficking, following Britain's agreement, after intense international pressure from the anti-opium lobby to prohibit the export of Indian opium into China. By banning the opium trade, the Chinese government had unwittingly paved the way for the rise of large-scale organized crime in China's biggest city. Just as the passing of the Volstead Act in the United States would bring millions to bootleggers, so Peking's prohibition of opium trafficking would open the door to unimaginable riches and influence for Shanghai's drug czars and their henchmen. This was dictated not only by the law of supply and demand, which gangster Meyer Lansky famously encapsulated as "If you have a lot of what people want and can't get, then you can supply the demand and shovel in the dough," but also by the political circumstances of the time, which saw China plunged into civil war and Shanghai itself controlled by a series of militarists, each of whom sought control of the port's vast opium revenues.

These militarists—warlords, they were called—had come to the fore in the vacuum created by Yuan Shi-kai's death in 1916.

With the disappearance of nominal authority, these former generals and bandits all commanded personal armies and competed fiercely with one another for control of various parts of the country. In the next decade, shifting alliances of these regional strongmen would gain control of Peking and a new figurehead would be pronounced head of the Chinese republic. Some of them, like the powerful northern general Wu Pei-fu, were Confucian-trained scholars as skilled at composing verse as at planning battles. Others, however, like the Manchurian warlord Chang, who had gotten his start helping the Japanese harass the Russians, were former bandit chiefs or soldiers of fortune whom ruthlessness, cunning, and the forging of alliances with one or other imperialist power had carried to the top. Within their own territories, which could range from a township to one or more provinces, they taxed their populations mercilessly and allowed their soldiers to pillage homes and rob local granaries when they couldn't afford to pay their wages.

In addition to the blight of warlordism, bandits infested the countryside. Gangs of bandits as large as warlord armies—in fact, many were the disbanded remnants of a defeated general's force—roamed the rural areas, looting and destroying what the warlords' "soldiery" had left behind. Few Europeans had firsthand experiences with either warlords or bandits, but in 1923, the whole world came to know just how dangerous the countryside was after a gang of Shantung bandits derailed the crack Blue Express on its way from Shanghai to Peking, taking two dozen foreign passengers hostage, among them Lucy Aldrich, a Rockefeller relation and daughter of a former Rhode Island governor. The women and children were released within a few days, but the male hostages were force-marched several hundred miles through the mountains to the bandits' lair. Only after the Chinese government paid a large ransom were they freed. The incident sparked a rash of similar train derailments and kidnappings of Europeans over the next three years, including one in 1925 perpetrated by the brother of the leader of the Lincheng bandits. Because of the number of foreigners involved, the story attracted international attention and even found its way to Hollywood as the inspiration for Josef von Sternberg's *Shanghai Express.* (Lucy Aldrich, who later wrote about her experiences for the *Atlantic Monthly,* had managed to bury her diamonds under a pile of rocks on the way to the lair. Months later, armed with a map drawn by the coolheaded heiress, a clerk from Standard Oil's Tientsin office retrieved the jewels.

From the depredations of the bandits and warlords alike, all those who could fled into the cities. More important, the opium prohibition made Shanghai a prize for warlords. Between 1916 and 1926, control of the city's Chinese areas would pass through the hands of so many different generals that even its foreign journalists lost track of their comings and goings. Possession of the Kiangnan Arsenal and the tax revenue on the Chinese municipality's business and commerce alone made Shanghai desirable to the militarists, but there was another, far more compelling reason for the militarists' endless scheming to wrest the port from a rival's hands: its vast opium revenues. Whoever controlled the Whangpu metropolis instantly commanded upward of six million dollars a month in protection fees from its contraband opium distribution racket, which took the form of a syndicate organized by the port's first warlord, Lu Yung-hsiang, a paunchy and affable minor general in Yuan Shi-kai's army. Military governor of Chekiang with jurisdiction over Shanghai, Lu ran his fiefdom from his headquarters in Hangchow. One of Lu's first acts upon assuming control of Chinese Shanghai was to establish a syndicate involving the Chinese opium wholesalers—a group known as the Swatow guild, because most of its members came from Swatow—to dominate the now illegal drug trade. In exchange for sanctioning the syndicate's operations and offering the help of the militarists in his Anfu clique in bringing opium from the interior to market, Lu received a cut of two Mexican silver dollars for every ounce of the drug landed. At the same time, Lu and the Swatow merchants enlisted the Big Eight Mob to protect their opium shipments, because a host of petty gangsters itching for their own supplies of the now scarce narcotic had taken to stealing the valuable cargoes wherever they could—while the consignments were in the harbor or when they were being transferred from one address to another. For its help, the Big Eight Mob was given its own slice of the syndicate profits.

It was at this point that Tu Yueh-sen formulated the plan of bringing all of Shanghai's drug trafficking under one organization's umbrella—namely, the French Concession Green Gang. It was a daring plan and one which undoubtedly had occurred to a number of other Shanghai mobsters, but only the big boss's weasel-mouthed lieutenant had the brains, cunning, and organizational skills to carry it out. Unlike Huang, who was essentially an old-fashioned secret society man who had a flair for crime, Tu, the nimble-minded child of the Pootung slums, had both feet planted in the modern world—and that included the world of corporate business on an international level. Indeed, the findings of the Chicago Crime Commission in 1919 that "our criminals apply business methods" and that "modern crime, like modern business, is tending toward centralization, organization, and commercialization" applied equally to the organization that would emerge under Tu's aegis.

Since the syndicate's formation, Pockmarked Huang's mob had relied upon the Big Eight Mob, to which Pockmarked Huang's organization was considered subordinate, for its opium supplies. Unhappy with the amount of opium the Big Eight Mob was able to send the Frenchtown mob's way, Tu began looking for an independent source of opium. At the same time, with Huang Jin-rong's consent, he formed his own personal organization of dedicated hoodlums and thugs, whom he put to work hijacking drug consignments protected by the Big Eight Mob. Through an alliance with a fellow gangster, Chang Hsiao-lin, Tu acquired the independent source of opium he needed. Chang, a huckster and extortionist, had arrived in Shanghai from Hangchow in 1919 and made a comfortable living running brothels, gambling houses, and even a bullring in and around the French Concession. His usefulness to Tu and Huang lay in his contacts with the local warlords, including Lu Yung-hsiang himself, whom Chang had met while attending a prestigious military academy in Chekiang (which he had subsequently dropped out of in favor of a career as a professional gambler and con artist). Through Chang, who subsequently joined the Frenchtown mob as a senior member, Lu granted the Frenchtown mob—for a cut, of course—its own supply of opium to be regularly delivered to Tu's men on the Chinese City's wharves by soldiers from the local garrison command.

In 1923 Tu's grand plan moved a giant step forward with an unexpected development—the Shanghai Municipal Council's launching of a major crackdown against drug trafficking. Embarrassed by sensational accounts in the foreign press revealing the vast extent of the Settlement's illicit drug trade, the council decided it was time to clean up the enclave's image. They appointed an incorruptible British assistant police commissioner, O. M. Springfield, head of a special antinarcotics squad. Hiring a network of informers, the squad was able to ferret out the locations of the Swatow wholesalers' warehouses and stage a series of spectacular raids. Springfield prosecuted drug traffickers so zealously that he doubled the number of drug-trafficking arrests during his campaign.

The Municipal Council's efforts to stamp out drug trafficking succeeded so well that one by one, Swatow wholesalers began shifting their operations into the French Concession and the Chinese City. As the antinarcotic squad's drive was reaching its height, the Frenchtown mob found itself confronted by an unexpected dilemma—one which, for Tu, was also his long-awaited opportunity. In the fall of 1924, Pockmarked Huang was arrested by Lu Yung-hsiang for ordering his men to beat up the warlord's playboy son, Lu Hsiao-chia, after the younger Lu had booed an actress—the crime boss's current paramour, in fact—in the midst of a performance at Huang's Golden Flower theater; so badly was the younger Lu assaulted that his bodyguards—who were so afraid of Huang's thugs they dared not interfere—carried their master's inert body to his carriage. Never having had his authority challenged, the Frenchtown capo was greatly surprised two days later when a group of Lu Yung-hsiang's plainclothes detectives seized him at an evening performance at the same theater, pushed him into a waiting car, and imprisoned him at Longwha on the city's outskirts— first giving him a taste of his own medicine with a savage beating.

The big boss's arrest presented the erstwhile fruit peddler with both a dilemma and an opportunity—one which Tu would capitalize on spectacularly. Lu Yung-hsiang was in no hurry to release his prisoner, but had hinted—through Chang Hsiao-lin, who had located Huang's captors—at welcoming a large ransom payment. Ingeniously, Tu brought together Shanghai's ten biggest opium wholesalers to solicit funds for Pockmarked Huang's release, but used the opportunity to pro-pose that the wholesalers contribute equally to the formation of a cartel to monopolize all of Shanghai's narcotics market. It was the old monopoly idea, but one on a far larger scale, as the total of the wholesalers' investments would make the cartel the largest illicit business entity Shanghai had yet seen. More-over, the total of the wholesalers' investments would create a pool large enough to enlist the support of the Shanghai garri-son command in bringing opium into the port. In addition, Tu could offer the wholesalers the Green Gang's citywide protec-tion, for by that time the Frenchtown Green Gang had become the city's preeminent mob, the International Settlement's anti-narcotics campaign having destroyed the Big Eight Mob's power base and sent its leaders into the French Concession to merge their organization into their former junior ally's.

Impressed by the scope of the operation Tu had outlined to them, the Swatow wholesalers agreed to the arrangement, furnishing him with $2.7 million in backing. With this sum, the Green Gang made its initial payment to the Shanghai garrison command—a transaction handled by Chang Hsiao-lin through his warlord contacts—while Tu met with the French Concession's top authorities to make yet another, equally critical deal: for regular and substantial payments to the top consular representative and to a committee of French businessmen, Tu was given a guarantee that the French authorities would close their eyes to all the drug trafficking conducted by the members of the monopoly.

With his proceeds from the opium wholesalers, Tu was also able to ransom Pockmarked Huang. But the positions of the two gangsters had irrevocably changed. Though Tu continued to refer to Huang as his "teacher," it was Tu who had raised the money for Huang's ransom and it was also his "pupil" who had orchestrated the opium monopoly. This, along with the fact that Huang had lost much "face" and much of his following after his humiliation, forced the crime boss to step down as the Green Gang's head in favor of a triumvirate consisting of himself, Tu, and Chang Hsiao-lin. Announcing his intention to "retire" from public affairs to pursue "philanthropic" causes, Huang Jin-rong retreated to his Frenchtown estate, where he did indeed engage in worthy endeavors (donating clothes to prisoners was a favorite project), but he kept an active hand in Green Gang affairs. Moreover, showing that he considered Tu and Chang his "brothers," Huang made a present of a large lot on leafy Rue Wagner in the French Concession to his two confederates so that they could build adjoining residences.

This "trinity of scoundrels," as the powerful triumvirate soon came to be called, established the Three Prosperities Company to take in and distribute the profits from their opium monopoly. Organized like any corporate entity, the Three Prosperities Company collected thousands of dollars a month from the city's sixty opium retail shops and a tax of thirty cents per pipe smoked in every one of Shanghai's opium dens—just a few of its direct sources of income from drug trafficking. In addition to overseeing the Green Gang's narcotics operations, the Three Prosperities Company also collected revenue from the organization's myriad rackets. Its profits—an estimated 56 million Chinese dollars a year—were distributed by the three bosses to their various underlings during the three most important holidays of the year, the Spring, Dragon Boat, and Mid-Autumn festivals. So all-encompassing were the company's concerns that Chinese eventually referred to it simply as the Big Company.

What made Shanghai work was the forging of bonds among the city's most important constituencies—the underworld, wealthy Chinese, and the holders of military power, that is, warlords. Tu, more than any other personality, was a master at negotiation. He also had vision, supreme cunning, and a gambler's sixth sense. By the end of 1924, by virtue of his orchestration of the opium monopoly and the protection he extended to Shanghai's vice and criminal rackets, he had emerged as an underworld power to be reckoned with. The *North China Herald* had already described the gangster in an open letter as "the chief loafer of the French Concession, an opium and arms smuggler [who] claims Portuguese citizenship, and pretends to be immune from arrest in the French Concession for whatever he may do."

Chang Hsiao-lin's position too had improved, for his warlord connections had served the gangsters well during the period of Huang's imprisonment, which also coincided with the most intense fighting yet around Shanghai, as rivalry among Kiangsu and Chekiang warlords for control of Shanghai's opium revenues reached such a pitch that the struggle was dubbed the "opium war." The Kiangsu warlord Chi Shi-yuan, a classicist with a small face and wispy mustache who spent hours perfecting his calligraphic style, started the conflict in September 1924 by declaring war against Lu Yung-hsiang with the following public statement: "I have a beautiful Sung vase, a precious thing which it would be sacrilegious to break. Inside the vase, a rat keeps climbing to the top and sticking out its head. Now I would dearly like to catch that rat and kill it, but I might break the vase. That would be a calamity. Yet, if I turn the vase upside down, the rat will run out and I can kill it. That is what I am going to do." Over the next two months, as the two governors' forces fought each other outside Shanghai, Tu Yueh-sen and Chang Hsiao-lin aided the Chekiang governor by supplying him with trucks and equipment; Tu even sheltered one of Lu Yung-hsiang's aides and Lu Hsiao-cha—the same Lu who had instigated Pockmarked Huang's fall—at his house on Rue Doumer before the two slipped off with the elder Lu on the *Shanghai Maru* for Japan.

A warlord of an entirely different sort, and one with whom the Green Gang leaders would find an instant affinity, was Shantung's gargantuan, shaven-headed, illiterate Chang Tsung-chang, whose sixty-thousand-man army of Shantung soldiers augmented by a contingent of White Russian army recruits next swept into Shanghai. The six-foot-seven "Shantung monster" had fought his way up from poverty by working in gambling dens in his native Shantung. The son of a witch and a trumpet player, Chang was the most feared and rapacious of the warlords. Critics were instantly executed, and he encouraged his men to hang the severed heads of their victims—"open melons," they called them—from telegraph poles throughout the province as an advertisement of their abilities. Chang Tsung-chang smoked only the biggest and most expensive Manila cigars and traveled everywhere with his enormous lacquered teak coffin. Notoriously fond of food and pleasures of the flesh, the Shantung behemoth consumed huge amounts of food, which he washed down with brandy and champagne, and maintained a harem of some three dozen Chinese and international beauties to which he was always adding new recruits—each of the foreign members of the seraglio was provided a washbowl with the flag of her country painted on its side.

Chang's sixty-thousand-man army had entered Shanghai in mid-January 1925 after defeating Chi Shi-yuan and sending the erstwhile Kiangsu governor packing for Japan along the same route as his predecessor. As this army approached Shanghai from the north, from the south came another army, sent by the swarthy Fukienese warlord Sun Chuan-fang. For nearly a month, the two forces faced each other in a standoff as refugees fleeing their sporadic fighting poured into the foreign concessions. At the same time, Chapei and the other Chinese areas were again occupied by a leaderless army—this time, Chi Shi-yuan's mercenaries. Just as with Lu Yung-hsiang's army, the armed horde extorted food and money from the Chinese merchants. The guilds' reluctant charity, however, did not forestall the worst looting yet seen in the Chinese districts. According to one foreigner, "shops were pillaged; residences . . . robbed of all their belongings," and "gangs of soldiers went from shop to shop, selecting articles of gold and silver after smashing in the doors, breaking the windows and taking everything that they could lay their hands on." But by early February, Chang Tsung-chang and Sun Chuan-fang had signed a pact to govern Shanghai together. Shanghai's two new conquerors then pulled back their forces and absorbed Chi Shi-yuan's leaderless men into their own forces.

The Green Gang bosses welcomed Chang Tsung-chang with open arms: the Shantung giant not only belonged to the Green Gang but had known Pockmarked Huang as early as 1911, when he served in a regiment Huang had put at the revolutionary movement's disposal. Soon after settling into his headquarters at the North Station, Chang Tsung-chang was joined by an ally and companion in debauchery—Chang

Hsueh-liang, the twenty-six-year-old opium-addicted son of the Shantung general's Manchurian ally Chang Tso-lin. For the two Changs, the Green Gang bosses threw elaborate banquets at which the intoxicated and often scandalous cavortings of the warlord and his wastrel friend sent, related one journalist, "a delicious shiver down the spine of sated, Bacchanalian Shanghai." At one boisterous dinner party, for example, held at the home of an important Chinese merchant, the lusty general sodomized a teenage male entertainer between courses with servants, guests, and Shanghai's most expensive sing-song girls looking on. Hardly an evening went by that did not find the northern duo roistering and carousing in the company of one of the gangster bosses at Shanghai's more opulent casinos and nightspots. Chang Tsung-chang agreed to the same arrangements the ganglords had made with his predecessors for a share of the profits from the opium trade in return for his protection. Under Chang Tsung-chang's rule, conditions were not as stable as before, however, as the general's officers fought among themselves over rights to the biggest opium consignments. One of these arguments even resulted in a pitched gun battle that left one junior commander dead and two wounded.

Chang Tsung-chang's tenure as Shanghai's satrap ended in mid-October, when Sun Chuan-fang broke the January truce by moving his forces against Chang and ousting him from his position as military governor. For his part, Chang seemed only too happy to have an opportunity to return to his northern seraglio and hardly bothered to put up a fight. A progressive— at least by warlord standards—and more open to influence by the cosmopolitan metropolis than his predecessors, Sun Chuan-fang combined all the Chinese parts of Shanghai into one municipality and appointed a Western-educated doctor of philosophy to the post of mayor. Eager to shed his rusticity, he exchanged his plain khakis and breeches for an elegant Second Empire frock coat with braided gold epaulettes and replaced his soldiers' tattered cotton uniforms and straw sandals with smart tunics and leather-soled shoes. But behind the surface liberalism, Sun Chuan-fang was still an old-fashioned warlord. Almost as soon as he arrived in Shanghai, he offered the Green Gang leaders his protection of their opium monopoly in return for the usual cut of their revenues, and by the end of the year he had appointed all three bosses to advisory positions at his headquarters.

By expanding the opium trade through the distribution of factory-refined drugs like morphine, heroin, and cocaine and expanding the marketplace to include South America, Europe, and the United States, Tu brought the Three Prosperities Company fat profits and extended his narcotics-trafficking activities outside China with tentacles into every part of the world to create a huge multinational cartel. Nor did he hesitate to use violence when necessary to protect his empire of vice and crime. One crusading journalist, Bertrand Lennox Simpson, discovered too late the consequences of crossing Tu when, after reporting the quantity and dollar amount of the opium chests stored in Tu's warehouses in the French Concession in an English-language newspaper, he was visited by a quiet, scholarly-looking Chinese in spectacles who handed Simpson a calling card, then "drew an automatic pistol from inside his long native gown and shot Simpson stone dead." Simpson's murder was but one of many—and of far more prominent men—the gang master ordered. Tu found that merely suggesting an untimely demise was enough to bring an opponent to heel. Patrons of Tu's casinos late in paying debts to the house manager, for example, often found a shiny mahogany coffin delivered to their door; it was an unmistakable warning, and most debtors immediately paid up—or left town.

One reason lawlessness flourished as blatantly as it did in the treaty port was the existence of three separate and rival jurisdictions—the International Settlement, the French Concession, and the Chinese territory, each of which possessed its own government and police. Lack of a central law enforcement agency meant that a thief could escape capture simply by crossing the street from one enclave into another, because the police in the district where he had committed his crime were prohibited from following him—at least while in uniform. Consequently, "for a uniformed member of the Force to trail a Chinese suspect near the Chinese Territory is . . . quite hopeless," one British policeman lamented. Armed robbers and kidnappers and other racketeers based themselves in one jurisdiction and committed their crimes in another, thereby neatly avoiding arrest or punishment. Similarly, gambling, prostitution, or narcotics operations closed down by the police could be back in business the next day simply by setting up shop in another, more receptive enclave.

The combination of multiple jurisdictions, an amoral atmosphere, and the existence of rich pickings for the criminally inclined all combined to make Shanghai an outlaw's haven. Because of its tolerance for vice, the port attracted more than its fair share of Europeans with notoriety or scandal in their backgrounds. Western lawbreakers, enjoying the added fillip of extraterritoriality, took liberal advantage of their protection to perpetrate a variety of illegal schemes. "No one asks why anyone comes to Shanghai," one of the characters in Vicki Baum's novel *Shanghai '37* declares. "One assumes they have something to hide." Most of the shady characters who found their way to the Eastern port were guilty of nothing worse than a run-of-the-mill swindle, but every so often, an internationally known criminal washed up in Shanghai. One of the most famous was Courtney C. Julian, a Canadian-born oil promoter who had convinced legions of American investors—including several prominent movie stars and moguls—to buy stock in his fraudulent oil wells. When the stock was discovered to be worthless, Julian fled to Shanghai. Because he was a Canadian citizen who had committed a crime in the United States, he could not be extradited. Telling Shanghai's American authorities to "go to hell," he proceeded to live the high life, spending lavishly on liquor and women. In the end, running out of both funds and friends, Julian took his own life by downing a bottle of sleeping pills.

In Shanghai, the law could be bent in ways beyond counting. Often, those in charge of enforcing the law were the very ones doing the bending. For a time, one of the most popular ways for a consul to build up his bank account in Shanghai was to sell passports or citizenship certificates to Chinese seeking to elude the arm of Chinese authority. The possessors of these documents supposedly could be tried or sued only in a consular court, not in a Chinese court. The "diplomats" selling these questionable passports represented countries with few, if any, nationals in China, such as Chile, Lithuania, Mexico, and Portugal. Indeed, the sole reason these diplomats were in China appeared to be to sell papers to criminals and lawbreakers. Business was brisk. "For one hectic period, a certain South American consul was selling citizenship rights to Chinese for two thousand local dollars and building up a string of 'protégés' among the drug and gun peddlers," related one newspaperman. Moreover, nearly every Shanghai gangster of any status found it obligatory to purchase a foreign passport. In the late 1920s, however, the diplomatic corps in Peking put its foot down on the entire scheme, revoking the consular privileges of the more notorious passport-sellers and nullifying the second nationalities of numerous less than respectable Chinese.

Foreign gunrunners and arms and munitions agents also hid behind extraterritoriality's skirts. When China became a signatory to the International Arms Embargo Agreement of 1919, a veritable horde of arms dealers descended on Shanghai hoping to unload their huge inventory of surplus World War I weapons on Chinese customers. Sinister-looking German, American, British, French, Italian, and Swiss arms dealers appeared in the lobby of the Astor House and Palace hotels to dangle fat catalogs of their wares before the eager eyes of any buyers. The members of this nefarious brotherhood openly flouted China's prohibition against arms trading—and without the interference of their consuls. Typical of the breed was a man described by a Shanghai journalist as "a well-groomed American with a Stutz roadster and a fat expense account, who sold tommy guns between cocktails at the country club and champagne parties at Del Monte, the city's gayest cabaret, conveniently located just over the boundary in Chinese territory. His tommy guns were just trade samples for the police forces. He had a two-million-dollar cargo of heavier stuff on a ship lurking in the Yangtze estuary." The high-living American and his fellow arms dealers made enormous profits supplying gangsters and warlords with everything from Mauser automatics—the gun of choice among criminals—to heavy field guns. As a result of the sudden abundance of weapons in China, the crime rate shot up dramatically during the 1920s, with armed holdups and kidnappings commonplace.

Consular protection also supported many of Shanghai's most popular lotteries and gambling establishments. Organized gambling flourished in the port on very likely the largest scale of any city in the world. Among Chinese, the passion for gambling approached a national disease. Countless families were ruined because of the head of the household's gambling habit, and stories of men throwing themselves into the Whangpu or otherwise committing suicide after a gambling loss were common. Even in imperial times, the government had attempted to ban gambling dens, but the taste for speculation—whether at cards, mah-jongg, lotteries, or cockfighting matches—could not be suppressed.

Both the International Settlement and the Chinese districts prohibited commercial gambling, but some of Shanghai's biggest and most lavish gambling operations did an enormous business year after year by claiming the protection of a foreign government that sanctioned gambling. By this means, the Portuguese and the Spanish consuls respectively sheltered highly popular Portuguese and Philippine lotteries in Shanghai, and casinos "owned" by a Spanish, Portuguese, or Latin American national openly flouted antigambling ordinances. Claiming extraterritorial protection enabled the International Settlement's most lavish casino, the Wheel, which was "owned" by a Mexican national, Carlos Garcia, to stay in business for years. A popular place for Shanghai society swells to while away the night, the Wheel had three roulette tables as well as a free buffet and bar. (For his elite clientele, Garcia spared no pampering; he even sent patrons home in chauffeured limousines and taxis.) Whenever the Wheel was raided by the Shanghai Municipal Police, Garcia "cheerfully paid his fine and went his way," said Shanghai chronicler John Pal, because the casino was so successful that he could afford to pay a fine every day and still not have an appreciable loss. If by chance the International Settlement's authorities managed to close him down, he simply opened up a new establishment in the same neighborhood.

At around the same time that the Green Gang was sinking its roots into Shanghai, the city's infamous nightlife was also being born. Incongruously, the Chinese City had the Bolshevik Revolution in Russia to thank for the first of what would be some three hundred cabarets at the peak of Shanghai's career as the jazz age capital of the Far East.

After the Bolsheviks took power in 1917, czarist loyalists, White Russians, waged a futile struggle against the Red Army for over a year before finally being cornered in their last stronghold in Siberia. When the Whites were finally ousted from Vladivostok, in 1919, the defeated supporters of the czar began pouring into China, and especially into Shanghai, in large numbers. They were hardly welcomed with open arms by Shanghai's caste-minded foreigners. Always careful to preserve the appearance of their superiority to the Chinese, the entrenched Westerners found their inundation by so many desperate and impoverished immigrant Westerners deeply embarrassing. While the better-off émigrés had brought jewels, heirlooms, and furniture that they were able to sell for funds and so survive temporarily, many of the newcomers had no funds and spoke no English, the lingua franca of European Shanghai.

A Russian Relief Society set up by the small group of Russians already in Shanghai sprang into action to provide food, clothing, and temporary shelter for the destitute arrivals. Nonetheless, the White Russians eventually had to find work. Some of the men among the first group of refugees to arrive in Shanghai had been professors or musicians in Russia, but most were Cossack officers or soldiers who had nothing to offer except their fighting skills. The Shanghai Volunteers formed its first paid regiment, a uniformed White Russian battalion, from these remnants of the czarist army, and the Shanghai Municipal Police hired many as policemen. Other Russian men became watchmen, janitors, riding instructors, doormen, groundskeepers, and bodyguards to rich Chinese or joined the warlords' armies as mercenaries. Failing to find even this kind of employment, a few Russian men even tried their hand at pulling rickshas.

Worse still, because the Russian imperial government had been dissolved and they declined Soviet citizenship, the White Russians had no extraterritorial protections—they, unlike the rest of the foreign community, were subject to Chinese law. Some turned to crime as burglars or pickpockets, but when arrested they were sent to the Chinese court—and if found guilty, to the Chinese prisons, where they received the same miserable treatment as Chinese malefactors. Others sank even further into degradation, joining the most desperate of the Chinese, the beggars, on public streets. "One sees them living under worse conditions than the poorest Chinese coolies," observed a foreign policeman. "Losing all self-respect, they cease to care whether they live or die, and when they have begged twenty cents from someone, they spend them on a concoction far worse than methylated spirits or even petrol. Having swallowed this awful stuff, they lie dead drunk in the streets until arrested by the police."

The sight of drunken Russians on the streets, their legs intertwined with those of Chinese mendicants, did much to destroy the prestige of the white man in China. Chinese found the behavior of the Russians unfathomable. "How fashion Russian man no got money so self can buy chow?" one American woman's amah asked her as they drove past a line of Russians waiting for food in a soup line. "My think Russian man b'long velly common—b'long [is] all same coolie." Hoping to shore up the white man's fast-sinking "face," a group of taipans tried to persuade the diplomats of the treaty powers to ship the émigrés en masse to Australia or New Zealand, only to have the idea rejected as impractical.

The female émigrées rescued their families from near starvation, and Shanghai entered the era of the nightclub, when Chinese and foreign entrepreneurs, taking shrewd note of the city's influx by white women in desperate need of employment, hired them as dancers and singers in the tawdry cabarets they were throwing up in Chapei. Barely more than one or two rooms in a tenement building where the walls had been knocked down to make room for a dance floor, a few small tables, and a Filipino band, these establishments were located in a warren of narrow alleyways that also housed brothels, opium dens, and gambling houses. The area soon came to be known as the Trenches for the brawls that broke out every evening over the favors of the new arrivals. Many of them were "blonde, beautiful, and bewitching in the eyes of young and exiled Englishmen and Americans," according to one writer. The Russian sirens were soon attracting the attention of not just the Western bachelors from the settlements but young Chinese blades as well, all of whom joined the sailors and marines in competing for the chance to twirl one of the "voluptuous vampires from Vladivostok" around the dance floor. "For these spectacles, the local Chinese gendarmes stood around the doorways every night, rifles slung across their shoulders, grinning at the goings-on," noted the same chronicler. "Cavortings like these they had never seen."

At first, the girls worked for drinks and commissions. Between dances, they did their best to persuade the customers to buy drinks—and while the hostesses were served cider or ginger ale, the drinks appeared as champagne on the bill. The hostesses mastered the few words of English necessary for survival. These included "Allo," "Good-bye," "Please," "You nice," and the all-important, "My prince, please you buy little Sonya one small bottle vine." Soon the girls were making enough money to take care of several refugees. "I knew of one little dancer who kept eleven adults going for months," said one female correspondent, who found most of the dance hostesses to be "nice girls" and "much better in family background, culture and character than their wealthy and important dance partners." Rather than bemoaning their fate, the Russians simply tossed their waved tresses and forged bravely ahead. "Some Asiatic fatalism in the Russian spirit enables a woman to lift her shoulders and with the old gesture say, 'Nichevo! It does not matter,' " explained Edgar Snow. "She puts a genuine gaiety into the experience and laughter on her lips."

Work as a barmaid or entertainer among a clientele that included the dregs of international society was not the worst fate that could befall the women. The least attractive or more unfortunate turned to outright prostitution. "Houses of prostitution sprang up like mushrooms and Russians formed the basic contingent," said Vera Akimova, a Russian revolutionary passing through Shanghai. Russian women also staffed the newly opened "massage parlors" on North Szechwan Road in Hongkew and on Avenue Joffre in the French Concession; massage, of course, was the least of the services the masseuses offered their customers. Like the dance hostesses, the Russian prostitutes served all comers, irrespective of race or color. You saw them, night after night, "standing at the entrance to their houses and inviting all and sundry to enter," said a policeman. Other Russian girls and women could be found at the "many low-class cafés and cabarets near by the dockside frequented by sailors and seamen of all nationalities." Russian streetwalkers, the lowest of the prostitute class, plied their trade in Hongkew, where Chinese as well as foreigners lived, and in the streets facing the Bund. They walked the "same beat for months and even years," said the policeman. And "in spite of repeated arrests, they still carry on in the same place."

The appearance of Russian women in brothels and as streetwalkers was yet another shattering blow to white prestige in China, so much so that the League of Nations formed a committee to investigate the problem of "white slavery in China." True, Shanghai had an oversupply of Russian hostesses and prostitutes, but nearly all of them had been forced into their professions by lack of other options. Indeed, many had come down to Shanghai from Harbin—a city known as "the distributing center of white women throughout the Far East" for its large numbers of Russian-staffed brothels and cabarets— in search of fresher opportunities. Not that overzealous brothel operators did not practice aggressive tactics in recruiting the more comely new arrivals to their establishments—more than one attractive Russian female, arriving alone at the passenger jetty, found herself offered a ride to a hotel by a chivalrous-seeming compatriot, only to find the "hotel" to be a whorehouse. Members of the League of Nations white slavery committee found "extensive prostitution among Russian girls and women" forced by competition with native prostitutes to "offer themselves to Chinese irrespective of the latter's social position." Decrying the Russian refugees' willingness to provide sexual services to lower-class Chinese as "disgraceful," the League maintained that such a situation could only "have a demoralizing effect on women and girls of other Western nationalities in China who are very often in the same unfortunate position as the Russian women and girls."

Not that male Shanghailanders had done without foreign ladies of easy virtue before the Russian invasion. Along the short stretch that included Kiangse Road behind the Bund and its curve into Soochow Road just behind the creek could be found "the Line," a neat row of brick houses making up Shanghai's foreign red-light district. The Line's history went back almost as far as the treaty port's, and its bordellos rivaled the best to be found in San Francisco or New Orleans for their luxury and hospitality. These establishments were run by legendary madams whose names were familiar to ship captains and merchants up and down the China coast—and, as from the nearby Public Garden, Chinese were barred from admittance. The most expensive of the Line's houses, at 52 Kiangse Road, was managed by a statuesque American, Grace Gale (or such was the name she took), whose cleverness and accomplishments could easily have made her the wife of a wealthy businessman at home, but perhaps an adventurous streak or a family scandal had made her come all the way to Shanghai. Gracie's stock in sin was American girls, at least a dozen of which she always had on hand at any particular moment. American women, in fact, formed the chief nationality along the Line; this was because a steamship ticket from San Francisco to Shanghai was half the cost of a ticket from Paris, London, or any other source of recruits to the trade. Indeed, the words "American girl" became so commonly associated with foreign prostitutes that every ricksha puller in Shanghai knew to take his fare to Kiangse Road once the words were uttered.

Gale approached her business with the same high regard for the quality of her merchandise that a jeweler would give his diamonds. She sent out engraved cards announcing the arrival of each new recruit and made regular trips to San Francisco for trunkloads of dresses to make her girls showpieces for the newest fashions. No ordinary bordello, Number 52 was furnished with Chippendale and contained what was reputed to be the most extensive English library in Shanghai. Some of the best meals to be had in Shanghai were served at the house's celebrated parties: Gale employed the former chef of the Imperial Russian Legation in Peking, who was as capable of whipping up crispy fried chicken as beef bourguignon—always accompanied by liberal amounts of the finest French wines. So powerful a draw was an evening event at "Gracie's" that no society lady could hope to attract one of the town's more eligible bachelors to a dinner when "the lads were planning an evening down the Line."

As the Moët flowed, antics in the drawing room became exuberant and uninhibited—as on the evening when redheaded "Lotus" from San Francisco danced "the cancan on a polished table top, with a champagne bottle hugged to her breasts and her magnificent hair shimmering halfway to her pink-nailed toes," as one appreciative celebrator recounted. Indeed, so much admiration did Lotus and her sisters in sin arouse among the Line's patrons that they regularly left their profession to marry well-heeled clients. Shanghai's madams took Cupid's incursions into the ranks of their employees in stride—after all, variety added spice to their trade. Besides, they always kept their eyes open for new "talent"—one madam, the mistress of the International Settlement's chief of police, approached a visiting Margaret Sanger in a tearoom to leave her card: the admiral of the British fleet, the madam informed the birth-control advocate, was dropping anchor in Shanghai in the next few days, and the demure-looking Sanger happened to be "just his type."

Hardly apologetic about their profession, the Line's always stylishly turned-out residents could be seen strolling down the Bund on any given day on the arm of young bankers or clerks, or dining in restaurants with prominent businessmen. However, the more straitlaced members of the American colony condemned the ladies of the night for "blackening the good name of American womanhood." They had even found a champion in the early teens in an American judge, Lebbeus Redman Wifley, who served subpoenas on the American prostitutes on the Line, threatening to jail them on vagrancy charges unless they left Shanghai. But the girls—or their madams—were one step ahead of the judge: instead of leaving port, they switched nationalities by marrying themselves to sailors to whom they had paid anything from one hundred to one thousand Chinese dollars for the privilege. No longer American citizens, they could pursue their professions free of Wifley's harassment. So unpopular did Wifley make himself with his many reformist campaigns that he was eventually sent back to the United States and replaced by a more tolerant jurist.

But Russian pulchritude succeeded where Wifley had failed. The Trenches were soon followed by dozens of nightclubs, cabarets, and dance parlors in the International Settlement and French Concession, which also featured the Russian women, by now well groomed and polished, as dance hostesses and floor show entertainers. Nightspots with floors shining for the foxtrot and entertainment provided by Russian orchestras sprang up on Bubbling Well Road and Avenue Edouard VII. For foreigners, the better cabarets offered a welcome alternative to club life and the stuffy tea dances at the Astor House Hotel and Majestic Hotel around which the foreign colony's social life had previously revolved. Nonetheless, the nightclubs catered chiefly to affluent bachelors, for which reason the Little Club advertised in a Shanghai guidebook that it offered "fifty charming fairies," while the Ambassador boasted of its "one hundred prettiest dance hostesses in all Shanghai." Their male clientele too was the reason why the cabarets staged lavish floor shows in which the girls performed everything from the Carioca to the Parisian Apache and dressed in the most risqué costumes the club owners could think of, from spangled harem costumes for a mock "Dance of the Seven Veils" to swimsuits.

Among the most popular of the dance revues was the Paramount Peaches, a team of a dozen Russian lovelies managed by Joe Farren, an Austrian who had begun his show business career in Vienna with a circus before drifting to Shanghai, where he found plentiful opportunities for his impresario abilities.

There were all kinds of nightclubs. Some were posh and expensive, like the ornately decorated Majestic Café with its high chandeliers, polished dance floor, and "American" orchestra as opposed to the Russian or Filipino musicians who performed elsewhere. Others attracted customers with their questionable locale or quirky offerings. Del Monte's, a dimly lit roadhouse café across a small bridge in the Chinese territory, specialized in predawn ham and eggs and was usually packed by three on any Sunday morning with everyone who was anyone in Shanghai; the same Russian waitresses who served the food also danced with customers for tickets and in a late floor show. At the Canidrome, right across from the dog-racing track, patrons could dance and watch greyhounds at the same time. St. Anna's Ballroom, not far away on Love Lane, had a miniature golf course. Outdoing its competitors as far as variety was concerned was the Carlton Café, owned by Al Israel, a former San Francisco saloon operator whom Prohibition had driven out of San Francisco. In Shanghai, Israel was known as the "Ziegfeld of the East" for the extravagant floor shows he staged with his own company of *artistes*. Israel also ran contest nights, awarding prizes to his guests for best or most elaborate costumes, chosen by popular vote; he also installed a movie projector in one part of the Carlton and staged boxing matches on his roof garden "bloody enough to call down the wrath of the Municipal Council." At the bottom end of the cabaret spectrum were the cheerful if cramped sailors' cabarets on Rue Chu Pao San, otherwise known as Blood Alley, behind the French Bund, where the girls behind the bar would shake dice with customers for drinks and dance to the music of a player piano.

Whether cabarets were "high class, low class or no class," as one Shanghai wag described them, the basics never varied. The hostesses, or "taxi dancers" as the girls working at the lesser establishments were called, danced for tickets—anywhere from ten cents to a dollar depending upon the quality of the club—and a share of all the drinks their customers bought. They sat around small tables to one side of the room, getting up to meet a customer halfway as soon as one approached. Afterward, "perhaps she might persuade him to buy her a drink," said an Englishwoman, describing the usual sequence of events. "And they would sit down and have a drink. Then they would dance a bit more and if they wanted to go and do other things, perhaps that was on the cards as well." Soon, every other man had a leggy Russian Venus as his mistress—or was looking for one. The advent of the Russian dancers spelled the end of the foreign-only bordellos, as love now came not only more cheaply but on a democratic basis as well; a man could support a mistress for a month on the cost of a single night at Number 52 and the Russians had dispensed with the color bar, instead distributing their favors to Occidentals and Orientals alike. "Love," said the wags, "came in only one color—green."

The Line's madams and its "American girls" were not the only casualties of the cabaret boom. The foundations of family life in the foreign colony were firmly shaken as husbands began divorcing their wives to marry the Russian entertainers and bachelors broke off engagements with fiancées back home for the same reason. And the Russians were only too eager to latch onto a foreign husband in order to secure a passport—as White Russians, the exiles were a stateless people. British passports were the most coveted, a circumstance which accounted for the higher incidence of divorces among British couples in

Shanghai. "The conduct of the pretty Russian women refugees in China has precipitated a crisis in the homes of British and American residents," opined the London *Daily Express*'s correspondent. "British wives in Shanghai declare that these fascinating rivals from Russia and Siberia, possessing no fortune other than face and figure, have lured husbands away from them and broken up their homes." One British judge told the correspondent that "most of the divorces he has tried recently have been [due] almost entirely to the fascinations of these Russian refugees who are characterized as 'real vampires' of the kind made famous in films."

The domestic turmoil also found its way into the local press, where British women "attacked the morals of the Russians and demanded their expulsion from China," with the Russians responding by calling the British wives "flat-chested, flat-footed, worn out by hunting, hockey and golf." Alliances between bachelors and the alluring émigrées were similarly frowned upon—employers went so far as to frustrate the wedding plans of such couples by transferring the employee to a branch office in a distant outpost.

In the meantime, Shanghai's nightlife was undergoing yet another revolution with the wholesale embrace of jazz by younger Chinese. From the moment the first nightclub opened, Chinese students and the sons of the idle rich had taken to the dance floors in such numbers that they outnumbered the foreigners. And after the novelty of dancing with White Russians wore off, they sought Chinese dancing partners. But the still powerful arm of Confucian propriety forbade any respectable girl to venture into anyplace as scandalous as a nightclub, no matter how sumptuously appointed the establishment or how many White Russian bouncers hovered at the door. To fill the gap, a group of enterprising Cantonese went into the nightclub business. They opened a string of cabarets featuring Chinese dancing girls, which quickly became so popular that they were drawing not just Chinese crowds but foreign sailors, soldiers, and tourists as well. The typical Chinese cabaret was even louder, bigger, and more brightly lit than the foreign ones. "It is usually decorated to the remotest corner, with perhaps a half a dozen incongruous and clashing types of Western ornamentation fighting for honors," remarked one Westerner. The orchestra was invariably Filipino and could be found ensconced "rather lackadaisically" on the bandstand, "pumping away at a tune-a-minute rate continuously between the hours of eight and two, three or four o'clock."

But the draw that soon had the Chinese dance palaces outnumbering the foreign ones was their Chinese taxi dancers and hostesses. The girls, "slim, self-possessed and self-sufficient to the *n*th degree," sat in rows on chairs next to the bandstand, "acting for all the world as if they were really just waiting for a street car and no amount of dance tickets could tempt them onto the floor." The taxi dancers' uniform was a dress that would become the signature of the modern Chinese female, the *cheong-sam* (long dress), to use the Cantonese term, or, in Mandarin, the *chi-pao.*

An adaptation of the Manchu Bannerman's gown—a long tunic with a slit along the sides that was worn over trousers—the new style *chi-pao* was a clinging sheath slit at the ankles—or higher—to reveal the once forbidden legs. Exactly who created the dress is unknown. One story has it that a Chinese actress who complained that she couldn't dance the newly introduced Charleston was advised by the bandleader of the Majestic Hotel orchestra to cut slits in her long dress. The actress was said to have caused such a splash on the dance floor that the rest of Shanghai's fashionable ladies followed her cue. The American writer and advertising agency owner Carl Crow speculated that Chinese women converted to the *chi-pao* upon realizing the superiority of their legs when Shanghai's foreign women began sporting the new flapper-style short skirts. Chinese females studied "the passable legs of the French women, the generally unattractive legs of the British and American, the fat legs of the German and Scandinavian, the atrociously ugly legs of the Japanese, and came to a sudden though centuries behind realization of the fact that here was an asset overlooked." Then, Crow continued, "they hit on a very happy solution, a long skirt with the left side slit to a point above the knee so that every alternate step revealed the contours of a beautiful leg. Old-fashioned fathers and a few jealous husbands raised the very devil about the scandalous style, but the girls liked it so well that the next season they slit both sides of the skirt."

Along with the skirt came leather high heels. Perhaps it had something to do with foot-binding, but for some reason, Shanghai's fashion plates preferred to wear the highest heels they could endure. As they had with the *chi-pao*, Chinese men welcomed the imported style in female footwear. Returning to Shanghai after studying in the United States, a student was delighted to find that "here, there, and everywhere on the streets high-heeled shoes adorned the dainty feet of young women." Whenever he heard "quick heels tapping the sidewalks," he thought of how "radically different" the new generation of women in China was from the old.

Clad in a *chi-pao* slit to the hips, her usually small feet encased in a pair of high heels, even the plainest taxi dancer was equipped—should she desire to do so—to dazzle her customers. The most popular girls always came late and, by custom, sat in the back row. Nor was it necessary for them to be overly proficient dancers; the chief requirements for being a top hostess were beauty and sex appeal. Any man who approached one of these haughty glamour girls with less than three or four dance tickets was likely to have them ripped up in his face. Nightclub managers coddled these women, relations between the two resembling those between "an opera impresario and a prima donna," as the notoriously temperamental hostesses were known to "quit on the drop of a watermelon seed." Like

Above: Pedestrians on Nanking Road. ***Below right:*** *Nanking Road, Shanghai's answer to Fifth Avenue and Oxford Street. The thoroughfare as it appeared in the late twenties with the spires of the Wing On and Sincere department stores in the background.*

Above: Panoramic view of the Bund. Among the buildings are (from left): the Hong Kong and Shanghai Bank with its distinctive dome; the Customs House with the clock on its tower ("Big Ching") prominent; the Palace Hotel; and the Cathay Hotel with its pyramid top (Victor Sassoon's penthouse suite).

Above: The first Shanghai Club, built in 1864, was typical of the colonial-style architecture that then dominated. The building was replaced with an even more solid-looking structure in the next century.
Left: Children at play in the International Settlement's "Public Garden." Chinese and dogs were not permitted to enter the park. *Below:* Crowds milling on a terrace at the Great World Amusement Center. To the right is a prostitute accompanied by her amah.

Above: One of the two opium hulks—dismantled sailing ships used to store the drug—moored to the Bund. From the opium trade's legalization in 1860 until Britain agreed to end importation of British Indian opium into China, these ghostly-looking structures marred the Bund's foreshore. *Right:* Shanghai's professional beggars were almost an institution. At one point they had a king (pictured here)—"a regal sort of personage in spite of his rags," said one who knew him. He trained aspiring mendicants, tried disputes, and made laws.

Above left: Sun Yat-sen, visionary revolutionary, and his wife, Soong Ching-ling, the second of Charlie Soong's remarkable daughters. (World Wide Photos) Above right: China's leading "strong man," Chiang Kai-shek, weds Shanghai belle Mei-ling Soong in a packed ballroom at the Majestic Hotel, December 1, 1927. "Don't marry that butcher," the bride's sister Ching-ling had wired her from Moscow. (World Wide Photos)
Left: Tu Yueh-sen, "Master of Shanghai." (Photograph taken in the thirties.)

Above: Blood was said to have flowed in Chapei's gutters for days after Tu Yueh-sen's gangster toughs slaughtered striking labor unionists and leftists in the "Shanghai massacre" of 1927.

Left: Police arresting two young suspected Communists in the aftermath of Chiang Kai-shek's 1927 coup.

Above: Another suspected leftist, possibly a student, being questioned by Nationalist soldiers on a Shanghai street. *Left:* American writer Emily Hahn with Mr. Mills, the Singapore gibbon that accompanied her to Shanghai's poshest social events. *Below:* A bevy of White Russian "bathing beauties" exposing their charms on the nightclub floor-show circuit.

Above: By the thirties, the Shanghainese had adopted Western notions of feminine beauty and sexuality. Here, a poster display of "modern" Chinese girls. *Left:* "There's only one race greater than the Jews, and that's the Derby," maintained Sir Victor Sassoon. The magnate owned a large stable of racehorses in Poona and Shanghai. *Below:* "Black Saturday"—August 14, 1937. Chinese planes accidentally bombed the busiest parts of the city, killing or wounding nearly two thousand Chinese and foreigners. It was the worst civilian carnage in a single day in World War II up to that point.

Above: Nanking Road outside the Palace Hotel on August 14, 1937. Left: Refugees streaming into Shanghai during the Japanase invasion. Below: The economic chaos. Inflation-wary depositors withdrawing their funds from the National City Bank of New York's Shanghai branch.

the most famous courtesans at the higher-class sing-song houses, a girl who rose to the top of the taxi dancing profession could expect to marry or become the concubine of a rich man. She might be photographed for the cover of a Chinese calendar, be gossiped about by Shanghai's tabloid-style "mosquito" press, or if she was very lucky—or had a well-connected patron—be signed up as an actress by a movie studio.

Such at least were the hopes of the scores of country girls arriving in Shanghai every year with the intention of streamlining themselves into Chinese-style flappers. A small industry had come to revolve around the training and upkeep of dancing partners for Shanghai's nightclubs. There were hundreds of dancing academies that trained girls to do the waltz, foxtrot, and tango; beauty parlors that marcelled their hair and taught them how to lengthen their eyebrows and powder their faces; and labor contractors who specialized in bringing potential taxi dancers into the city—for payments of upward of fifty dollars from the girls. True, taxi dancers could earn anywhere from a hundred to a thousand dollars a month, far more than they could expect to make as factory or domestic workers. But once the novelty of the nightclub setting wore off, the dancers found the work grueling and tedious. Occasionally, a taxi dancer did indeed strike it rich, but for the most part, Shanghai's five to ten thousand professional dancers had few real alternatives once their looks had faded. Moreover, organized crime had its tentacles in the nightclub business, so the girls frequently worked under pimps who forced them into prostitution.

Despite competition from Chinese taxi dancers, the old-fashioned teahouses still flourished, but the sing-song girls too found themselves adapting to modern tastes. The entertainers added Western melodies sung to Chinese lyrics to their repertoires of Chinese opera arias, exchanged their loose Chinese gowns for the sleeker *chi-pao,* and went to their appointments in rickshas "lacquered to a mirrored gloss" and brilliantly lighted by battery-powered headlamps fore and aft. While the more traditional sing-song girls could still be summoned from teahouses, now many made the leading Chinese hotels their headquarters. Every evening, they would stop by to see what "calls" they were to make for the evening. Then, "from hotel to hotel and restaurant to restaurant, these little butterflies of Oriental song dashed through the milling crowds responding to calls with all speed in order to collect as many appearance fees as possible in a night." Often, as one sing-song girl was arriving, another was leaving, because it was common to invite several entertainers to brighten up a party.

The taxi dancers, like much of the Shanghai public, took their cues from Hollywood. The female entertainers as well as shop girls and college students learned American slang from James Cagney, styled their hair like Jean Harlow, and aped Mae West's walk. From the moment that motion pictures—"electric shadows" (*dian-ying*), as the Chinese called them—appeared in Shanghai at the turn of the century, Chinese flocked in such numbers that the city supported more than a dozen first-run movie theaters. So important were Chinese movie audiences that each of the top Hollywood studios maintained a publicity and distribution office in Shanghai, in this way ensuring that *Honeymoon Express, The Law of the Lawless,* or *So This Is Paris* opened in Shanghai only shortly after its American premiere. By the early 1920s, a few Chinese entrepreneurs, all from Shanghai, had begun turning out a domestic crop of movies. The Ming Hsing (Star) Company, perhaps the most successful, was started by the head of an amateur theatrical troupe, Chang Shih-chuan, whose uncle happened to overhear two foreigners — who had just acquired film equipment—discussing in a hotel their search for Chinese actors. Imitating their foreign competitors, these Shanghai-made productions tended to be escapist fare—comedies, melodramas, and historical romances. Despite their lack of experience and their limited financing, these movie companies took on the same glamorous aura that surrounded Hollywood's biggest efforts. "Ambitious young men and women flock to Shanghai's studios, looking for fame and fortune," reported one American correspondent. "Willing to work for rice money in hopes of getting a break," they "haunt the studios." And when some drop out, "others take their places."

The stars of Shanghai's movies grew to be every bit as famous as the big names of the American screen. They appeared on magazine covers, became public idols, and set the tone for fashion. But for many, as with their Tinseltown counterparts, success led to unhappy, even tragic, personal lives. There was, for instance, Chou Hsuan, a slender, milky-faced woman dubbed "Golden Voice" by her fans. She was an orphan who worked as a serving maid, but her talent at singing and dancing won her a part as a character whose experiences paralleled her own in *Street Angel*, a film regarded as one of the classics of Chinese cinema. In the film, the actress played a prostitute and street entertainer victimized by men. Chou's life was much the same: overworked by the studios and exploited and abused by the movie moguls, she attempted suicide and eventually was committed to a mental institution.

Far more sensational, however, was the life of the actress called "China's Garbo"—Ruan Ling-yu. The daughter of a poor Cantonese mechanic who died when she was a child, the slender, waiflike Ruan was raised by a devoted mother who saved every penny from her job as a housemaid in order to send her daughter to school. At seventeen, in 1927, Ruan sought work as an actress to relieve her mother of her support. An air of sadness and mystery—while living with the family that employed her mother, she had been raped by their son—made Ruan an instant success. The actress went on to star in twenty-six more films in the next nine years. In 1930, as Chinese moviemakers were beginning to address the country's pressing social and political questions, Ruan left the commercial-minded Ming Hsing Company to join the more progressive Lianhua Film Company.

There, her roles of victimized women echoed her own history much as Chou Hsuan's did. In *The Goddess*, one of her most celebrated parts, for example, she played a mother who, unable to find any other work, becomes a prostitute so that she can send her son to school. In 1935, despairing over gossip in the mosquito press about her personal life, Ruan took an overdose of sleeping pills. Her suicide note said only, "Gossip is a fearful thing." Lamenting her death in an essay, the great writer Lu Husan assailed those who drove the actress to suicide.

If the problem of women's oppressed position appeared to preoccupy some of Shanghai's most talented filmmakers, it was because the issue so urgently required addressing. To be sure, Chinese women had long been freed from the purdah of the inner courtyards and no longer hobbled on mutilated feet. The breaking of these feudal chains began with the 1911 Revolution. Girls were encouraged to enroll in modern schools to become educated citizens and also to participate in athletics to make their bodies strong, as their patriotic duty. "Girl students" in their utilitarian school uniforms were fixtures at Shanghai political rallies and even marched in military drills at radical schools. The more earnest of these New Women made no concessions to the old ways. Some, like Chiu Chin, a celebrated revolutionary and early feminist, even went so far as to dress in Western men's suits—complete with fedora. Far more common than the militant "emancipated woman," however, was the urban sophisticate who bobbed and waved her hair, shod her unbound feet in leather high heels, and revealed her natural contours in a figure-clinging *chi-pao*. To outsiders, these Europeanized females appeared to epitomize the New Woman. But in fact, such women tended to be society women, concubines, or entertainers, that is, women whose livelihood or support depended upon catering to men—a situation that placed them squarely in the old society's sexual caste system. For a woman to forge a different path, to become a Chinese George Eliot or Marie Curie, for example, was even more daunting.

For the educated female coming of age in China during the turmoil of the 1920s, the problem had no clear solution. But if there was anyplace where a woman could grapple with the issue, it was Shanghai. To the citadel of progressiveness and the capital of style came women seeking emancipation and excitement, many of them graduates of the modern girls' schools that had sprung up throughout the country. Some became students, surviving on small remittances from their families; some took part-time jobs as salesgirls or teachers in workers' schools. They often had intellectual or artistic ambitions and belonged to the city's decidedly left-wing bohemian circles. One could see them strolling down North Szechwan Road and stopping in at a Chinese teahouse to debate philosophy, politics, theater, free love, and feminism. Their heroine was Ibsen's Nora, a woman who gives up being her husband's "doll" to make her way alone in an unknown world. But, as all too many found, except for teaching jobs in girls' schools and factory work, "respectable" jobs for women were almost nonexistent. The alternatives for independent females were jobs as domestics, actresses, or entertainers, or those linked in one way or another to the sexual services industry. By the 1920s, moreover, in addition to the traditional brothels and teahouses, this area had expanded to include masseuses, female "guides," and striptease performers.

Of course, not all women allowed themselves to become victims. The clever ones used their sexuality to their advantage. Ironically, perhaps the best-known performer of the part of Nora on the Shanghai stage was a not particularly talented actress from Shantung who took several names, the last being Chiang Ching. The slender, dark-eyed woman who would become the future Madame Mao arrived in Shanghai in the 1930s to try her luck in the city's theatrical and film world. A string of liaisons already behind her, the flirtatious ingenue would have many more ahead of her as she boldly advanced her career in the time-honored manner of ambitious actresses everywhere. Her forthright ways were a far cry from the days when a woman blushed if a man seemed enthralled by a glimpse of her satin-shod feet. Instead, Chiang Ching was the kind of woman who would go to an expensive restaurant, order "only a cup of tea or a bowl of steamed rice" and give the general impression that she was "waiting for a man friend, old or new." And, more often than not, "a man would come in to join her," as biographer Ross Terrill wrote. Women like Chiang Ching were all too aware that they had taken their chances by coming to Shanghai, the most cruel and mercenary of cities. Success was a possibility, but so was failure, and for a woman that meant resorting to "selling the skin and the smile," as the Shanghainese put it.

Whether there was any future for the Chinese Nora after she left home was a subject that absorbed the attention of the most important writers of the period. In Lu Hsun's story "Remorse," a young woman whose refrain is "I am my own mistress; none of them has any right to interfere with me," returns to her native village, then dies following her lover's loss of a job. In an essay on the same issue, Lu Hsun concluded that starvation, prostitution, or a return home was the independent woman's most probable fate. A beautiful prostitute, Chen Pai-lu, kept by more than one lover in a luxurious apartment is the "heroine" or main character in playwright Tsao Yu's *Sunrise*. Bearing a close resemblance to the modern call girl, Chen eventually takes her own life after she fails to prevent a young girl who comes into her care from falling into the hands of a brothel keeper. The seeming intractability of the obstacles that lay before women seeking social and economic freedom compelled the writer Ting Ling to ask, in 1941, "When will it no longer be necessary to attach special weight to the word 'woman' and raise it specially?"

It was Ting Ling who shocked traditional sensibilities by writing boldly and directly about romantic and sexual feelings and the struggle between men and women. Her groundbreaking short story "The Diary of Miss Sophia" recorded the thoughts of a woman driven mad by passion for a handsome cad. "I ought to forget everything and pack myself off again to start my life over," confesses the tubercular, self-absorbed Miss Sophia. "I should make myself good with either a pen or a gun even if its purpose is just my own vanity or to win the praise of some shallow audience. All for that man's soft hair and red lips. . . ." In the end, Miss Sophia achieves a bittersweet triumph over the object of her obsession by rejecting his advances. Bleakly, she concludes that "life has been my own toy, I've wasted enough of it away. I'm going to take the train southward and waste what's left." When Ting Ling's heroine goes south, it is, we assume, to Shanghai.

The modern metropolis attracted not just women confused about their roles in modern society, but men as well. To Shanghai came students returning from Japan and abroad as well as graduates of the modern schools that had sprung up throughout the country since the 1911 Revolution. The treaty port, which supported scores of newspapers, magazines, and journals as well as major publishing companies, was the one place in the country where it was possible for intellectuals to support themselves as journalists, essayists, or fiction writers. Moreover, opportunities existed not just to make a living writing serious literature or journalism but to contribute to the large number of publications specializing in gossip or light amusement for the urban masses. Shanghai had a large number of tabloids, known as the "mosquito press," which probed the lives of public figures, be they movie stars or magnates. So prominent was their place in the Shanghai press that, as one scholar notes, their "skirmishes in court or with hired hoodlums in the streets became themselves items of journalistic interest." Items intended for "idle amusement" also filled the back pages of even the more serious periodicals—articles about a scenic spot in China or a new style in Western hats or a poll asking male readers to answer the question, "What was the first thing you said to your bride on your wedding night?" Also catering to the public appetite for light entertainment was the flourishing of a genre of fiction, the "Mandarin duck and butterfly" school, which offered the public pure escapism whether the work was a tale about a knight errant in traditional China or a modern detective story.

While the young bourgeois intellectuals who filled the coffeehouses on Szechwan Road or audited classes at the leftist Shanghai University might have cast a jaundiced eye on the tabloid press and the Mandarin duck school of fiction, the flourishing of such journalism and literature reflected rising rates of literacy and changes overtaking the society as a whole. Certainly Shanghai's demimonde of students, writers, artists, actors, and actresses was the very first to adopt the newest trends and fashions. Here is one writer's description of a 1920s "girl student," as progressive young Chinese women were called: "Her hair has been cut by half. To her loose short hair is fastened an ivory butterfly [ribbon]. Her breasts inside her snow-white gauze shirt are very flat; obviously she is wearing a tight brassiere. Under her short and open black silk skirt are a pair of short legs in white silk stockings." Nor was the girl student's male counterpart behind her in modishness. Though it was fashionable for modern Chinese men to wear Western-style trousers and leather shoes beneath their old-fashioned scholar gowns, the most style-conscious men went to far greater pains. Here is an example supplied by the critic Leo Ou-fan Lee from a 1926 writer's description of a returned Chinese student. He "wears a stiffly ironed western suit. The folds of his suit are like iron wires. His shining and pointed leather shoes are of low cut, revealing gleaming silk socks. Under his hard collar hangs a silk cravat, which is placed in front of his pongee shirt. His hand holds a 'civilized stick' and, as he steps inside the front court over the stone lintel, he takes off from his head a brand-new straw hat."

Young progressive Chinese aped Western youth not just in their choice of clothing but in their personal lives as well. Rebelling against arranged marriages, filial piety, old-fashioned family, and all the other conventions of traditional society, they experimented with the concept of "free love," joined leftist organizations, handed out flyers promoting strikes and boycotts, and attended lectures by the likes of Bertrand Russell, John Dewey, or Margaret Sanger. In Shanghai, students and intellectuals could lead freewheeling bohemian lives. They might live in boardinghouses or buy their midday meal from a streetside cook, yet they still enjoyed the privileges that come from being intellectuals, as their education afforded them a measure of respect not given to a merchant or worker. Moreover, most of Shanghai's students and intellectuals were the sons and daughters of the scholar-gentry. Though the class was deeply in decline, their children nonetheless had inherited their parents' sense of obligation to lead society in one way or another.

In the hothouse milieu of Shanghai's literary intelligentsia, men and women of letters enjoyed a uniquely glamorous position. Their world, just as competitive as the avant-garde circles of Paris or New York, was one of gossip, literary backbiting, and hopes of having a novel published or an essay or short story placed in one of the better journals. The novel, in particular, had acquired a new respectability among the younger generation. In the old culture, novels had been associated with the storytelling tradition of the lower classes and dismissed as frivolous. But Western translations of fiction by Balzac, Dostoevsky, Chekhov, and Tolstoy were eagerly absorbed by Chinese students, and the novel or novella was fastened upon as a vehicle for expressing their own confusion about personal and social transformation.

The acknowledged giant of Chinese letters was Lu Hsun.

He had gone to Japan to study medicine but decided to commit himself to becoming a writer after seeing photographs of Chinese collaborators watching their own countrymen being decapitated by Japanese during the Russo-Japanese War. (The dead men executed had acted as spies for the Russians.) Appalled at the lack of courage displayed by the spectators, and taking it as symbolic of the dangerous passivity of the nation as a whole, Lu Hsun hoped to show the Chinese the nature of their weaknesses before it was too late. His *Diary of a Madman,* which depicted the Chinese as a cannibalistic people who "eat" their own, won him his first acclaim, but even more powerful was his most famous work, *The True Story of Ah Q,* in which the protagonist rationalizes his failures as success, retreats into the glories of his past to escape the reality of the present, and thrives—and bolsters his sense of inferiority—by bullying others. By satirizing the character of Ah Q, exposing his dishonesty and self-delusion, Lu Hsun was speaking of China itself. "Savage as a lion, timid as a rabbit, crafty as a fox" is how the writer derogated his country and countrymen.

Lu Hsun became the leader of a loose association of China's most prominent modern writers. He championed literature in a realistic vein that dealt with society's ills. He therefore strongly criticized one of the smaller groups that grew out of the association, which emphasized "art for art's sake." Known as the Creationists, the members of this clique modeled themselves after the Western romantics and wrote about such themes as romantic love, breaking away from the restrictions of family, and the need for personal freedom. They had read and studied Keats, Byron, and Nietzsche and valued, they said, the individual above all else. Members of this school wrote in a confessional vein, their fiction often being thinly disguised autobiography.

One of the founders, the Japanese-educated Yu Ta-fu, for instance, wrote about his love of nature as well as his sense of sexual frustration—which he equated with China's powerlessness. Another leading Creationist was Hsu Chi-mo, a poet whose lyrical, if overly emotional, verse about love and despair won him a large following among young people. Hsu's romanticism extended from his poetry to his personal life. The scion of a Chekiang industrialist family, the handsome, talented Hsu went abroad to study first at Columbia University in the United States, then at Cambridge in England. Against his family's wishes, Hsu gave up banking and economics for poetry. Having divorced his first wife while in England, he returned to China, where his emotion-laden verse about love and romantic agony won him the adulation of a youthful readership. His celebrity increased all the more when he married a Chinese socialite with whom he had become infatuated while she was married to a military officer. "I know and only believe in myself," the poet wrote. "To my mind, democracy is only individualism universalized. The spirit of real democracy lies in an individual's self-awareness and self-improvement." Hsu died young, killed at age thirty-two in an airplane crash while flying from Shanghai to Peking.

Had Hsu lived, perhaps he might have abandoned what Lu Hsun belittled as the Creationists' "roguish and dilletantish" ways. Sadly, the May Fourth generation of Chinese writers were not afforded the luxury of placing their art before society's needs. One by one, these avatars of individualism were forced to come face-to-face with the sobering political reality of China in the late 1920s and 1930s. Art for art's sake would soon give way to art for "art for life's sake" and revolutionary literature.

THE SHANGHAI MASSACRE

Paradoxically, the river that gave the poorest of the Shanghainese life was also its river of the dead. Soochow Creek
was the first place where newly arrived immigrants from the
most destitute parts of China made their home upon arriving
in the great port. On the waterway, too, floated barges containing piles of coffins awaiting their return to the homes of
the deceased farther up the creek. The artery was not only a
link to their homes for many of Shanghai's native immigrants
but, in many cases, home itself. On thousands of sampans
jammed against one another like thick ice floes, a multitude
of Chinese lived: some were born, grew up, married, raised
families, and died on sampans. Here were children tethered
to sampans by a piece of rope, watched over by older brothers
and sisters scampering over the wooden planks that served as
walkways between boats. Men who lived in the sampan colonies
earned a living, if they were lucky, as wharf coolies, or by fer-

rying passengers with small loads—vegetables, eggs, ducks, or other comestibles—across the creek. Their wives added what little they could to the family's income by gathering rags to make cloth soles or patching and darning garments for the coolies without families for a few coppers in return.

If ever a downtrodden working class existed, it was Shanghai's. While the World War's prosperity had created a golden age for the city's Chinese industrialists, it had also spawned China's first authentic proletariat: a workforce of 300,000 impoverished men, women, and children who lived in slums as abysmal as any to be found in the world. These slums, which had sprouted on the edges of the industrial areas, consisted of row upon row of flimsy tile-roofed mud-and-bamboo houses in which a single room was shared by two or more families so that each house accommodated several families. In "boarding-houses" or "dormitories," other workers paid one yuan a month for the privilege of occupying a cubicle barely large enough to lie down in, while those too poor to afford even this minimal degree of privacy shared the floor of a room with as many as fifteen other "tenants," the sleeping figures piled on top of one another in the winter. Most appalling of all were the shantytowns along the banks of the Soochow Creek and the Whangpu, where the poorest families lived in conditions so squalid and unsanitary that health officials periodically forced the residents out and burned their dwellings to the ground lest an epidemic break out. The scores of peasants driven by rural destitution into Shanghai provided employers with a huge and instantly replenishable supply of labor, a situation that enabled employers to pay low wages and still have more applicants than jobs. Moreover, as the meager pay seldom enabled a worker to meet his living expenses (the average factory worker in 1920 earned anywhere from six to fifteen yuan a month, but minimum expenses for a single person were twelve yuan), nearly half the workers were permanently in debt; they borrowed from pawnbrokers and moneylenders who did a thriving business advancing money at a standard interest rate of 125 percent.

In the years since the failure of the 1911 Revolution, a new generation of politically active intellectuals had come to the fore. The business of creating a strong, independent, and democratic China was still unfinished. In 1919 the ever combustible tinder of Chinese nationalist feeling was ignited by the news, reaching Peking by telegraph on May 4, that the Versailles Treaty called for the handing over of Germany's former leased territories in China to Japan, with the full acquiescence of the warlord government. In Peking, thousands of students took to the streets in the largest and most violent demonstration yet seen in the capital, incensed at the government for caving in to its pro-Japanese ministers and stunned by the hypocrisy of the Allies, who had raised China's hopes that the "unequal treaties" would be abolished and Chinese sovereignty restored. Fueled by disillusionment with Western diplomacy and outrage at China's continued humiliation by outsiders, the protest marked the beginning of the watershed May Fourth Movement, which would profoundly reshape Chinese literature and intellectual thought over the next decade.

The Versailles arrangements angered not only the Peking students but Chinese everywhere, and within days, demonstrations took place throughout China. In Shanghai, scene of the largest, best-organized protests of all, shops closed and sixty thousand workers walked off their jobs the day after news of the Peking demonstrations arrived; and in early June, Shanghai's students and merchants organized a nationwide boycott of Japanese goods so effective that at the end of the month, the Peking government released thirty-two arrested students, dismissed the three pro-Japanese officials, and instructed its delegates at Versailles not to sign the treaty.

From that moment on, Shanghai became the movement's center as the exponents of its various currents made their way there. Among these was the man who had had perhaps the most galvanic influence upon the protesters, Chen Tu-hsiu, former dean of the literature department at Peking University, who had spent three months in jail for helping his students distribute anti-Japanese literature and had then been dismissed from the university. Chen's arrival in Shanghai was, in a way, a homecoming, as it was there, three years earlier, that he had made a name for himself as editor of a groundbreaking magazine, *New Youth*, in which he articulated, better than anyone yet had, the beliefs and aspirations of a new generation of educated Chinese youth. In his opening salvo, Chen called for the abandonment of the "old, rotten and useless" values of China's past, which were to be replaced by "fresh" and "vital" ideas from the West: freedom of speech, of choice, and of political opinion; the right to be an individual independent of one's family; equal rights for women; and an end to Confucianism.

There could be little doubt that *New Youth* had struck a resonant chord with the Chinese intelligentsia when it published the work of a twenty-six-year-old former doctoral student of John Dewey's, Hu Shih, who proposed the replacement of the stilted and abstruse classical form of written Chinese, *wen-yan*, with the colloquial *pai-hua*, or "plain language," that could be understood by the common people. Hu's suggestions struck an overwhelming response among younger writers, and seemingly overnight, hundreds of newspapers and magazines entirely in the vernacular began rolling off the presses. The impact upon literature was just as great, as the most talented young writers of the day—men and women like Lu Hsun, Mao Tun, Guo Moruo, and Ting Ling—wholeheartedly embraced the common speech in their essays, novels, short stories, drama, and poetry.

In the wake of this literary revolution came a churning of ideas in other realms as well. Still grappling with the question of how China might throw off its twin yokes of imperialism and warlordism, Chinese intellectuals watched the unfolding of events in Russia following the Bolshevik overthrow of the czarist regime with deep interest. Both Russia and China, after all, were large, agrarian-based countries that had been defeated in war by Japan and suffered from attempts by the Western powers to intervene in their affairs. Disillusioned with Western liberalism, the new wave of radicals yearning for a solution to China's ills thought they had found the prescription in Marxist socialism. At the time of the May Fourth outburst, Marxism's leading Chinese exponent was Peking University's librarian, Li Ta-chao, who held meetings of a Marxist research society in his cramped office with a handful of adherents to the new ideology drawn from radical circles. Among the group's most dedicated members was Li's young library assistant Mao Tse-tung, the impecunious, brooding son of a Hunanese farmer, who had never heard of Marx or Engels until he was taken under Li's wing.

Part of Li's attraction to Marxism, one which his protégé shared, was its emphasis upon the critical role of the rural masses in fomenting revolution, for Li, like Mao, had sprung from peasant roots. Nonetheless, the first front on which the battle for socialism in China would be fought was not the countryside, but Shanghai, home to China's largest industrial proletariat. It was also in Shanghai that Chen Tu-hsiu, who had started a Shanghai Marxist study group, was visited in the French Concession by an agent of the Comintern (Communist International), the organization that Lenin had founded to propagate the revolution worldwide. The agent volunteered the Comintern's services in helping the Chinese to build a Communist organization, an offer Chen accepted. By the next year, enough members had been recruited that a national "congress" could be held: in July 1921 twelve delegates representing a total of fifty-nine members in China and Japan gathered in a deserted schoolroom in the Bo-wen Girls' School on Rue Wantz in the French Concession. With a Comintern representative standing impatiently by, the young delegates—all in their twenties or thirties—plotted the course of the Chinese revolution. Four days into the proceedings, a stranger was detected lurking outside the building. Suspecting a spy, the group hastily shifted venue to a lake outside Hangchow, reconvening in a houseboat.

In this meeting of gangly intellectuals was born the political organization that would truly revolutionize China. While many of these "founders" would soon drift out of the party into other camps, those who remained constituted a tough, determined, and resourceful core. Returning to their home provinces, they offered their help to the trade unions that had already begun forming throughout China and played a leading role in the instigation of several strikes that broke out among railway workers, coal miners, and seamen the next year in Hunan, Hupeh, and the south. Shanghai's Communist organization, however, was the largest and most effective: trading in their long gowns for blue cotton trousers and jackets, the uniform of Shanghai's workers, Communist organizers attended workers' meetings, ran schools for factory workers, set up trade unions, and encouraged strike action. Several Communist-instigated strikes broke out throughout Shanghai in 1921 and 1922, the largest of them a strike at the British-American Tobacco factory in Pootung and another involving the twenty thousand female employees of the silk factories in Hongkew and Chapei. Both strikes were eventually broken by Chinese police and soldiers of the local warlord authorities; they also closed down the Communists' labor headquarters in the International Settlement, forcing the new party underground.

Conditions were appalling for workers. On top of miserable wages, the laboring population endured wretched working conditions. Workdays in the factories averaged twelve hours, usually from seven in the morning until seven in the evening. (The standard ranged from ten hours a day at the Chinese-owned Commercial Press to fourteen hours a day at Jardine, Matheson's Ewo Company silk-weaving mill and at the Japanese-owned match factories.) Some enterprises employed workers twenty-four hours a day, running twelve-hour day and night shifts. The work week lasted seven days, with Chinese New Year the only holiday observed; even then, laborers seldom rested, as their foremen and overseers demanded that they perform a variety of chores and services. Most laborers lived in fear of incurring the wrath of their foremen—for a careless mistake, a laborer might lose an entire day's wages. To keep their jobs, moreover, workers were obliged to present their superiors with frequent gifts; even to secure their jobs, many had to invite their immediate superiors to expensive dinners at restaurants.

Into the grimy red-brick buildings of Yangtzepoo, Chapei, and Hsaioshatu, employers jammed as much machinery and as many workers as possible. The lighting was always dim and the air suffocatingly hot, as few of the factories had windows. Many of these enterprises were housed in flimsy old tenement houses, the owners often knocking down walls to expand into the neighboring building. Anywhere from fifteen to one hundred employees could be crowded into such makeshift premises—along with machinery—and fires frequently broke out. In one of the more notorious of these incidents, one hundred women died inside a blazing silk filature because the door to the building had been locked from the outside by the owner—who, like many factory operators, kept his employees virtual prisoners while they worked. The accident rate too was high, because of improperly installed machinery or simply a lack of attention to basic safety measures. One teenage mill worker died when her fingers got entangled in a machine that had not been equipped with a standard protective casing. Eye and hand injuries occurred as a matter of course in silk-weaving factories, as workers were frequently struck by the pointed shuttle of their looms as they bent over their work. Other health hazards resulted from simple greed. In match factories, where young children also worked, a kind of phosphorus that had been banned from European factories at the end of the nineteenth century continued to be used instead of the more expensive red phosphorus despite the fact that it caused painful skin inflammations. In addition to these youngsters, toddlers and babies could also be found on the factory premises, because mothers had nowhere else to take their children. Sometimes babies lay sleeping on the floor, looked after by tiny children.

Long days, monotonous work, and inadequate nutrition all contributed to poor health and exhaustion among industrial laborers, women and children in particular. Tuberculosis was endemic to the working class, as were occupational diseases. Particularly appalling from a health and hygiene standpoint were conditions in the silk filatures. In these airless factories, no ventilation whatsoever, even on the hottest days of summer, was allowed, as the slightest draft could damage the delicate silk threads. Women spun the actual silk, but small children, often as young as six, were given the task of loosening the silk from the cocoons by stirring the cocoons in vats of boiling water. "Women and children grow very skillful in keeping their hands out of the water, yet they are loose-skinned and parboiled, for fingers must of necessity be continually dipped in," noted one visitor to a silk filature. "Then, too, the Chinese women overseers, passing constantly up and down the lines, occasionally punish a child's inefficiency, or supposed laziness, by thrusting the little hand into the bubbling caldron." All the workers, children included, invariably stood while they worked. Compounding their discomfort was the steam rising from the vats, which covered everyone in sweat, and the horrible stench rising from the mounds of dead cocoons on the floor. In the match factories, conditions were similar. There, little children, "some hardly more than babies," related an American reporter, "stood twelve hours a day before trays filled with matches, their small hands working like lightning as they filled match-boxes. A foreman carrying a short stick walked back and forth along the aisles."

Many women and children were virtual prisoners of the factory operators. Their freedom had been signed away by parents or relatives whom destitution had driven to affixing their signature—more often thumbprint—to labor contractors who paid them a fixed sum for custody of their young women and children for a period of three to four years. During that time, the women and children became, said one chronicler, "wards of the subcontractor, who provides them with food which is poor, clothing which is meager, and shelter which is crowded. He charges them for these services, which must be worked off before they leave his employ." These additional "expenses" often added two or three years to the contract worker's period of servitude, and afterward, "the health of the workers is so broken that they are no longer employable and others are found to take their place from the always plentiful supply." Children, usually boys, also came into the labor market through the apprenticeship system. Instead of working in factories, the boys worked in shipyards, tanneries, oil mills, and printing businesses, and, as in contract labor, they were given only the barest food and shelter.

Even more marginal than the 150,000 men, women, and children employed in the factories was the remainder of Shanghai's proletariat, 150,000 ricksha, dock, and warehouse coolies—the word "coolie," which means "bitter strength" (*kwei-li*), applied to the unskilled male worker who earned his living by the sweat of his brow. Readily identified by their universal garb of straw sandals, an old jacket—if they were lucky— and ragged blue trousers tied at the waist with a piece of string, coolies performed work in China that elsewhere was done by animals or machines: they shouldered backbreaking loads on the docks, groaned behind the spokes of nonmechanized pile drivers, and pushed, pulled, and shoved a variety of vehicles through the city's streets. In Shanghai, coolies either roamed the docks in search of work on a transportation crew or became wheelbarrow or ricksha coolies. Wheelbarrow coolies carted anything from freight to a clutch of factory girls on their way to or from work on Chinese wheelbarrows, which were constructed with a wheel in the center so that the coolie could keep his balance. The work was hard but not as physically taxing as pulling a ricksha, which so exhausted even the strongest man that few ricksha coolies lasted in their business longer than four years. "Heart trouble and China's inveterate foe, tuberculosis, carry off the majority," noted one Shanghailander. "Perspiring freely, even in winter, after a hard run, then waiting, it may be an hour, for another 'fare,' in the penetrating wind or chilling rain, with no extra covering for their thinly clad bodies, the coolies are in a condition to succumb readily to disease."

For their labors, the ricksha men seldom earned more than ten cents a day, barely enough to buy cheap-grade rice from a street vendor, as the real profits from the ricksha business were made by the companies that owned the rickshas and their subcontractors. Shanghai's largest ricksha company, the French-owned Flying Star Company, for example, rented its rickshas to a major subcontractor for seventy cents a day, who in turn rented the vehicle to a minor subcontractor for ninety cents a day. For a dollar a day, the last contractor would rent out a ricksha to two or three coolies who used the ricksha in shifts. "On top of that dollar, the pullers had to put up the cash for traffic fines or for a broken fender," explained one foreigner. "If the dues were higher than the coolie's earnings of the day— and they often would be—the contractor did not care. He wanted his money just the same. And heartbreaking were the scenes enacted at the depot, with a special employee who carried a tremendous cane for beating the coolies into 'confessions.' They were always under the suspicion of having hid some of their earnings away, and at times, perhaps they had." Not only the ricksha contractors but the International Settlement's Sikh policemen abused the pullers: it was common to see one of these red-turbaned giants drag a coolie away from his ricksha and beat him with a club for a minor traffic infraction.

The contrast between the abject poverty in which most of Shanghai's population lived and the conspicuous luxury enjoyed by its privileged class was one aspect of Shanghai that many arriving in the city for the first time frequently commented on. But its rich Chinese and longtime foreign residents felt few pangs of conscience for those whose misery made their ease and abundance possible. "The streets are crowded with hungry, sullen, half-starved people and among them roll the sedans and limousines of the wealthy Chinese, spending fabulous sums on pleasure, food and clothes, wholly senseless to others," wrote the writer Pearl Buck after a visit to Shanghai, which she likened to Bourbon Paris on the eve of the French Revolution. While Buck blamed the wretchedness of the poor on the "moral weakness of the upper classes," others pointed a finger at foreign imperialism. Shanghai's foreign enclaves conveyed, declared American journalist Vincent Sheean, an "instant impression of pompous and rather purse-proud arrogance. The confrontation of European power and the swarming, fluid, antlike life of poverty-stricken Chinese is more obvious here than anywhere else in China."

In the Communist movement, these and other members of Shanghai's swollen underclass found the promise of better conditions and, more important, a channel for their anger. By 1925, the Shanghai Communist organization had grown considerably, thanks to an infusion of members from Shanghai University, a former teachers college which a student revolt had turned into a training ground for radicals, and to the return to China of students who had gained valuable experience organizing trade unions in Europe as part of a work-study program financed by Chinese radicals. In Paris, the Chinese students had formed a European branch of the Chinese Communist Party, from whose ranks a number of party luminaries would emerge. To Shanghai came two of these returned students, Li Li-san and Liu Shao-chi, who had helped coal miners in eastern Hunan launch their first strikes before being dispatched to Shanghai. Li, a tall, large-boned Hunanese with a razor-sharp mind and, said writer Enid Candlin, the ability to "whip up a crowd of rather apathetic, stolid persons into a frenzy," set about rousing the proletariat, while Liu, dour, serious, and destined to be Mao's second-in-command, took charge of day-to-day details and kept in touch with the Comintern.

The killing on May 15, 1925, of a Chinese worker and Communist organizer by the Japanese foreman of the Japanese Naiga Wata mill during a strike set off a chain of tragic and momentous events that would sharply increase the new party's strength. By failing to prosecute the Naiga Wata foreman and instead arresting six workers staging a protest at a memorial for the slain worker a week later, the Municipal Council provoked a gathering on May 30 of some three thousand sympathizers on Nanking Road. Shouting anti-Japanese slogans and waving banners that read "Take back the concessions" and "Down with imperialists," the crowd marched down the thoroughfare toward the Louza police station in protest. It was a repeat of the 1904 riot at Louza Station, but this time a young lieutenant was left in charge of the station as the police commissioner went off for a long lunch at the Shanghai Club. As the crowd approached, the panicked officer shouted a warning that he would shoot unless it dispersed. Ten seconds later, not giving the protesters time to respond, he ordered his men to fire. Forty-four shots rang out, killing eleven and wounding many others.

Instantly, the formerly anti-Japanese protest became transformed into a public outcry against foreign privilege and the unequal treaties. The Nanking Road victims became the "May Thirtieth Martyrs" and their massacre the floodgates for an outpouring of fury against Westerners not seen since the days of the Boxer Rebellion. After seven decades of foreign exploitation, the patience of the Chinese had worn to a thread, re-vealing, in the words of one Westerner, "an amount of hostility that astonished even the most experienced observ-ers." In the International Settlement, foreigners who appeared on the streets risked being beaten, cursed at, or spat upon from the balconies over shops and stores. The next day, seizing the initiative, the Communists called for a general strike and formed a branch organization, the General Labor Union, to direct the strike, with Li Li-san as its chairman. The strike began on June 1, and over the next few days, the city's Communist leadership brought 117 unions representing more than 200,000 workers to join the General Labor Union. More important, Li had secured the sponsorship of the General Chamber of Commerce, whose rich industrialists had agreed to underwrite the workers' strike pay: resentful of their foreign competitors and the special privileges they enjoyed, these rich bankers and businessmen were only too pleased to show their patriotism by cutting into the Japanese and Western firms' profits. By June 16, employees had walked out of every Japanese- and British-owned enterprise, and the International Settlement's municipal services nearly shut down. "The ships in the docks were immobilized and the goods left standing; the telephones ceased to function and foreign newspapers ceased publication," related one correspondent. There was "nothing but a skeleton staff left at the power station in the International Settlement."

The strike spread like wildfire to twenty-eight other cities, and the slogans shouted by marching students and workers were even more virulently anti-imperialistic than in Shanghai as more Chinese blood was spilled in the streets of Hankow, Nanking, Chungking, Ningpo, Amoy, Chinkiang, and Wangh-sien by British and Japanese soldiers firing at unarmed demonstrators. The worst incident of all took place in Canton, where British and French militiamen fired at a great parade of students, workers, and soldiers demonstrating in front of the

Shameen concessions; they killed fifty-two and wounded one hundred. In retaliation, Communists and labor leaders organized the most massive anti-British strike and boycott yet as Chinese workers in Hong Kong left their jobs en masse, crippling Hong Kong for an astonishing sixteen months. The collective protests following the Shanghai shootings became known as the May Thirtieth Movement. A watershed in the history of relations between foreigners and Chinese, the movement frightened Westerners as nothing had before. Missionaries in the interior, suffering harassment as in the Boxer Days, fled into the foreign concessions, but even there, despite the presence of the treaty powers' gunboats and soldiers, they felt a none too subtle menace. "I could not believe it," declared one shocked American. "The Shanghai I knew and enjoyed . . . had suddenly vanished. I was living in a strange, unfriendly world thousands of miles from nowhere." The upheaval had made it unmistakably clear that the days when Chinese could be cowed by a display of Western firepower and gunboats were over. In the words of one Shanghailander, "the beginning of the end had come."

In Shanghai, the call for abolition of foreign privileges and the unequal treaties was louder than it had ever been before. At monster meetings attended by thousands of ordinary Shanghainese—the students wearing black armbands in mourning for their dead comrades—the strike leadership drew up a list of seventeen demands for the Municipal Council. The most important were withdrawal of all foreign land and naval forces from China, abrogation of consular jurisdiction, Chinese representation on the Municipal Council, and freedom of speech and assembly for the International Settlement's Chinese. But in the palatial building of the Shanghai Municipal Administration, the taipans of the Municipal Council, meeting around their green-baize-covered conference table, were not yet ready to see Chinese entering their clubs through the front door or occupying seats beside them. Moreover, while their own factories, businesses, and banks were closed, they saw the same Chinese capitalists who called for an end to Western privilege pulling in the profits of their enterprises—which were unaffected by the strike. While they could comprehend the striking laborers only as pawns of Bolshevik agitators, they understood their counterparts on the Chinese General Chamber of Commerce far more clearly.

On July 6, at the suggestion of the manager of one of the British cotton mills, the Municipal Council shut down the electric current from the Shanghai Power Company in Yangtzepoo to the Chinese factories in the International Settlement and Chinese territory. Exactly as the taipans had anticipated, this brought the Chinese businessmen and industrialists to their knees. They broke with the General Labor Union and withdrew their financial support, pressuring other wealthy contributors to do so as well.

That brought the strike to a halt. By August, its funds depleted, the General Labor Union negotiated a settlement with the Japanese authorities that called for monetary compensation to the slain Naiga workers' families as well as improvements in wages and working conditions at the Japanese factories. Small as these concessions were, they represented a gain for Shanghai's workers. More significant, the tumultuous events following the Nanking Road shootings—the May Thirtieth Movement—catapulted the heretofore obscure Communists into sudden prominence. Scores of workers and students flocked to its banners; from nine hundred members at the beginning of May, the growing organization's rolls expanded to ten thousand by the end of 1925.

The explosion of support for the May Thirtieth Movement demonstrated not just the strength of antiforeign feeling among Chinese masses but also disgust at the country's continued degradation by the parade of generals in Peking. To even the most rabidly foreign-hating Chinese, it was obvious that China could not wrest back its rights from the Western powers until it had cleared its own house of the scourge of warlordism. In 1923, the Communists had joined forces with the Kuomintang in a "United Front" pledged to reunify the country and oust the Peking warlords. That year the Comintern had offered Sun Yat-sen assistance in his campaign to seize China back from the Peking generals and restore the Kuomintang to power. Sun accepted the offer, having vainly sought the backing of the treaty powers and been spurned by each. Since returning from Japan in 1917, he had led one failed attempt after another to revive his revolutionary government in Canton but had always failed and been forced to beat a hasty retreat to Shanghai's French Concession. There, Sun and Comintern representatives negotiated their agreement. Sun was only too happy to accept the Comintern's funds and advisers, but he balked at a coalition between the Kuomintang and Chinese Communists. Fearing, and rightly, that the Comintern's truly militant members sought to gain control of the Kuomintang by infiltrating it with Chinese Communists, he allowed Communists to join only as individuals.

Within months of the Kuomintang-Comintern agreement, Russian advisers, weapons, and much more began flowing into Canton, the base of Sun's "southern government." Most of the Russians' activities were concentrated on the creation of a disciplined and reliable military force through the establishment in 1924 of the Whampoa Military Academy outside Canton; to instill a sense of commitment to their political mission, the cadets heard lectures by a slender, bushy-browed Communist by the name of Chou En-lai, recently returned from managing the party's affairs in France. Chou, suave and persuasive, was Whampoa's deputy political director and a popular figure among the students—so much so that a number of the cadets soon afterward joined the Communists. Chou's superior at Whampoa, the man whom Sun and the Russians had chosen to head it, was a man who, three years later, would put a price of eighty thousand Chinese dollars on Chou's head. This was

Chiang Kai-shek, the reckless bravo of the Shanghai Revolution who had won his revolutionary stripes as Chen Chi-mei's right-hand lieutenant.

Since those heady days of intrigue, Chiang Kai-shek had climbed up the ladder of Sun Yat-sen's revolutionary organization to become his chief military aide. To do so, he had been forced to control his quarrelsome nature and stubbornness. He would undertake an assignment for the party, only to have a falling out with one or another officer and leave in a huff. On one occasion, Sun sent Chiang a chastening letter, advising the short-tempered younger man to curb his "fiery temper which often leads to quarrels and renders cooperation difficult. As you are shouldering the great and heavy responsibility of our party you should sacrifice your ideals a little and try to compromise."

During his absences from Canton, Chiang usually took himself to Shanghai, where he could expect political counsel and financial aid from Chang Ching-chang, the Kuomintang fundraiser and millionaire curio dealer who had befriended him after Chen Chi-mei's assassination. Chang Ching-chang had joined with other Shanghai businessmen and bankers to start the Shanghai Stock and Commodities Exchange, partly to fund the Kuomintang. He gave Chiang a job on the exchange as a junior broker. Initially Chiang appeared successful at this work, but at one point he accumulated such large losses from over-speculation that Chang Ching-chang stepped in to pay off his debts.

Through his benefactor too, Chiang took on a second wife. At fourteen, Chiang had been married to a girl from his native Chikow three years older than himself. She had borne him a son and had remained in Chikow. But Chiang had long alienated himself from his wife by his womanizing in Tokyo and elsewhere. His new bride was a shy fifteen-year-old, Chen Chieh-ju, a childhood friend of Chang Ching-chang's new young wife whom Chiang had first seen at Chang's house.

Taken with the tall and slender teenager, who looked older than her age, Chiang pursued her. But Chen, frightened by Chiang's aggressive attentions, spurned him. Known for his "intense dissipation" and ability to "disappear for months . . . into the houses of sing-song girls" during his days as Chen Chi-mei's comrade, Chiang surprised those who knew him by his determined efforts to win over the reluctant young woman. ("Everyone says that I am given to lust," Chiang had once confided to a friend. "But they do not know that this is a thing of last resort, in a state of utter depression.") In her memoirs, Chen described how Chiang waylaid her shortly after their introduction. As she emerged from Chang Ching-chang's house, Chiang stood "like a sentinel" at the front gate. Chiang was "flushed from the wine he had drunk, and he looked so very red," recalled Chen. "He came forward to ask why I was leaving so early and where I was going." When she failed to reply to his question, he persisted. In her words:

"'Where do you live?' he asked anxiously. I thought it was none of his business, so I purposely told him a wrong number. 'Eighty-eight Tibet Road.' Actually, my house number was 33 Tibet Road.

"'Then I will take you home!' he said determinedly.

"'No, no,' I protested excitedly. Then he stood in front to bar my way."

Chiang pursued the resistant Chieh-ju for two years until she finally agreed to marry him on December 5, 1921. Once married, however, Chen became Chiang's devoted wife, traveling everywhere with him and assisting him as a secretary and English translator in much the same way that Soong Ching-ling had become Sun Yat-sen's indispensable partner.

After his marriage, Chiang's career advanced meteorically. On Chang Ching-chang's advice, he left his brokerage job in June 1922 to go to Canton to help Sun Yat-sen at a critical point in his fortunes. A Kwangtung warlord who claimed to be Sun's ally had betrayed him, leaving Sun alone and in a vulnerable position in Canton. Chiang gained Sun's trust by making the dangerous journey to Canton to join the revolutionary and the scattered remains of his support. For two months, Sun insisted on remaining on one of his last gunboats outside Canton in the hope of reinforcements arriving from a friendly general. Chiang steadfastly stayed by his side. The troops never materialized, but the new attitude of his formerly rebellious junior officer impressed Sun. The next year, he sent Chiang to Moscow to learn about Soviet military methods, appointing him, upon his return, head of the Whampoa Academy and of the party's military organization. In less than a year, Chiang had leaped from the periphery of Sun's staff to one of the most important positions in the Kuomintang.

Sun Yat-sen's death in March 1925 in Peking, where he had gone in hope of allying himself with one of the northern warlords, unleashed a furious jockeying for power among his lieutenants. Assassinations and secret cabals eliminated all but Chiang and Wang Ching-wei, a longtime associate of Sun's. Wang had made a name for himself in 1910 after attempting to assassinate the prince regent, but failing. In the subsequent trial, he managed to talk his way out of an execution, supposedly because one of the judges had been taken by his charm and dimpled good looks—for which reason Wang acquired the lifelong moniker "Baby-Faced Wang." But Wang Ching-wei had allied himself with the left wing of the Kuomintang, on which side also stood Soong Ching-ling and the Kuomintang's Comintern adviser, Mikhail Borodin.

The alliance between the Communists and the Kuomintang had always been an uneasy one, but open conflict had been avoided during Sun's lifetime. In July 1925, in an attempt at showing party unity, the Kuomintang had proclaimed itself the Nationalist government of China. But dissension broke out as Kuomintang conservatives, frightened at the growing infiltration of the party by Communists, demanded their expulsion. Chiang Kai-shek too distrusted the Communists but deftly steered a middle course between the two factions. In March 1926 he cleverly cleared the way for his ascension to the top party position by claiming to have discovered a plot against his authority and imposing martial law on Canton without consulting Wang Ching-wei. The latter, catching Chiang's drift, speedily departed for France.

On July 27, 1926, Chiang Kai-shek, newly appointed commander in chief of the Nationalist Revolutionary Army, launched Sun Yat-sen's long-dreamed-of military campaign, his Northern Expedition, to retake China from the warlords. Though outsiders doubted the crusade's chances of success, the Nationalist forces swept into Changsha in August, Wuhan in September, Nanchang in November, Foochow in December, and Nanking in March 1927. The swiftness of these victories was attributable less to the prowess of Chiang's forces than to the fact that Communist cadres—trained by Chou En-lai—had worked in advance of the army's entrance to encourage strike action and the storming of police stations and the local warlord's offices, and so by the time the Nationalist soldiery arrived, all resistance was over: the local warlord, explained one foreign correspondent, had "vowed his love for nationalism and his long unpaid solders joined Chiang Kai-shek's army."

Tensions between the Kuomintang's left and right wings had seen its conservatives split from the party, while the leftists—among their leaders was Soong Ching-ling—and their Russian advisers moved the capital of the Nationalist government to Hankow in November. Also to Hankow went thirty-year-old T. V. Soong, whose skillful reorganization of the Kuomintang's finances had earned him a position as the party's minister of finance. Foreign correspondents soon dubbed the city "Red Hankow" for the ardor with which the revolutionary spirit thrived in the city: huge parades of celebrating citizens wound their way down through Hankow's main streets almost every day, while factory owners found themselves faced with either acquiescing to the labor unions' demands or closing. Then, in January, a mob worked up to a pitch of anti-imperialistic fervor rushed the British Concession, overcame the British marines guarding it, and forced the British consul to agree to the unprecedented—the return of the British concession to Chinese control. Antiforeign rioting in Kiukiang in February and in Nanking in March led to the British surrendering their concessions in those ports as well.

In Shanghai, home to some seventy thousand foreigners, a nervousness verging on panic prevailed. Western women and children jammed the port's outgoing ships after the Nanking incident, while a dozen nations rushed in forty thousand troops—two men for every Westerner and Japanese in the International Settlement and French Concession—to prevent a repeat in the Whangpu treaty port of the events in Hankow. In a matter of days, foreign Shanghai had become an armed camp: soldiers and members of the hastily called up Shanghai Volunteer Corps dug trenches and erected barbed-wire barricades protected by sandbags along the borders between the foreign and Chinese areas. Seven-foot-high steel-picketed gates went up along the roads leading into the Chinese district. During the day, sentries guarded the gates, and at night, when a curfew was imposed on the foreign areas, the gates were shut. The barricades calmed fears about a sudden attack by the Kuomintang army, but they could not stop the showers of anti-imperialist leaflets that fluttered down to Nanking Road from the rooftops of Sincere's and Wing On to be "grabbed by eager hands." Nor could they prevent the ever larger crowds from gathering around the student and labor orators who mounted doorsteps in every neighborhood to call forth in forceful and impassioned tones for the abolition of the concessions. More evidence of the strength of popular support for the Nationalists lay in the sudden appearance of the Kuomintang flag from balconies, attic windows, and rooftops throughout the foreign areas. Even the Chinese police who were called in to break up the knots of people gathered around the street speakers did so with a noticeable absence of enthusiasm. "Their heart was not in their job," said one Westerner.

Fearful as they were of the arrival in Shanghai of the Nationalist army, the prevailing sentiment among foreigners was, as expressed by the Municipal Council, that the International Settlement and French Concession should be "preserved at all cost" and that all efforts to abolish the foreign enclaves would be fought "to the last ditch."

Though their complacency had been punctured by the events downriver, Shanghai's foreigners were unable to comprehend either Chinese demands for sovereignty or Chinese hostility toward Westerners. They suffered from the "Shanghai mind," an outlook characterized by a myopia to all but events directly affecting foreign interests in China. The term "Shanghai mind" was coined by Arthur Ransome, a British journalist, in an article for the *Manchester Guardian* that chastised Shanghai's foreigners for their blindness to the true condition of China. Ransome's piece, written as he followed the course of the revolution in 1926, became a classic of its kind—and also aroused the enduring fury of Shanghai's foreigners. "These people 'think imperially,' " Ransome declared. "They look round on their magnificent buildings and are surprised that China is not grateful to them for these gifts, forgetting that the money to build them came out of China." Reserving particular condemnation for his fellow Britons, he pointed out that it was only because of the port's trade that the British in Shanghai prospered, yet they "forget that it is the trade that is valuable to England and not the magnificent buildings which big profits and small taxes have allowed them to erect." Then too, blind to the decline of imperialism since the World War, Shanghai's diehards regarded the Boxer Rebellion "as the last important political event" and continued to demand military contingents from their home countries whenever their interests were threatened. "Europe is very far away from them and China, at their very doors, seems almost as far," Ransome concluded. "They seem to have lived in a comfortable but hermetically sealed and isolated glass case."

Ransome's astonishment at the arrogance of the port's foreigners would be echoed by other Occidental visitors to Shanghai. The roving American writer Vincent Sheean, who passed through Shanghai on Ransome's heels, described the International Settlement as a place where its foreigners "considered that they had built Shanghai out of nothing" and "frankly asserted themselves as a superior race, designed by nature to make money out of the Chinese." Those who had "lived here free of taxes, amassing comfortable fortunes, had little to say in favor of the Chinese," said the English aesthete Harold Acton in the mid-1930s. At the Shanghai Club, he found the tone of conversation "intensely anti-Chinese, and when I ventured to protest, I was just told I was not qualified to have an opinion. Thirty years—sometimes more—without troubling to learn the language, and these 'Old China Hands' pickled in alcohol considered themselves supreme authorities on the country and the people." "In Shanghai one finds most flamboyantly and conspicuously the Westerner who hates the Chinese," noted the American foreign correspondent John Gunther in the 1930s. "*He* has done the Chinese an injury, that is, sucked the wealth out of him; for this he cannot forgive China."

But renegades, foreigners who backed the Chinese and called for a strong China and an end to the unequal treaties, could be found. The most vocal were Americans, and generally Americans associated with the *China Weekly Review,* a newspaper put out by John B. Powell, a friendly, owlish-looking Missourian who smoked a corncob pipe. Of a decidedly populist bent, J. B., as he was usually known, employed foreign and Chinese reporters alike and gave many an American in China his first newspaper job. Powell had arrived in China in 1917 to work for the *Review* when it was founded by Thomas Millard, another Missourian. Though different from Powell in his taste for sartorial splendor and prowess on the dance floor, Millard condemned imperialism, in particular British colonialism. (For refusing to side with the British at the outbreak of World War I, he was forced to sell an earlier Shanghai newspaper, the *China Press*, in 1915 to Chinese interests.) Though not opposed to foreign commercial interests in China, he criticized Westerners who opposed change that interfered with their profits and the continuation of their privileged lifestyles.

Millard went to Peking to become an adviser to the Peking government in 1922, selling the *Review* to Powell, who continued his advocacy of a strong and independent China. The *Review* flourished despite its frequent criticism of the policies of Shanghai's leading foreigners because of its wide influence in China, particularly among Chinese, who avidly read each issue. Chinese businesses consequently advertised heavily in its pages. Both Millard and Powell had championed Sun Yat-sen, and when the Nationalist army marched out of Canton, the *Review* applauded the event as the auspicious birth of a "New China." Chiang Kai-shek, for his part, appreciated the *Review*'s support, so much so that in the 1930s his government bought up large quantities of each issue to mail abroad. For his pro-China policies, Powell was always ruffling feathers among his fellow foreigners. After calling on Shanghai's foreigners to voluntarily give up their extraterritorial rights, Powell was asked by Shanghai's American Chamber of Commerce to give up his membership.

Nor did Powell ever say a word of complaint when a brash new reporter on his staff, yet another Missourian, this one named Edgar Snow, penned a blistering editorial rebuking the British owners of the building at Number 4 on the Bund, where the *Review* had its offices, for its policy of having a "foreigners only" elevator. Snow sparked such heated debate over the issue in Shanghai's foreign newspapers that the building's landlord had no choice but to change his policy to avoid more unfavorable publicity. A few months later, however, the *Review*'s landlord got his revenge by refusing to renew the newspaper's lease. As a result, the newspaper moved to a nearly windowless suite of rooms down the street on Avenue Edouard VII. In years to come, Snow would champion the Communists—as would many other foreigners in China—while Powell remained a staunch supporter of Chiang Kai-shek and the Kuomintang. Though no lover of the Communist cause, Powell knew Chiang Kai-shek well enough to discern that he was not a Communist and predicted that Chiang would "split with his 'Red' allies."

Apprehensions that the "Red wave" was not far from Shanghai's door were hardly eased by a renewal of labor activism. In October 1926, emboldened by the success of the trade unions in Hankow, laborers in Shanghai deemed the time ripe for liberating their city from the authority of Sun Chuan-fang, the warlord of Shanghai and the surrounding areas, but their plan was thwarted by one of Sun's subordinates, who quickly dispersed the strikers and beheaded twenty suspects. A second rising was attempted four months later at the end of February 1927 just after Chiang Kai-shek's troops had entered nearby Hangchow. Though 350,000 workers had been mobilized, this effort too failed, because the Communist leadership had been hoping to coordinate the rising with the entrance of Nationalist troops from Hangchow. The army never appeared, but a brutal repression began even before the strike was over. Through the streets of the Chinese areas filtered public executioners—large, fierce-looking men dressed in black with chains wrapped around their waists and "great broadswords" in their hands—followed by squads of soldiers who either shot or beheaded strikers or anyone distributing leaflets. The victims, after being marched to a prominent spot, wrote one American reporter, "were forced to bend over while their heads were cut off. Thousands fled in horror when the heads were stuck on sharp-pointed bamboo poles and were hoisted aloft and carried to the scene of the next execution." As many as two hundred people—including bystanders caught reading the leaflets—were said to have died in this manner. As a further gruesome warning, the heads were put in bamboo cages and hung on telephone poles on the busiest streets in the Chinese areas. "Relatives recognized their dear ones, moaned and cried, women knocked their heads on the ground," wrote another eyewitness. "Unclaimed, decapitated corpses lay in the square. People inhaled the stench of corpses."

Among the orchestrators of the aborted second rising was Chou En-lai, who had been dispatched to Shanghai in December by the Communists to give direction to the workers. Deeply disturbed by the insurrection's bloody aftermath, Chou tightened his control over the Communist underground, trained and equipped a militia of five hundred workers for armed warfare, and oversaw the infiltration of the warlord's army in preparation for a third and last uprising. Chou saw his opportunity on March 20, after Chiang Kai-shek's forces had scattered Sun Chuan-fang's armies and sent the warlord fleeing north. In the wake of Sun's departure, another warlord, the Shantung general Chang Tsung-chang, had moved down the Shanghai-Nanking railway and taken over the Shanghai area. But Chang, a beefy-faced former wharf coolie called the Dog Meat General for his savage methods, was even more detested than his predecessor.

Judging the timing ripe for insurrection, Chou called for a general strike and assault against local government forces to begin on March 21. That day, Shanghai shut down even more completely than it had during the May Thirtieth strikes as 800,000 workers answered the call to strike: lights went out, streetcars stopped, cotton mills and department stores shut their doors, mail and cables went undelivered, and the wharves stood empty and quiet. At the same time, a workers' militia armed with Mausers spread out into all parts of Chinese Shanghai to take over the police stations and local military stations. Resistance melted away as "soldiers and policemen tore off their uniforms and surrendered arms and ammunition." The hardest fighting took place at the North Station railway in Chapei, where Chang Tsung-chang's mercenaries had set fire to houses in the vicinity, and along Paoshan Road, where from behind barricades the workers returned their fire; from an armored train car, the Shantung men lobbed shells into the streets as the car moved up and down the railway tracks. By the evening of the next day, however, their ammunition was exhausted, and the warlord's soldiers hoisted a white flag over the station and dispersed under the cover of burning houses into the Chinese district. With that, all of Shanghai except for the International Settlement and French Concession had fallen to the workers. Having conquered the citadel of capitalism for the revolution, the trade unions took over the key municipal buildings, set up a provisional "citizens' government," and began policing Chinese Shanghai's streets, as in the course of the insurrection they had acquired a large cache of weapons. To the jubilant workers, Chou declared that their victory proved "that the working class is the most revolutionary and that it can take the leadership of the expedition against the warlords. . . . A new revolutionary democratic power can be established."

The euphoria was short-lived. Threatened by labor's sudden power and frightened by the possibility of social revolution, Shanghai's bankers and businessmen found a savior in Chiang Kai-shek, whom they offered three million dollars to suppress the labor movement and set up a rival Nationalist government in Nanking. Chiang had always been opposed to including Communists in the Kuomintang but had quietly bided his time, professing friendship for Moscow while he built up his power base. When Borodin ordered him to continue the Northern Expedition toward Peking, he deliberately disobeyed, taking the Nationalist army coastward, toward Shanghai. In the citadel of capitalism and imperialism could be found Chang Ching-chang and other financiers from the same province, member of the powerful Chekiang clique, which could secure for Chiang the financing he required to declare his independence from the Nanking government.

Throughout February, delegations of Shanghai businessmen came to Chiang at his winter headquarters in Nanchang to dicker with him over his price for crushing the labor movement. In this they had the support of the Municipal Council, which had broken all precedent to invite the leaders of the Chinese General Chamber of Commerce to a dinner where the Chinese capitalists offered to join hands with the foreign taipans in restoring "peace and stability." The Chinese capitalists took the opportunity to assert their demands for equality by demanding representation on the Municipal Council. In reply to remarks by Sterling Fessenden, the council's American chairman, about the common troubles the foreign and Chinese business community faced, Yu Hsia-ching, the head of the Chamber of Commerce, acknowledged "the exceedingly tense situation," adding, "It is no exaggeration to say that spontaneous combustion is apt to take place at the slightest provocation which may quickly lead to a worse conflagration than that of last year. For our respective and common interests we must by all means prevent it." Of course, the Chinese sought a restoration of order, he declared, "but speaking frankly, we do not care to have it at 'any price.' "

Slowly, Shanghai's taipans and consuls were being forced to address the grievances of the city's increasingly outspoken native business interests. In January, for example, the foreign consuls bowed to pressure by the foreign ministry to create the Shanghai Provisional Court, where Chinese magistrates tried the International Settlement's Chinese cases; this eliminated the foreign-dominated Mixed Court. The Municipal Council would begin to meet the native business community's demands three weeks later, when the admission of three Chinese members to the Municipal Council was approved by the foreign taxpayers. Though the General Chamber of Commerce would reject that offer as insufficient, it was the beginning of a new relationship between the city's foreign and Chinese magnates.

Among those calling on Chiang at Kiukiang was Pockmarked Huang, the Green Gang boss, who was an old acquaintance of Chiang's from his Shanghai days. Huang had come to offer Chiang the Green Gang's assistance in securing Shanghai for his forces in exchange for protection of the Green Gang's opium monopoly. The gangster and military chief's relationship dated back to the days of the 1911 Shanghai rising, when Huang had supplied gangsters for use in the revolutionary force commanded by Chiang's mentor, Chen Chi-mei. Chen himself was said to have been a member of the Green Gang, and Chiang was inducted as well into the gangster fraternity. Huang and Tu Yueh-sen had watched the cold-eyed military man's progress with interest and decided that he was a better man to protect their illicit rackets than the austere Communists. Before he left Nanchang, Pockmarked Huang had offered his "younger brother" Chiang the use of his racketeers in suppressing the trade unions and extracted a promise of protection of the Green Gang's opium operations.

By the time Chiang made his triumphal entrance into Shanghai on March 27, the stage was set for one of the great countercoups of history. Even as Chiang professed his friendship for Moscow, hundreds of Green Gang thugs were mustered into a purportedly pro-labor organization, the Society for Common Progress, to compete with the Communist-led General Labor Union, and units of the Nationalist army sympathetic to labor were being transferred out of the area. To all those involved in the final arrangements for the suppression of the Communists it was apparent that Tu Yueh-sen, not Pockmarked Huang, was in charge of the assault, as Tu summoned one worthy after another to Huang's residence to make last-minute arrangements. From the French consul and police, Tu asked for five thousand rifles and enough ammunition to supply his needs, and of Sterling Fessenden, the Municipal Council's American chairman, the gangster chief asked permission to move a convoy of his armed toughs through the International Settlement into Chapei. Never before had the city's foreign officials acceded to such a request from any Chinese force, but Fessenden believed the situation dire enough to warrant breaking precedent. That same day, he obtained the backing of the other members of the Municipal Council. And so foreign Shanghai and the forces of the underworld, joining hands, were ready to ambush the left.

The sound of shotgun fire from somewhere in the French Concession followed by the shrill whistle of a gunboat at four in the morning on April 12 signaled the beginning of Chiang's purge of the Communists. Fifteen hundred Green Gang toughs, dressed in blue uniforms with white bands on their arms bearing the character meaning "labor," descended upon the trade unions' strongholds at some twenty-five points, from the General Labor Union's offices in Chapei to the workers' militia's headquarters in west Shanghai. They conducted a wholesale slaughter of the pickets and arrested their leaders. They traveled in trucks and armored cars supplied by the British military. At each point, the same scene was repeated— squads of gangsters stormed their stations, rained gunfire on the pickets, then disarmed them. Caught completely off guard, the workers fought back desperately, especially at the Commercial Press's huge plant, the Communist command center, where four hundred students and laborers fended off both Tu's men and Nationalist soldiers for six hours. To those taken captive, Tu's hired guns showed no mercy. Prisoners were taken out into the street to be shot or beheaded on the spot or marched to Lunghwa for summary execution. "Heads rolled in the gutters of the narrow lanes like ripe plums," reported one witness, "and the weary executioners wielded their swords with the monotonous rhythm of *punka wallahs*." At the South Railway Station, a scene of particular barbarism, men were "fed alive into the fireboxes of locomotives."

The following day, 100,000 citizens gathered in pouring rain to present a petition to the local Nationalist military commander. Still not grasping the import of the attacks on their positions, they were so confident that the soldiers would not dare shoot them that they placed women and children at the head of a procession marching down Paoshan Road. But shoot the sentries did, killing sixty-six and wounding 316, and they arrested hundreds. "On Paoshan Road, they were ambushed by troops," wrote one witness. "From concealed nests, machine guns poured lead into the crowd. When it broke and ran, leaving behind scores of bodies, soldiers chased the workers into the alleyways and houses and bayoneted them and smashed their heads with rifle butts." Then, "walking up and down the street, they kicked the bodies in a search for the injured. Others were still dragging their victims from alleyways. Coolies were already on the scene, tossing corpses into trucks." The dead and the wounded were mixed together in the truckloads of victims carried away from the scene. The carnage continued as Tu's plainclothesmen and Nationalist soldiers went from house to house ferreting out more suspected Communists and labor leaders, and in the International Settlement, police supplied with lists by Chiang's spies rounded up even more. Given no trial, the suspects were tortured in order to elicit the names of underground comrades, then shot after dark. Every evening for weeks to come, residents along the road to Lungwha heard military trucks rumbling toward the Nationalists' headquarters, knowing that their passengers were bound for their graves. Men were often forced to dig their own graves, but particular cruelty was meted out to females, especially as the repression spread to Hunan and Canton, where every woman with bobbed hair was seized as a radical. "The girls' bodies were always horribly mutilated," said a female Communist who escaped capture in Hunan. "After girl students were beheaded, their heads were put into men's coffins, and the gendarmes said: 'You have your free love now!' If girls and men happened to be killed at the same time their heads were exchanged on the bodies."

Chiang had succeeded in smashing the city's labor movement and suppressing its Communist organization, but it was at the cost of a bitter and bloody vendetta with the Communists that would last over two decades and ultimately end in the Nationalists' defeat. As it was, the "Shanghai Massacre" had already taken a heavy toll in lives—between five and ten thousand Shanghainese were believed to have perished in the three weeks during the purge and its aftermath. Several of the Communists' top leaders had been caught up in Chiang's antileftist net in Shanghai, including Wang Shou-hua, the General Labor Union's head (who had been murdered by Tu Yueh-sen's henchmen shortly after he arrived at Tu's house for a dinner engagment on the eve of the coup), and one of Chen Tu-hsiu's sons, an organizer of Shanghai's ricksha pullers. Chou En-lai would have been arrested at the Chapei headquarters of the Nationalist army, where he had gone to protest the assaults against the workers on April 13, had it not been for the intercession of an officer sympathetic to the Communists whom Chou had known at Whampoa. Afterward, deftly dodging the police, who had posted his photograph at all the train stations (Chiang had put a reward of eighty thousand dollars on his head), Chou escaped upriver to Hankow.

While the Green Gang helped spread the "White Terror" throughout the lower Yangtze and south in Canton, Chiang set up his own Nationalist regime at Nanking. The Wuhan government scathingly denounced Chiang for his "treachery" to the party, but there was little question that Chiang would prevail: behind him, he had not just the Kuomintang's right wing but the Shanghai financiers and the foreign powers, which had hastened to recognize the Nanking regime once Chiang had aligned himself with the forces of capitalism and law and order.

More important, Chiang controlled the Nationalist army. Under pressure of an economic blockade from the Western powers, the Wuhan leadership began splintering, and by August it had expelled the Communists and Soviet advisers as a prelude to a rapprochement with the Nanking regime.

Almost alone in her condemnation of the cowardly about-face was Soong Ching-ling, who, horrified at her colleagues' betrayal of Sun Yat-sen's alliance, condemned the party's "counterrevolutionary" leadership. So that none would mistake her views, Ching-ling soon left Wuhan for a self-imposed exile in Moscow for the next several months before traveling on to Germany to join other Chinese revolutionaries in planning an independent Chinese party aligned with neither the Kuomintang nor the Communists. After her departure, the remnants of the Kuomintang left wing were free to reunite with the right wing in Nanking, but the two sides could not agree on Chiang's role in the government. In August, Chiang abruptly resigned from his posts to "tend to my mother's grave," he told reporters. His reason, however, was to give the squabbling politicians time to realize how indispensable he was to their government. Chiang had calculated correctly. Barely six months later, he would be invited back to Nanking to again command the army and appointed to the Kuomintang's Central Executive Committee.

During Chiang's absence from the government, Shanghai's bankers and industrialists had breathed a collective sigh of relief. After bankrolling his coup, they thought they had paid their debt to him, but much to their dismay, he demanded further funds to pay his troops and continue his military campaign. When they refused, he used extortion and intimidation, the same coercive tactics that his mentor Chen Chi-mei had employed so effectively in 1912. His "reign of terror" began with the arrest the new chairman of the Chinese General Chamber of Commerce, Fu Tsung-yao. Chiang's agents accused the businessman of being a "counterrevolutionary." Fu responded by transferring as much property as he could to foreigners before fleeing to Dairen; the rest of his property was then confiscated by the government. Other warrants for arrest and actual arrests followed. Even Jung Tsing-ching, the great textile and flour magnate, was jailed on charges of corruption and aiding warlords and released only after he had paid Nanking 250,000 dollars.

Where the arm of the "law" could not reach, Tu Yueh-sen's services were called in. A kidnapping wave of unprecedented proportions hit the foreign settlements for a dozen weeks from the end of March until mid-June as one wealthy Chinese after another was spirited away by Tu's "plainclothesmen" and held for ransom. The victims were many and various: the three-year-old son of the director of Sincere's; the fifty-eight-year-old comprador of a Chinese trading company, who was "forced at gunpoint into a Ford motorcar by three kidnappers . . . leaving Li's ricksha puller behind to report the crime," according to one chronicler of the crime wave; a wealthy Soochow merchant who was seized as he was stepping "into his gray Austin, having just enjoyed a stop at the public baths, when four men with pistols pushed him into the back seat, threw out his chauffeur, and sped off"; "an executive of a Chinese insurance company who was shot and killed in his automobile during an attempted kidnapping."

With such dire threats hanging over their heads, few businessmen dared resist when Nanking announced the sale of government bonds and "apportioned varying quotas" to Shanghai's largest concerns. Representatives from the finance ministry went from one company or association to another "requesting" bond purchases. "The Nanyang Tobacco Company, for instance, was ordered to give five hundred thousand yuan; the Nantao Electric and Gas Works, three hundred thousand yuan; and the Sincere Company Department Store two hundred fifty thousand dollars." Yet another means of squeezing merchants for money was to fine them for violating a government-organized boycott of Japanese goods (in protest of

Japanese military activity in Shantung). Green Gang "inspectors" called on every shop and business "levying fines and blackmail on all and sundry of the merchant classes—both millionaires and small shopkeepers being found guilty of 'assisting Japanese imperialists,' " reported the American consul, Edwin Cunningham, who also noted the appearance of wooden cages bearing the signs "Cages for Rent to Foreign Slaves" on Chinese streets close to the foreign areas. Numerous merchants were arrested and held at Chiang's military headquarters at Lungwha until ransoms of up to 150,000 dollars were produced.

Through these decidedly unorthodox fund-raising measures, Chiang accumulated a war chest of some fifty million dollars. Once again, Tu Yueh-sen and his gangster fraternity had rendered him invaluable aid. For putting down the threat from labor, the "Al Capone of the Orient" had already ascended to unaccustomed heights of celebrity among grateful foreigners. He became "the deliverer . . . a hero to the European women of Shanghai and acclaimed a pillar of society." For his help in securing Shanghai and milking its moneymen, Tu was decorated by Chiang himself at a ceremony in Nanking and named a "major-general" in the Nationalist government. Though merely honorary, the appointment nonetheless signified the unique position the criminal kingpin occupied in the regime. Though his government was opposed to opium, Chiang split half the profits from narcotics traffic by appointing Chang Hsiao-lin, Tu's associate, head of an Opium Suppression Bureau whose avowed purpose was to eradicate the drug traffic by seizing and destroying the contraband while requiring all addicts to register with the bureau. In fact, the bureau enabled the Green Gang to monopolize the opium traffic—the confiscated opium found its way back into the marketplace and the bureau charged addicts the going rate for their opium. In 1931 Tu himself became head of the bureau. The absurdity of Tu's position—to be both China's biggest opium importer and the man charged with suppressing the drug—was not lost on him; in 1936, on the occasion of Chiang's fiftieth birthday, he presented the Generalissimo with a brand-new airplane which he had christened "Opium Suppression of Shanghai."

Recognized by the Nanking government, the master of the underworld now sought a position in the "upperworld" as well. This was accomplished with ease, as Tu had more money and power—the only two commodities that Shanghai respected—than anyone else. With his money, he became a banker and philanthropist. His first bank, the Chung Wai Bank, located in a spanking new modern building on Avenue Edouard VII, served as the gangster's business headquarters as well. (A bulletproof elevator took Tu up to his private offices on the second floor.) Never wanting for funds, the Chung Wai Bank did a brisk business selling directorships to wealthy businessmen who wanted Tu's protection. Within five years of assisting Chiang in his rise to supremacy, Tu had accumulated more directorships and chairmanships on banks, exchanges, and companies than any other Shanghai businessman. Because of his influence and ability to solve problems, Tu's help was frequently solicited by important Shanghainese in delicate situations. "Businessmen and rich heirs especially valued their association with him, for it meant protection from certain dreaded evils: kidnapping, paternity and breach of promise suits; estate disputes; and recovery of debts incurred by heirs," observed one of Tu's biographers. Tu also had access to the mail of everyone in Shanghai through his control of the post office workers' union. As he was so often asked to rescue the rich and prominent from one embarrassment after another, he came to know a great deal about their personal lives—which only enhanced the general fear in which he was held.

Chiang ceased using Tu's toughs to extort funds from Shanghai's magnates six months after bringing into his government T. V. Soong, the Wuhan regime's erstwhile finance minister and the man who had put Sun Yat-sen's finances in order for the Northern Expedition. This feat, along with Chiang's bolstering of his credentials as Sun Yat-sen's rightful heir, was accomplished through his marriage, on December 1, 1927, to Soong Mei-ling. The engagement, contracted during the period of Chiang's short-lived "resignation," was a brilliant political move. By announcing his impending marriage into the family of the widow of the sainted Sun Yat-sen, Chiang not only lifted himself from being one of the many contenders for the "Father's" mantle to his clear successor, but boosted his standing among foreigners as well: they could only view his acceptance by Shanghai's foremost Westernized Christian family as a sign that he was friendly to the West. As shrewd as was the alliance, it had been conceived of not by Chiang but by one equal to him in manipulation—Soong Ai-ling. Charlie Soong's shrewd and indomitable eldest was "always the matchmaker, planner and builder of the family wealth," said one of her Chinese contemporaries. "Would it not be a brilliant coup to marry off her youngest sister, Mei-ling, to the powerful Commander-in-Chief of the Nationalist armies? 'We can use this man,' she said. And immediately went about convincing the recalcitrant Mei-ling that such a marriage would be in the interest of all, especially the House of Soong."

Ai-ling had proposed the plan to Chiang as early as March, after Chiang had asked for her help in gathering support for his Nanking regime. If Mei-ling had any doubts about the suitability of the provincial soldier with the country accent as a husband, they speedily vanished with the success of his counterrevolution. Moreover, marriage to the general now touted as "China's man of destiny" assured her what she had found wanting in her previous suitors—a position on the public stage. Ai-ling had used her considerable persuasive skills to press T. V. Soong into abandoning Ching-ling in Wuhan to lend his talents—and his contacts with the Shanghai bankers—to the Nanking regime. Only one obstacle remained—obtaining the permission of Mei-ling's mother. But before he could approach the redoubtable Madame Soong, Chiang sent his second wife, Chen Chieh-ju, to the United States in the company of two of Chang Ching-chang's daughters and had Tu Yueh-sen handle the financial arrangements. Then he went to Japan, where Madame Soong was vacationing with Mei-ling, to confront the matriarch, who had made clear her disapproval of the match. Even more opposed to the idea was Ching-ling, who, upon hearing the news of her sister's engagement, had telegrammed from Moscow, "Don't marry that Bluebeard!" Ching-ling knew well that even in marriage, Chiang was an opportunist, as he had tendered an offer for her hand through an intermediary shortly after Sun Yat-sen's death. In Japan, Madame Soong, hearing that Chiang had pursued her to Japan, fled all the way to the other side of Japan. But Chiang followed her. Finally, with Ai-ling at his side to plead his case, Chiang persuaded Madame Soong of his suitability as a son-in-law and promised to convert to Methodism.

To the nuptials, "the outstanding Chinese marriage ceremony of recent years," declared the *Shanghai Times,* came thirteen hundred guests, including nearly every foreign diplomat in Shanghai and the commanders of the British and American fleets. They gathered in the Majestic Hotel's ballroom, decorated to resemble a foreign-style church and hung with huge bells of massed white chrysanthemums. More flowers and ferns lined a red pathway leading to an altar dominated by a portrait of Sun Yat-sen flanked on either side by the Chinese and Kuomintang flags. When Chiang appeared at the head of the room, stiff in an English-style cutaway, the audience broke into applause. Then, to the furious whirring of newsreel cameras, Mei-ling entered in a gown of silver and white georgette, diamonds in her ears and her head covered by a lace veil adorned with orange buds. The orchestra played "Here Comes the Bride," as T. V. led his sister down the aisle. After many speeches and bows before Sun Yat-sen's portrait, Mei-ling and

Chiang posed for photographs, she looking alert and decidedly unsubmissive, and he, said one foreigner, "weary beyond words."

From Peking, Chiang brought Sun Yat-sen's remains to Nanking. They were to be placed in a tomb behind a gleaming marble mausoleum on Purple Mountain high above the city which the Ming emperors and the Taipings had made their own capital. Now it was the seat of a new and fortified Kuointang government, one which the foreign powers had not hesitated to recognize. On June 1, 1929, the day Sun's remains were formally placed in the crypt, Chiang bowed before Sun's coffin, announcing his completion of the Northern Expedition. His pleasure in the event, attended by all Nanking's officials and its entire diplomatic contingent, was marred only by the fact that Soong Ching-ling, who had been persuaded to return to China for the burial, had soundly denounced him before leaving Berlin and on every step of her way toward Nanking.

She went back to Shanghai, installing herself in the modest gray brick house on Rue Molière that Sun Yat-sen's followers had given him in 1916 and that was the only worldly possession he could claim upon his death. Soong Ching-ling would leave for Berlin soon after her brief stop in Shanghai. In 1931 she would come back to Shanghai for good. Then the shutters on the Rue Molière house would be kept shut on the street side, because it was constantly under surveillance. Chiang Kai-shek's secret police had it kept it under discreet watch night and day. His agents kept track of Soong Ching-ling's comings and goings and recorded the names of all those who entered. And there were many. Through her door came all of China's important writers and intellectuals, along with nearly every liberal foreign luminary to visit China, from George Bernard Shaw to Rabindranath Tagore to Agnes Smedley, for Soong Ching-ling had taken on the highly dangerous cause of publicizing the Kuomintang's repression of its leftist critics.

But in August 1929, Soong Ching-ling had not yet left Shanghai for Berlin. On August 1, International War Day, she fired off a telegram to the European press blasting Chiang Kai-shek for his lies and betrayals. Ten days later, a Kuomintang official, a former associate of Sun Yat-sen's, called on her. "If you were anyone but Madame Sun, we would cut your head off," he warned.

"If you were the revolutionaries you pretend to be, you'd cut it off anyway," she curtly rejoined.

C
H
A
P
T
E
R
6

ENTER THE DWARF BANDITS

Never was Shanghai's allure greater than at the beginning of the 1930s. Hong Kong's views might be more magnificent, Peking's monuments more ancient, Yokohama's climate more salubrious, and Singapore less expensive. Perhaps the natives in the provinces were more cordial, the accents in Soochow more pleasing, or the food better in Canton, but ask any Orient-bound traveler his prime destination and the answer would invariably be "Shanghai!"

For a moment, imagine what met the eye of newcomers to the "Paris of the Orient" in its heyday. After passing nondescript ranges of warehouses, docks, cotton mills, foundries, and shipyards, you knew that Shanghai was just around the bend by the progression of unlovely sights heralding the approach of a metropolitan center: huge billboards mounted on stilts touting cigarettes and Chinese miracle curatives, work sheds piled high with lumber and scrap metal, and range after range of grimy warehouses and dockyards. Finally, the city's harbor comes into view. Dominating the river is a line of gray-and-white warships—the watchdogs of the treaty powers. Riding loftily at anchor for nearly a mile in the middle of the river, these cruisers, destroyers, minesweepers, and other nautical mastodons seem almost to shout: "I am a colonial power." The Union Jack flies high above a British P&O mail steamer and the Stars and Stripes flies above an American merchant marine ship, while the Italian Lloyd *Triestino* and Japanese Nippon *Yusen Kaisha* freighters exchange toots. Swimming alongside these mastodons are an astonishing variety of smaller craft, everything from tugboats to junks with magnificent bat-winged sails. There are two-storied Noah's Ark boats, high-pooped lorchas with wondrous painted eyes, flat-bottomed blunt-nosed fishing boats, and the ubiquitous mat-covered sampans.

Then, a sharp turn to the left, and the most famous skyline east of the Suez looms suddenly into view—a solid front of imposing granite and marble buildings above a boulevard and grassy promenade where the pedestrians appear as mere insects. The edifices on the International Settlement's Bund outdo those of many a European and American capital for sheer ornateness. Built in a hodgepodge of styles—everything from Moorish to Italian Neo-Renaissance—they incorporate enough Doric and Ionic columns, friezes, bas-relief sculptures, balustrades, turrets, domes, cupolas, and clock towers to satisfy the most enthusiastic student of Western architecture.

These palatial buildings, erected in solid and approved Anglo-Oriental style, had been raised in celebration of the British imperium and the spirit of Western commercial enterprise. "What pangs of regret and remorse ought to be awakened among these proud, unenlightened men, when, in their moments, if any, of honest reflection, they cast their eyes upon this 'Model Settlement,' and perceive that a handful of outer barbarians have done more than they themselves, with their highest efforts, have achieved anywhere in their own wide

Empire during all the untold centuries of its fame," mused British photographer John Thomson, displaying a self-satisfaction shared by his fellow foreigners. But those less enamored of the West's lust for conquest—and not all of them Chinese—saw the Bund as emblematic of the artificiality of the foreign settlements in China. Its mongrel mix of architectural styles, for one, struck the Sinophilic writer Harold Acton as a "ponderous parody" of authentic Western thoroughfares; the ornate structures, he said, "do not look man-made: they have little connection with the people of China; they are poisonous toadstools raised by anonymous banks, trusts and commercial firms. Imposing from the river, but essentially soulless: no court or government had designed them and given them life."

To walk the length of the Bund was to encounter Shanghai at its most vibrant. The street was alive with noise and movement. Horns honked, whistles blew, bells jingled, peddlers barked, mendicants whined, and small hucksters cried. Vehicles of every description—pushcarts, pony carriages, bicycles, rickshas, wheelbarrows, motorcycles, automobiles, buses, and trucks—streamed down the roadway in a mad rush as throngs of pedestrians jostled one another on the crowded thoroughfare. The barking of ricksha pullers competing hotly for fares pierced the air while here and there, jogging coolies, their muscular shoulders supporting bamboo poles weighted with baskets containing everything from squawking geese to vegetables to earthenware jars, shouted at the top of their lungs for the crowd to make way.

On both sides of the Bund, the sidewalk and the grassy riverbank, gathered the most bizarre agglomeration of humanity to be found anywhere on earth: world-weary sophisticates crossed paths with wide-eyed peasants from the countryside; roistering sailors with dapper, aloof Englishmen; silk-gowned Chinese merchants with penniless White Russian emigrés. Wherever one looked, the ordinary rubbed up against the bizarre and fantastic: bejeweled, exquisitely groomed Chinese matrons stepped past ragged beggars ostentatiously displaying their sores; nimble pickpockets darted around *ancien régime* ladies tottering unsteadily on their shrunken "lily" feet; gilded, enamel-haired courtesans riding in brightly lit rickshas passed alms to monks in flowing black robes; cigar-smoking midgets crying "Cheap sale" made way for silent blind men tinkling wooden hammers against brass gongs; scruffy urchins chased after startled tourists yelling their ubiquitous cry, "No mama, no papa! . . . No whiskey soda!"

"Everywhere in Shanghai, one jostled adventurers and rubbed shoulders with people who had no inkling how extraordinary they were," said a mesmerized Harold Acton of perhaps the most polyglot spot on earth. The Whangpu metropolis absorbed the exotic with a spongelike facility. It took strangeness for granted, never asking for passports or visas; the port rejected no one, not the peasant fleeing his burned home and ravaged fields to make a pittance in the city's mills or to beg in its streets, not the demoralized White Russians who arrived in Shanghai penniless and speaking no English, not the Jewish refugees from Hitler's Europe to whom the rest of the world had shut its doors, not ex-bandits and retired warlords, not political revolutionaries with prices on their heads, and certainly not an international assortment of criminals and fugitives from justice who found this Oriental "Paradise of the Adventurer" a comfortable spot in which to lie low—or to run a scam.

Where it started, at the Garden Bridge on the Soochow Creek, the Bund curved for one majestic mile along the riverbank before ending alongside the greasy, cobbled waterfront of the old native quarter, the Chinese City. The Bund lay between two powerful symbols of the Western presence in Shanghai—the fortresslike buildings of the British Consulate on the north near the Soochow Creek and the foursquare, columned Shanghai Club to the south. Between these two "bookends" ran a solid line of similarly imposing colonial structures—in addition to the Hong Kong and Shanghai Bank; the Chartered Bank of India, Australia and China; the Yokohama Specie Bank; the Glen Line Building; the *North China Daily News* building—and the headquarters of such powerful "blue-blooded" firms as Jardine, Matheson and David Sassoon and Company.

First, you passed the large and well-tended grounds of the British consulate, at whose entrance turbaned, black-bearded Sikhs stood rigidly on guard. Directly opposite the consulate lay a park bordering on the riverfront, upon whose wrought-iron gate, legend has it, the notice "No Dogs and Chinese Allowed" was posted. In fact, those with sharp memories say no such sign existed: instead, two notices were posted on the gate, one reading "No Dogs Allowed," and the other, "Only for Foreigners." (An exception was made for Chinese nursemaids accompanying their white charges.) In the end, the upshot was the same—Chinese, if not canines, resented their exclusion from the misnamed Public Garden.

Over the Bund towered Sassoon House, the tallest building on the "magnificent mile," built by Victor Elice Sassoon, descendant of the family of Iraqi Jews whose antecedents had once served in the capacity of bankers to Baghdad's caliphs. Included in Sassoon House was a hotel facing the Bund, the Cathay. The ten-story ultramodern structure had been envisaged by Victor Sassoon—"Sir Victor," as the horse-loving *bon vivant* was called—as a monument to his extravagant personal taste and as tribute to his family's exalted name. The building resembled nothing less than an elaborate architectural Sphinx, its extended ferroconcrete body supported by a towering green pyramid beneath which projected, like a peering eye, the semicircular window and balcony of Sir Victor's penthouse suite.

Anyone who was anybody, it was said, sooner or later passed through the Cathay's revolving doors. Into a lobby of rose-and-gray marble and black pillars and ceilings you went, past Art Deco frescoes, past the long mahogany reception desk manned by a British-accented Chinese concierge in tails and striped pants, around a corner into a splendidly vaulted Tudor-style hallway to ascend a black marble staircase or up the caged elevator to any one of 214 rooms and suites or nine "Apartements de Luxe." Sir Victor, connoisseur of all the good things in life, had intended the Cathay to be the last word in luxurious hostelries, and so it was. You summoned drink waiters, room boys, maids, valets, and launderers simply by lifting the telephone (an innovation yet unknown in Europe's finest hotels), and you bathed in vast marble baths with silver spigots in purified water piped in from Bubbling Wells Springs outside the city. Swank society met for highballs in the Horse and Hounds bar, dined in the Grill Room, then danced rhumbas and fox-trots on the hyacinth-scented rooftop restaurant until the wee hours of morning.

If the Cathay was Shanghai's stronghold of chic, the massive Hong Kong and Shanghai Bank was its temple to Mammon. Fronted by a vast Corinthian-columned entranceway and surmounted by a colossal white dome, the bank's palatial edifice provided an appropriately stately setting for the most powerful financial institution in the Far East. Its octagonal entryway, faced in marble, featured a mural for each of the bank's eight locations—Calcutta, Bangkok, London, New York, Paris, Tokyo, Hong Kong, and Shanghai. Its name synonymous with financial stability and prestige, the bank had been founded by a group of local taipans who had obtained the virtually unlimited backing of British banking partners and, by financing new ventures, had catapulted Shanghai to its position as Asia's commercial and financial giant. Though it was called the Hong Kong and Shanghai Bank, there was no doubt in anyone's mind that the bank's headquarters were not on the rocky offshore island but beneath the great gray pile at Number 12, the Bund.

Just as all great Chinese houses were protected by lions— the symbol of power and prosperity—so the bank was guarded by two magnificent ones of bronze. The crouching larger-than-life-size beasts held themselves in a position of vigilant alertness. Among the superstitions attached to these figures was that rubbing their feet brought good luck. Hopeful passersby were to be seen lovingly burnishing the lions' already gleaming paws. Ribald wags maintained that the lions, both males, had been known to roar whenever a virgin passed but because of the scarcity of virgins in Shanghai they had long been silent. By virtue of their potent symbolism, they suffered from the mysterious twists and turns of China's history. When the Japanese invaded Shanghai during World War II they removed the lions, intending to ship them to Japan and melt them down for scrap; they were prevented from doing so, however, by the U.S. Navy's blockade of the exit to the Yangtze. After the Japanese surrendered, the lions were located and returned to the bank. These icons of capitalism enjoyed another fifteen years in place, withstanding the frantic last days of Kuomintang rule and lasting through even the first decade of Communism. But during the Cultural Revolution of the 1960s when Red Guards surged through the streets of Shanghai—the Cultural Revolution's headquarters—the statues vanished again; today, they are in crates in the Shanghai Art Museum.

To the left of the bank rose the less ornate but equally dignified facade of one of the Hong Kong and Shanghai Bank's most valued customers, the Shanghai Customs House. Though plainer than its neighbors, the Customs House was hardly less visible. Travelers could make out its famous tower with its large-faced clock—the "Big Ching," as locals referred to it—from afar, long before the rest of the Bund came into view. Though officially an arm of the Chinese government, the Chinese Maritime Customs Service was administered by foreigners on behalf of the Chinese authorities. To Chinese, the Bund was the creation of outsiders; and the Customs House, more than any other part of the foreign-made waterfront, represented China's subjugation by outsiders. Nonetheless, the customs service was run on an honest and efficient basis, so much so that the receipts it forwarded to Peking eventually made up more than a third of the Chinese government's annual revenue. This success was due in great part to the service's longtime head, Robert Hart, an Irishman who rose from modest circumstances to become one of the most powerful foreigners in China—a man so trusted by the dowager empress, T'zu-hsi, and her councillor, Prince Kung, that they referred to him as "our Hart."

Few Westerners could claim Hart's degree of familiarity with the Chinese—and, naturally, not all of them aspired to. The bastion of those who sought to maintain as much distance as possible between themselves and the Chinese was the exclusive, all-male Shanghai Club. Standing at Number One, the Bund, the club occupied an imposing stone building whose heavy double doors were flanked by Greek pillars. Within its ornate, dark-paneled premises reeking of cigars, leather, and brandy, one might—if English and of approved social standing—retreat when the East pressed too close. If you turned to the right upon entering the large black-and-white-tiled lobby, you could take the caged elevator upstairs to the small restaurant and bar upstairs, but most members turned left in the direction of the Club's celebrated Long Bar, which, Shanghailanders boasted, was the world's longest bar. An unwritten rule was that taipans occupied the end of the bar closest to the large bay windows that faced the Bund, while newcomers stood at the opposite end. Residents measured their social progress by how far they had managed to inch along the hundred-foot stretch of dark, polished mahogany. A businessman knew he had arrived when one day—months, even years, after first setting foot in the Shanghai Club—he found himself at the Long Bar's window side swilling gin with Shanghai's best.

A few yards past the Shanghai Club, where the Bund met the Avenue Edouard VII, marked the end of the International Settlement and the beginning of the French Concession. Here, narrowing as it changed into the Quai de France, the Bund gave way to a scene of gritty commerce. All was chaos and bustle as crates thudded onto gangplanks, foremen bellowed out orders, shipping clerks rushed about with bills in hand, and files of blue-trousered stevedores jog-trotted endlessly between the wharves on one side and the red-brick godowns on the other. One had to step lively in this crowded precinct to avoid being overrun by a fast-moving wheelbarrow or splattered by lurching water carriers. Piled high on the docks were bags, barrels, and bundles of everything, seemingly, that went into or out of the Celestial Empire, from sandalwood and kingfishers' feathers to soybeans and kerosene oil. Certainly among the most aromatic of Shanghai's districts, the waterfront reeked of a pungent combination of sweat, rotting garbage, fish oil, and garlic from the braziers of the many itinerant cooks who wandered the wharves, preparing instant meals of sizzling noodles and steaming rice and bean curd for a few coppers. Other peddlers, from tea and pastry vendors to traveling seamstresses and barbers, patrolled the dockside, and their shrill cries added to the general din.

Equally at home on the Bund were the city's professional beggars. To make themselves appear all the more pitiable, they faked wounds, using pig's blood, or made themselves even dirtier than they already were by smearing themselves with mud, or even deliberately maimed themselves. Female beggars frequently picked up corpses and slung them over their chests as props in making their appeals. For a time, the two beggars who occupied the sidewalk in front of the Palace Hotel at the corner of the Bund and Nanking Road were so familiar to Shanghailanders that they had nicknames: one, a man who had driven a nail into the top of his shaven skull—a nail that held a lighted candle—was dubbed "Light in the Head," and the other, a woman who cried without pause and so copiously that small pools formed around her hunched body, was called "the Weeping Wonder." To see, in the evening, a group of beggars "trooping home to their mat sheds, with the day's earnings securely stowed away on their dirty persons, is something to be remembered," recalled one Shanghailander. Still, not every mendicant had willingly chosen the profession. Some had been deformed when young by parents who were professional beggars, and others had lost their hands or feet at the command of some cruel magistrate. Then too, many Chinese, especially refugees driven into the city by poverty or civil distress, were driven to begging to survive.

Slightly off the Bund, but not far enough away to escape the noise and commotion along the docks, gaped the dark opening of Blood Alley. On this dingy neon-lit strip, familiar to sailors of all nationalities, flourished more than a dozen boisterous cabarets and tawdry sailors' haunts through which nightly streamed some five to ten thousand seamen, smugglers, crooks, prostitutes, dance hostesses, and thrill-seeking tourists. Blood Alley came by its nickname because of the regularity with which brawls broke out among its rowdy patrons—usually over the favors of one or another of the Russian dance hostesses. The seamen most eager for a fight were British and Americans, who "took boxing lessons not only to qualify for appearances in the ring but in order to make a good showing in barroom brawls." And however much the Brits and Yanks blackened each other's eyes with zest, they gamely joined forces when German, Italian, or French sailors appeared on the scene. The ensuing bottle-throwing, furniture-smashing melee was usually settled by the arrival of the French Concession's Annamite police, but on at least one occasion, foreign diplomats were summoned from their beds to negotiate an armistice between the two camps.

From dusk until early morning, Avenue Edouard VII was filled with aggressive ladies of the night. "Kidnapped bedfellows were taken to small hotels around the corner," Percy Finch related. "When the police appeared along the International Settlement side of Avenue Edward VII, the girls ran across the street into the more broad-minded French Concession until the patrol, making a pretense of duty, had passed. It was more than your virtue was worth to walk downtown after the movie or even to take a ricksha. The girls turned highwaymen and snatched customers from traffic." With Chinese customers, especially newcomers from the countryside, the prostitutes were even more aggressive. Spotting a country bumpkin, two or three girls would work together, said another Westerner, "in a concerted onslaught, grasping the victim firmly by the clothing and doing their best to work him into a doorway or other place where they can compromise him to the extent that he loses face if he doesn't accede."

Shanghai was nothing if not a city of contrasts. For all its modernity, Nanking Road still belonged to China. You could never be sure who or what you would run into. Right off the most crowded part of Nanking Road, not far from one of the great department stores, you could step into a temple that looked for all the world as if it had been in the same spot for thousands of years. Behind a dirty stone wall fronted by a wooden gate, you entered a courtyard to see a few shaven-headed monks tending to the incense burner, and inside the temple a worshiper or two lighting red candles in front of an altar. On feast days, the same courtyard would be jammed with peddlers, tooth-pullers, itinerant cooks, bird dealers, and professional scribes seated at rickety tables penning love letters or bills for the illiterate. When you left the temple, closing its wooden doors behind you, the sound of Nanking Road's roaring traffic pulled you back into the twentieth century.

The great artery ended in a swirl of fierce traffic at its juncture with Thibet Road, one of busiest parts of Shanghai because of the confluence of several main streets at the green oval that formed the racecourse. Here were grandstands, a racetrack, and the stately clubhouse of the Shanghai Race Club. But dominating the area was an enormous concrete building encircled by balconies and topped by a five-story minaret. This fantastic creation was the Great World, a teeming labyrinth of theaters, distorting mirrors, shooting galleries, magicians, jugglers, acrobats, fortune-tellers, and much else, patronized both by the Chinese masses and thrill-seeking Europeans.

No one establishment said more about Shanghai during its last decades of semicolonialism than this hodgepodge of the most déclassé elements of East and West. The brainchild of a medicinal millionaire, Huang Chu-jiu, the Great World was built in 1916 to provide a place where the city's "common folk," in Huang's words, could have a good time. Huang, the owner of a chain of drugstores, had earlier made a fortune selling a concoction that he claimed enhanced the mental faculties. A master of marketing, Huang put a picture of a rich Jewish friend on the label—an endorsement that sent sales soaring, as what genuine Shanghainese could not respect the financial acumen of the Sassoons and other members of Shanghai's prosperous Sephardic Jewish community? Huang had started the Great World after selling out his interest in two earlier amusement centers, the New World and the Small World. The Great World outdid its predecessors in every way, pulling in huge crowds from the day it opened. In the Great World's churning wake an assortment of smaller pleasure palaces tried to imitate Huang Chi-jiu's success, but none succeeded. "There was the Tachien World, the youngest and most modest," explained one Chinese chronicler. "The New World, which is not as successful, and lost some of its audience and the Little World, which, despite the name, boasted of having the most number and varieties of entertainment."

The Great World's success soon aroused the envy of another Huang—Huang Jin-rong, at the time Shanghai's biggest racketeer. Deciding to add the Great World to his own empire, the gangster took advantage of Huang Chi-jiu's overspeculation in the real estate market to sour his other investments. The businessman was brought to the brink of ruin, and in 1931 he sold the Great World to the racketeer. From an innocent enough resort for the middle and working classes, the Great World changed into a notorious vice spot, a place which no male could walk past without "feeling a feminine hand tugging at his elbow" or, worse, finding himself dragged in the direction of the Great World's entrance by a posse of prostitutes and their amahs in a manner which one American described as "the Chinese equivalent of a football tackle." No young girl dared enter the establishment unless she was a member of the world's oldest profession, and impressionable young men were not permitted past the first floor. Swarming with prostitutes, thieves, gamblers, and petty gangsters, the Great World soon came to be regarded, in one historian's description, as a "Shanghai in miniature, a concentration of all the city's warts and blemishes." "Obscene dramas and cabaret shows of vile, or at the very least, indelicate taste were staged there," recorded one visitor. And a French journalist recalled "seeing a manager complacently pointing to his premier sideshow attraction—a pregnant girl of six!"

The pulse of the Great World after its takeover by the underworld was fast and raunchy. Joseph von Sternberg immortalizes it for us in a colorful, albeit liberally embellished account in his memoir, *Fun in a Chinese Laundry*, and in the early 1930s his best-known Hollywood foray, *Shanghai Express*, had film audiences all over the world—except perhaps in Shanghai—wondering what Marlene Dietrich really meant when she said, "It took more than one man to change my name to Shanghai Lily." The director found the Great World's six floors to be

> seething with life and all the commotion and noise
> that go with it, studded with every variety of entertain-
> ment Chinese ingenuity had contrived. When I had
> entered the hot stream of humanity, there was no
> turning back had I wanted to. On the first floor were

gambling tables, singsong girls, magicians, pickpockets, slot machines, fireworks, bird cages, fans, stick incense, acrobats and ginger. One flight up were restaurants, a dozen different groups of actors, crickets in cages, pimps, midwives, barbers and earwax extractors. The third floor had jugglers, herb medicines, ice-cream parlours, photographers, a new bevy of girls, their high-collared gowns slit to reveal their hips, in case one had passed up the more modest ones below who merely flashed their thighs; and under the heading of novelty, several rows of exposed toilets, their impresarios instructing the amused patrons not to squat but to assume a position more in keeping with the imported plumbing. The fourth floor was covered with shooting galleries, *fan-tan* tables, revolving wheels, massage benches, acupuncture and moxa cabinets, hot-towel counters, dried fish and intestines, and dance platforms serviced by a horde of music makers competing with each other to see who could drown out the others. The fifth floor featured girls whose dresses were slit to the armpits, a stuffed whale, story tellers, balloons, peep shows, masks, a mirror maze, two love-letter booths with scribes who guaranteed results, "rubber goods" and a temple filled with ferocious gods and joss sticks. On the top floor and roof of that house of multiple joys a jumble of tightrope walkers slithered back and forth, and there were see-saws, Chinese checkers, mah-jong, strings of firecrackers going off, lottery tickets, and marriage brokers. And as I tried to find my way down again an open space was pointed out to me where hundreds of Chinese, so I was told, after spending their coppers, had speeded the return to the street below by jumping from the roof.

If, instead of turning from the Bund onto Nanking Road, you continued along it, crossing the smelly Soochow Creek via the Garden Bridge, you would find yourself in Hongkew, the former unofficial American concession before it joined with the British to form the International Settlement. Hongkew's best-known landmark was the Astor House Hotel, the center of foreign social life before the coming of the Cathay and its ilk. Four large neo-Renaissance brick buildings linked together by stone passageways, the Astor House took up an entire block just off the Garden Bridge. Managed by a retired ship captain who ran it as a ship, the hotel had corridors painted with portholes and *trompe l'oeil* seascapes and rooms decorated like cabins; there was even a "steerage" section with bunks instead of beds at cheaper rates. Meals, for which formal dress was expected, were announced by trumpet fanfares. Americans favored the Astor House because of its venerable namesake in New York, "The finest service in the world," a seven-year-old Brooke Astor was told by her father, a naval officer, when her family stopped in Shanghai in 1911. "When we went up to our rooms I saw a long, long hall with a man dressed in a white skirt and blue jacket beside every second door," she reminisced in her memoirs. " 'Who are all these men?' I asked Father. 'They are the "boys," ' he answered. 'And when you want your breakfast or your tea, just open the door and tell them.' "

On the other side of the road from the Astor House stood the Russian, German, American, and Japanese consulates in appropriately imposing edifices. Of these, the Russian consulate, built just before the czarist government's fall, was the most heavily fortified. The huge four-story structure had massive iron gates surrounding all the windows on the first floor. This precaution became useful for the consulate's next occupants, for Shanghai's White Russian community would occasionally assemble outside the Red consulate and attempt to storm it. Only a short walk away from "Consulate Row" was the Hongkew market, Shanghai's biggest market, where farmers brought their fowl and produce to sell every day, and, a little farther on, Little Tokyo, the Japanese part of Shanghai. Here, you could buy kimono cloth and bonsai trees or dine with a party of friends in a private tatami room in one of the area's many sukiyaki restaurants. Then too, Hongkew boasted the Shansi Bankers Guild, the most sumptuous of all Shanghai's guild houses. Its most popular room was a theater whose ceiling was equipped with "a curiously shaped dome in which it is possible to see oneself upside down."

As the 1930s began, Shanghai was entering the peak of its prosperity. It was bigger and richer than ever and flush with its success. The port had ascended to fifth-largest in the world. Through its portals went 51 percent of China's foreign imports and 30 percent of its exports. Foreign businesses had invested more than three billion dollars in the City of Mudflats, the largest outside investment in any city in the world. Into the big Chinese banks on the Bund, grinning coolies had trundled on wheelbarrows some five billion Chinese dollars in silver, nearly five times as much as the same bank vaults had contained after the World War, thanks to the Nanking government's new policy of keeping its silver reserves in the four big Chinese banks, the Bank of China, the Bank of Communications, the Central Bank, and the Farmer's Bank. Industrial enterprise flourished too as new factories, producing everything from celluloid to soap to meet the demands of the metropolis's growing and ever more sophisticated population, sprang up in Yangtzepoo and the outlying districts. Downtown, real estate prices tripled in only five years to make an acre of land anywhere near the Bund more expensive than the choicest acre along Fifth Avenue or the Champs-Elysées.

The inauguration of the Nationalist government in Nanking had brought with it a stronger Chinese administration in Shanghai, beginning with the creation of a Greater Shanghai Municipality in 1927. The municipality combined all the Chinese parts of Shanghai into one and was administered by a mayor appointed by the central government. Three years later, the International Settlement's foreign taxpayers voted to allow five Chinese members to be seated on the Municipal Council. This was a hard-won triumph for the Chinese, who had rejected an offer of three seats in 1927, holding out for five. With the addition of the Chinese representatives, the British lost their majority on the council. They were loath to give up this long-standing dominance but saw that unless they made a conciliatory gesture to the Shanghainese, they stood to lose everything; the Chinese councilors, all of them powerful businessmen or bankers with ties to the Nanking regime, could mount a campaign for the all-out rendition of the foreign settlements to Chinese authority. Already the Nanking government had pressed Britain into giving up its concessions at Hankow and Kiukiang, and the major Western powers had agreed to lift the fixed tariff, a much-hated reminder of China's semicolonial status.

But on the issue of the return of the major concession areas and relinquishing extraterritoriality, Britain and the other foreign powers refused to budge. They claimed that they could abandon extraterritoriality only when China's law courts and code had been modified to match Western legal standards to ensure the protection of their nationals. When the Kuomintang's National Revolutionary Army had swept up from Canton into Nanking, it had won its popular support by promising an end to warlordism and foreign imperialism. Chiang Kai-shek, the commander of that army, and now the leader of the Nationalist government, could make a fair claim to having achieved the first part of the Kuomintang's pledge. On the question of forcing the treaty powers to renounce their special privileges, however, Chiang was hardly in a hurry. He had become preoccupied with the suppression of the Communist Party, whose remaining members had taken refuge in Kiangsi and had formed an army. Unable to put aside his hatred of the Communists, Chiang let the matter of aggressively pressing the Western powers to renounce the unequal treaties lapse as he concentrated most of his energies on the annihilation of his old enemies.

Ultimately, Chiang Kai-shek's pursuit of his old vendetta would be his undoing, as he was even willing to let the country be eaten away by a far more dangerous opponent: an expansionist Japan. In the sixteenth century, when Japanese pirates had made forays on the towns along China's coast, Chinese had dubbed the Japanese the "dwarf bandits." However short their physical stature, by the end of the nineteenth century the inhabitants of the "island nation" were challenging the other treaty powers for supremacy in Shanghai. Fewer than four hundred Japanese had lived in Shanghai before 1890, but, stimulated by the Treaty of Shimonoseki, which brought industry to Shanghai, and by the even greater spur of the World War boom, their colony grew to twenty thousand by 1920. The 1920s saw the greatest growth yet, and by 1930 their population far surpassed that of the British, who up until then had been the treaty port's largest foreign group. Moreover, the Japanese were making demands for control of the International Settlement. The Japanese, a treaty power since 1895, had pressured the reluctant Municipal Council into granting it first one, then two representatives on the Municipal Council, and once the body grew to fourteen members with the addition of the Chinese councillors added in 1930, the Japanese began agitating for an additional seat. In addition, the Japanese insisted upon patrolling the Japanese district with their own Tokyo-trained police force; they were made an auxiliary force of the Shanghai Municipal Police.

Economically too, Nippon's presence in the Chinese port could not be ignored: Japan's investment in Shanghai approached a billion yen and the Japanese exported to China via the Whangpu port more than 124,000 bales of cotton, alongside an ever-growing variety of other goods, from coal to chemicals. Also, the Japanese owned the largest number of factories of any foreign country in Shanghai—thirty cotton mills alone were owned by the Japanese, twenty-five more than the British could claim. Except for a few heads of the most prestigious Japanese companies like Mitsubishi and Mitsui, who had their offices in the International Settlement, most of Shanghai's Japanese lived in Little Tokyo, the Japanese colony in Hongkew not far from the Japanese consulate. Little Tokyo had Japanese schools, businesses, and restaurants. Here too were Japanese geisha houses and brothels. The latter were licensed and maintained for the exclusive use of the Japanese in Shanghai. Foreigners seldom ventured into Little Tokyo except to have sukiyaki parties in one of the many Japanese restaurants, and, aside from the clerks who worked at the offices of Mitsui, Mitsubishi, the Yokohama Specie Bank, or the Nippon Yusen Kaisha shipping line in the International Settlement, the Japanese seldom left Hongkew. But the Mitsui taipan, Mr. Urabe, who also sat on the Municipal Council, made a point of inviting important Shanghai businessmen and diplomats for a spring garden party at his house in the French Concession when his cherry trees were in bloom.

Japan's blatant imperial ambitions regarding China, however, were stirring ripples in the seemingly cordial relations between Shanghai's Chinese and Japanese. The Japanese invasion of China would not officially take place until 1937, but its prelude took place on September 18, 1931, with a small bomb explosion on the tracks of the Japanese-owned South Manchurian Railway in Mukden, the capital of Manchuria. The Japanese army, which had most likely planted the bomb, used the incident as a pretext for occupying the province, the entirety of which was under Japanese control by December. The Manchurian warlord Chang Hsueh-liang, who was in Peking at the time (being cured of his opium addiction), sought Chiang Kai-shek's advice, but the Generalissimo, who wanted to preserve his fighting units for his anti-Communist campaign, advised nonresistance. This remained his policy when the Japanese reconstituted Manchuria into a puppet state, the Republic of Manchukuo, naming the deposed Manchu "boy emperor," Pu-yi, as its head.

Though Shanghai was thousands of miles away, its response to Japan's action was one of intense nationalistic passion against the Japanese. The city's business leaders and activists organized an instant and highly effective anti-Japanese boycott. Japanese products from toys to bicycles had been popular among the Shanghainese. But now shopkeepers removed them from their shelves, and no Chinese dared set foot in a Japanese-owned business. Japanese goods merchants had ordered a few weeks earlier were refused and left to pile up in the Japanese shipping firms' godowns. Japanese ships found it impossible to unload their cargoes, and passengers were prevented from disembarking by pickets along the docks. Many Japanese residents began leaving Little Tokyo for their homes as well because of the difficulties of obtaining food and other supplies; Chinese grocers and shopkeepers refused to serve Japanese. (Anyone caught doing so risked grave repercussions, from a physical beating to the boycotting of his business.) By the end of December, the boycott organizers had dealt a crippling blow to Japanese economic interests in Shanghai. During only three months of the boycott, the volume of Japanese goods brought into Shanghai dropped from 29 to 3 percent of the city's total imports, while most of the Japanese-operated factories either closed permanently or suspended production.

Violence erupted on January 18, 1932, when a Chinese crowd attacked five Japanese monks chanting on a street in Chapei. The monks were members of the militant pan-Asian Buddhist Nichiren sect and had been sent into the Chinese area to create an incident. One of the monks died and two were wounded. Three days later, the Japanese consul general delivered an ultimatum to the Chinese municipality's mayor, Wu Te-chen. He demanded the arrest of the Chinese responsible for assaulting the monks, the breakup of the anti-Japanese organizations, and an end to the boycott in ten days; otherwise Japanese forces would occupy Chapei. Even as Wu Te-chen, Chiang Kai-shek's personally appointed mayor, agonized over his response and consulted with Nanking, the Japanese navy had brought in reinforcements and its bluejackets were massing along the border between Hongkew and Chapei. It was clear to everyone that whatever Wu's decision, the Japanese naval command had decided to invade Chapei. On the afternoon of January 28, Wu accepted all of the Japanese consul general's demands, even closing down the offices of the anti-Japanese boycott association.

But Admiral Shiozawa, the Japanese naval commander in Shanghai, had not even bothered to read Wu's reply before sending his forces into action. That same evening, an elite unit of four hundred Japanese marines in their distinctive white leggings and white caps staged a parade in front of their naval headquarters in Hongkew to cheers from a large crowd of Japanese residents. Bowing toward Tokyo, they yelled "Banzai," then climbed aboard eighteen military trucks accompanied by armored tanks to begin their assault on Chapei. Their principal target was the extensive yards of the North Railway Station, which was protected by the Nineteenth Route Army, an intensely nationalistic independent army of sixteen thousand southerners formed during the fiery first days of the Northern Expedition before Chiang Kai-shek had come to power. The troops were commanded by a tall, soft-spoken Cantonese, Tsai Ting-kai, who had been in and out of several Kuomintang factions. Chiang Kai-shek had warned Tsai not to fight the Japanese and even ordered the army out of Shanghai. However, Tsai and his independent-minded soldiers could not stomach the idea of allowing the Japanese to take Chapei without a fight. A large part of the force had already left Shanghai, but as soon as it became clear that the Japanese intended to attack the city, they returned en masse to throw up barricades and sandbags around North Station and dig in.

The fighting started almost immediately, with the Japanese bluejackets shooting with their heavy artillery into North Station from five hundred yards. Admiral Shiozawa fully expected North Station to fall, as he boasted, "within three hours, without a single shot being fired." Much to his surprise, the Chinese army valiantly resisted. The battle for Chapei lasted for five weeks, during which time the sturdy Nineteenth Route Army had humiliated Shiozawa into summoning heavy reinforcements from Japan. It was at this point that Japan introduced the world to checkerboard bombing, the same large-scale, indiscriminate bombing of a civilian population that would be seen a few years later in Guernica, Coventry, and Dresden. From the landing decks of their cruisers off Hongkew, Japanese seaplanes daily skimmed across Chapei, releasing their deadly black cylinders over its buildings from a height of three hundred feet. Under the continuous shelling, nearly 85 percent of Chapei's buildings were destroyed. Churches, schools, hospitals, and factories all went up in flames. Some ten thousand civilians would die in the conflict—far more than the military casualties. "For the first time," reflected one writer, "the world could marvel at the results of combined artillery and aerial bombing in a thickly populated peaceful city."

While the hundreds of thousands of refugees who had fled into the International Settlement from the battle zone huddled in camps set up by the Chinese municipality in the Chinese areas and the Nanking government retreated toward Loyang, Tsai Ting-kai's troops continued their heroic defense. The army had received much aid and moral support from the Shanghainese, who had donated money, food, and clothing. But without reinforcements or ammunition from the Nationalist government, the Chinese forces were steadily losing ground. "I want the world to know that we are doing our best to resist the Japanese and that we will fight as long as our ammunition lasts," General Tsai announced to a group of correspondents at his field headquarters along the Shanghai–

Nanking railway tracks, where the tracks were pitted with bomb craters and steel freight cars stood "ripped open like sardine cans" from Japanese bombardment. Though Tsai had not said a word about Chiang Kai-shek, it was a silent appeal to the Generalissimo for help.

No assistance came. As a result, at the beginning of March, the Nineteenth Route Army, its original thirty thousand men reduced to sixteen thousand, began dropping out of North Station. At the same time, negotiations were under way for a truce. On May 5, both sides agreed to a demilitarization settlement that called for Japan to remove all its troops from Shanghai except for its garrison units and for the Chinese to keep their troops outside a thirty-mile radius of the city's limits. When the Nineteenth Route Army departed from Shanghai shortly after the truce's signing, they left as heroes. Their example had buoyed the patriotic spirits of not just Shanghai's citizens, but Chinese everywhere. (The Filipino overseas Chinese, for one group, had sent Tsai a donation of several thousand dollars.)

The Japanese, for their part, claimed to have achieved a victory in Shanghai. If so, it was not just an expensive and time-consuming one, but a stunning blunder to boot. Japan had hoped to maneuver the other imperialist powers into approving its annexation of Manchuria, but the ingloriousness of the "Shanghai Incident," as the Japanese called the invasion, had dashed all hopes of such acceptance. Japan's embarrassment was compounded by the presence in Shanghai of the biggest press corps east of the Suez, which in words, photographs, and newsreels conveyed the horror of the world's first modern urban war to Americans and Europeans. The single most powerful image from the Shanghai fighting was the picture of a burned baby, arms outstretched, wailing on a stretch of deserted railway track, taken by Paramount News's H. S. "Newsreel" Wong. It outraged so many Americans that it contributed to the mushrooming of a campaign to pressure the United

States government to instigate sanctions against Japan. Americans began to view the Japanese as "butchers" and "murderers." At a cocktail reception he held for the foreign press aboard the Japanese flagship, the *Idzumo*, shortly after the end of hostilities, Admiral Shiozawa bitterly complained to Hallett Abend of *The New York Times:* "I see your American newspapers have nicknamed me the Babykiller." Then, with a defiance in his voice that surprised the correspondent, who had always found Shiozawa kind and sympathetic, he added: "They should give me some credit. I used only thirty-pound bombs, and if I had chosen to do so I might have used the five-hundred-pound variety."

The admiral's remarks hinted that Shanghai might face another attack by the soldiers of the Rising Sun in the not-so-distant future, but Shanghai's businessmen did not allow themselves to contemplate the possibility too deeply. Instead they immersed themselves in rebuilding their badly damaged trade and industry. It had been all of five years since Shanghai last saw bloodshed, with Chiang Kai-shek's purge of the Communists, and, indeed, it would be five years later that the Japanese would return to take their vengeance upon the cocky, belligerent city.

In the meantime, Shanghai celebrated its escape from yet another brush with catastrophe. True, Chapei had been nearly leveled, but already shopkeepers were returning, the wreckage was being cleared for new construction, and plans were afoot for widening streets and constructing a modern civic administration building and new schools and hospitals.

While Chapei rebuilt, a face-lift of a different sort was taking place elsewhere in Shanghai as the International Settlement and French Concession were acquiring a host of thoroughly modern hotels, apartment buildings, and offices. Unlike the bulky gray monuments that dominated the Bund, the new buildings were thoroughly modern Art Deco towers that would not have looked out of place in Berlin or Chicago.

All of Shanghai's "smart" living was in the penthouses on top of buildings like the Yangtze Insurance Company on the Bund or Cathay Mansions on Rue Cardinal Mercier in the French Concession, in the same neighborhood as the French Club and the Lyceum Theater. Fashionable Shanghailanders had abandoned their mansions for luxury apartment buildings with large windows, air-conditioning, high-speed elevators, restaurants, garages, and room boys who could be summoned with the press of a bell. Many of the buildings had restaurants, shops, theaters, and even a nightclub on the ground floor. Foreign bachelors and young couples favored the modern hotel-apartments like the China United or Medhurst Apartments that had also gone up in the central district and provided foreign-style meals and room service.

As early as 1932, Shanghai's skyline already bore the distinctive stamp of a man who had made Shanghai his legal domicile only a year earlier. This was Victor Elice Sassoon, "Sir Victor" as all Shanghai knew him, the witty, idiosyncratic, and cynical chairman of E. D. Sassoon. The previous year, he had astounded the financial world by transferring all of the companies associated with the Sassoon empire out of Bombay, headquarters of the family firm for almost one hundred years. By incorporating all his companies in the British crown colony Hong Kong while buying up thousands of dollars' worth of the choicest parcels of real estate in Shanghai, the tycoon moved his base to the Far East, doing so largely to avoid the onerous taxes demanded of him by the postwar British tax collector. Under their breath, Shanghai's British taipans called the magnate a "tax dodger," but if Sir Victor was willing to sink his millions into Shanghai, it was a good augury for their own businesses. Long before he actually moved to Shanghai, Sir Victor had already demonstrated his faith in the value of Shanghai real estate by buying Arnhold & Co., an old British firm whose most attractive asset was the Cathay Land Company, ownership of which gave Sir Victor control of a number of apartment buildings and a hotel in the International Settlement as well as choice housing estates in the French Concession. An even more breathtaking coup was his acquisition of Silas Hardoon's most valuable landholdings upon Hardoon's death in 1931, by forming a public company to buy up the deceased magnate's most important sites on Nanking Road and elsewhere for eighteen million Chinese dollars.

The massive Art Deco edifices that Sir Victor put up throughout Shanghai quickly became landmarks. It was impossible to cross the Soochow Creek, for instance, without one's eyes passing over the soaring bulk of Broadway Mansions, a twenty-story sand-colored apartment building that sat on the western side of the Garden Bridge. Its opposite number was the even bigger Embankment House, a gray, curving building on the eastern side of the bridge. Shanghai's largest apartment building, Embankment House occupied a quarter mile of the creek's frontage. It had a swimming pool and offered the residents of any of its 194 apartments fresh drinking water from an artesian well. In the French Concession, Sir Victor's Cathay Mansions with its top-floor restaurant soon had an equally elegant neighbor in Grosvenor Gardens, another luxury apartment building, this one with a garden. Back in the International Settlement, the Cathay Land Company had also put up the more modest Metropole Hotel and Hamilton House at Kiangse and Foochow roads.

Of all the property that Sir Victor owned, none was more valuable than the triangular block between Nanking and Jinkee roads on the Bund. Here, at a cost of one million pounds, he built the Cathay Hotel, the finest hotel in the Far East, and behind it Sassoon House, his business headquarters. The last word in luxury, the Cathay had air-conditioning, water piped in from Bubbling Well Springs outside the city, bright red-flocked wallpaper, and built-in mahogany wardrobes in every room. The most luxurious foreign shops in Shanghai were to be found in the shopping arcade next door in Sassoon House.

Fashionable Shanghai met in the Horse and Hounds bar near the Nanking Road entrance, in the Tower Restaurant twenty floors above Shanghai, or in the Rooftop Garden. Sir Victor's own preserve was his dark-oak-paneled penthouse suite, which afforded him a 360-degree view of the city. The Cathay had glamour and excitement. One never knew what movie star or celebrated writer might be spotted in the hotel's gilt-and-Lalique lobby. One of the first celebrities to spend the night at the Cathay was the playwright Noël Coward, "tall, elegant and obviously made-up," according to a teenager who wandered into the hotel specifically to take in the sights. (Coward spent four days in the Cathay's best suite nursing the flu and writing *Private Lives*; afterward, the suite was named after him and a plaque put up in his honor.) Everyone famous who came to Shanghai always passed through the Cathay's revolving doors—even those staying at the less expensive and un-air-conditioned Palace or Astor House.

Sir Victor Sassoon cut a large figure in Shanghai society, heartily indulging his appetite for parties, good food, women, and horses. Of this last passion, the magnate had famously quipped, "There's only one race greater than the Jews, and that's the Derby." Determined to breed his own Derby winner, he owned some one hundred racehorses, many of whom were kept in a private racecourse he had built in Poona, outside Bombay, which included not just stables but bungalows for his trainers and jockeys. One of the most familiar sights in Poona was the hatless and monocled Sir Victor, wrote Sidney Jackson, "in morning clothes and carnation, always looking nonchalant and faintly contemptuous as he limped into the winners' enclosure, leaning on a silver-mounted stick while he held his horse's reins in the other hand." In Shanghai too, Sir Victor bought up all the best China ponies, and he always turned up at the race meets in the most important seat—and invariably with a stylishly turned-out female on his arm.

Though handsome and debonair, the magnate could walk

only with the aid of two sticks, because of a World War accident (he was one of the Royal Air Force's first fliers) that had left him maimed in one leg. He was so self-conscious of the handicap that he vowed never to marry, as he had persuaded himself that "nobody would ever marry him except for his money and position." Just before he died, he married his nurse, but in the interim, he had a healthy—some said voracious—appetite for women. His suite had not one but two bathtubs, for, as he once confided to a friend, he liked to share his bed, but never his bath. His taste tended to pretty chorines and actresses. Whenever a particular light opera company toured Shanghai, for instance, the troupe always departed less "one or two selected ladies from the chorus" who found their way onto Sir Victor's payroll as "temporary members of his secretarial staff." Women were intrigued by the magnate "partly because of his wealth, partly because he is an enigma that piques their curiosity," explained one socialite, Hui-lan Koo, who was thrilled when Sir Victor presented her with two dozen pairs of French silk stockings upon their first meeting, only to discover later that, said Koo, "this was his invariable routine with any lady to whom he was even vaguely attracted." When he was truly fond of a lady, Sir Victor could be truly extravagant. To the writer Emily Hahn, whom he considered a kindred spirit, the millionaire made a gift of a shiny new blue Chevrolet coupe.

In his penthouse suite and in his villa far out on Hungjao Road near the golf course and airfield, Sir Victor hosted parties so lavish and outrageous that many of them became legendary. At his shipwreck party, guests came dressed as if they were abandoning a sinking ship onto lifeboats. The first prize was awarded to a couple who came draped in a shower curtain with nothing but a small hand towel between them; they explained that they had been taking a shower together when the ship's alarm went off. Equally famous was the circus party, to which the most respectable citizens in Shanghai came dressed as acrobats, tightrope walkers, clowns, performing animals, and striptease dancers, while the host himself looked every inch the ringmaster in top hat and scarlet coat and with riding whip in hand.

His wealth and exotic pedigree notwithstanding, Sir Victor was considered not quite their equal by some foreigners. This was true in particular of the English, who derided him behind his back at the same time that they partook of his hospitality. Overhearing Sir Victor refer to England as "home" in a discussion with a dinner partner about the easiest way to travel to London, a fellow diner interrupted from across the table, "Don't you go by camel?" Certainly the prevailing anti-Semitism of the British community accounted for much of their dislike of the tycoon. For others, it was envy of his millions. Still others resented his evasion of the British tax collector by the wholesale transfer of his assets from India to Hong Kong and Shanghai. And the prudish, or again the merely envious, disapproved of his fondness for attractive women.

Knowing that not all of what passed as Shanghai "society" welcomed him, Sir Victor enjoyed tweaking its nose. A lover of practical jokes, at one party he poured the contents of a bottle of crème de menthe down the back of a particularly starchy member of the British consulate's staff. He went to even greater lengths to make a point when he and a group of friends were told that a table was not available for them at one of Shanghai's swankiest nightclubs. (Outraged, he was said to have shouted, "Don't you know who I am? I am Victor Sassoon!" before storming out.) He got his revenge by building Shanghai's first air-conditioned nightclub on Bubbling Well Road, located close to not only the nightclub that had rejected him but the ultra-snobbish British Country Club, which had long refused admittance to Jews. The nightclub was called Ciro's, but wags dubbed it "Sassoon's sing-song house."

Because they were shut out of the British Country Club, Shanghai's Jews opened their own club, the Jewish Country

Club, on property owned by the Kadoorie family. Nor was Sir Victor alone among the city's wealthy Sephardic Jews in the lavishness of his hospitality. At Marble Hall, his gigantic mansion on Bubbling Well Road, Sir Elly Kadoorie held lavish parties in his eighty-by-fifty-foot ballroom, the biggest in town. Its sixty-five-foot-high, ornately embellished ceiling was hung with eight chandeliers, whose combined total of 3,600 colored lightbulbs could go on and off to change the ballroom's lighting scheme from pink to red to blue at a moment's notice. Black marble fireplaces topped by mirrors reaching nearly to the ceiling dominated the ends of the room. Elly Kadoorie, who had made his fortune in merchant banking, rubber, and utilities, was an avid dancer and particularly loved the tango. Marble Hall was the scene of magnificent balls attended by the elite of Shanghai. Whenever one of these gala affairs was held, the mansion was brilliantly lit from one end of its 225-foot verandah to the other and the line of cars driving up to its statue-lined walkway brought the traffic on Bubbling Well Road to a crawl. Elly Kadoorie and his two sons, Horace and Lawrence, who were equally sociable, knew more than a bit about comfortable living, as they owned the Hongkong and Shanghai Hotels chain, which operated, among others, the Majestic Hotel, which had been Shanghai's most luxurious hostelry before the Cathay's arrival.

In a city whose social life was already noted for its frivolity and bibulosity, Sir Victor's presence only enhanced Shanghai's reputation as the pleasure capital of the Orient. Luxury round-the-world cruises, inaugurated in the mid-1920s, had put the city firmly on the tourist map, and even in the midst of a worldwide depression, every ocean liner disgorged hundreds of tourists. "Such crowds at the night clubs! Such cocktail parties given! Such wine consumed, and curios bought, and promises made of future hospitality in other ports!" remarked Emily Hahn of the giddy, over-the-top atmosphere that engulfed the town whenever an ocean liner weighed anchor. "We, the residents, sat there in our Eastern city and watched the world bring us amusing books and news and people."

For foreigners and rich Chinese alike, Shanghai in the 1930s was a place of riotous abundance where there seemed no end or limit to the pleasures that money could buy. Despite Japan's invasion of Chapei, it was still the heyday of the foreigner in China. The Great Depression had barely touched Shanghai, and the city still enjoyed what everyone agreed was the best nightlife on earth. By 1932, some 48,000 foreigners representing fifty different nationalities lived in Shanghai. In addition, there were anywhere from 25,000 to 50,000 White Russians.

By any accounting, this made Shanghai the most international city in the world, yet the various nationalities chose not to mix, but to rigidly maintain their "home" identities. Unlike other cosmopolitan cities in the world, Shanghai was one place where the different races and nationalities stayed resolutely apart. "New York, Paris, Berlin and Vienna can point to a medley of races," observed Edgar Snow. "But in Shanghai, there is for the most part no mixture; that is the phenomenon. Here, generation after generation, the British have stayed British, the Americans have remained '100 percenters.' " The British played cricket and lawn bowls on the racecourse in crisp whites, and men and women dressed to the nines promenaded on its shady green park just as they would have in London. They held sailing regattas at Kiangwan and organized paper hunt chases in the rice paddies west of Shanghai, worshiped in the Gothic recesses of Trinity Cathedral, designed by Sir Gilbert Scott, and counted the formal balls celebrating Empire Day and British holidays as the high points of their year. Americans, for their part, gathered at the Chocolate Shop on Bubbling Well Road for ice-cream sundaes or at Jimmy's, a restaurant run by an ex-marine that served the best sirloin steaks and chili in town. They picked up stateside newspapers at Kelly & Walsh, the American-owned bookstore on Nanking Road, played golf at the Columbia Country Club, the suburban outpost of the American Club, and sent their children to the Shanghai American School on Avenue Pétain, where the main building was designed to resemble Independence Hall in Philadelphia.

The Russian émigrés, too, had become a distinct community. Though they still remained at the bottom of Shanghai's white pecking order, the more resourceful of them had managed to set up restaurants and shops along Avenue Joffre—and in so doing, turned Frenchtown's main thoroughfare into a "Little Moscow." Here one found establishments, all small and inexpensive, serving borscht, beef Stroganoff, and blinis and featuring small orchestras playing Viennese waltzes, and balalaika players and violinists strolling from table to table in the intervals. The waiters and musicians with "dismal émigré vodka-drowned expressions" wore sashed Russian blouses and real Cossack boots, and they "rolled as they stepped, like cavalrymen," recalled Helen Snow. At least one such restaurant could be found on every block of Avenue Joffre. Russian conversations could be heard on every street corner and Russian melodies drifted out of doorways and windows. Deft in matters of style and aesthetics, the émigrés opened up dress and lingerie boutiques, haberdasheries, photo studios, beauty parlors, perfumeries, and florist shops along Avenue Joffre. When a census discovered upward of fifteen thousand Russians in Shanghai in 1927, Russians were added to the police forces of both the International Settlement and the French Concession; the Shanghai Volunteers also had its own Russian regiment, the corps' only paid force and the first to go into action whenever trouble threatened. A dozen Russian Orthodox churches appeared, including the magnificent Mission Church on Rue Henri, whose gold onion-shaped domes could be glimpsed from far away and became one of the Concession's most distinctive landmarks.

These cosmopolitan elements mingled at the Cercle Sportif Français, or French Club, the most sophisticated gathering place in town. Its opulent French neoclassical building, built in 1926, had a roof terrace, formal tennis courts set in a garden with fountains, indoor and outdoor swimming pools, and a ballroom with the best sprung dance floor in Asia and an enormous stained-glass skylight. Because of the paucity of French nationals in Shanghai, the club drew its membership from the rest of the foreign community. It had Britishers, Americans, Scandinavians, Belgians, Germans, Finns, Spaniards, Italians, Brazilians, and Portuguese, among other nationalities. Women, too, were allowed to join, though the membership was limited to forty, and there was always a waiting list. At five o'clock, members were already collecting for cocktails in its ornate grill room, where the sign behind the bar might read "Plat du Jour: suprème de Volaille Casanova" and the frescoed walls bore framed pictures of French dignitaries. In addition to the women in evening dress and men in gleaming linen suits, there was always a sprinkling of officers in gold braid and service ribbons at the bar. "The types fascinated me," recalled Edna Booker. "An enormous man with a rubicund face and a series of red chins was a rich planter from Batavia. The tall Britisher with only one arm was an adviser to a Chinese warlord. The bronzed chap next to me was an American from Manchuria who had married the most beautiful dance hall girl in Harbin."

European and Chinese society met at the fashionable nightclubs, in particular the Paramount in the St. Georges area. Shanghai's largest nightclub, the Paramount was located in an Art Deco building whose stained-glass windows were illuminated every night by the lights from the ballroom. The Paramount, like the Park Hotel's fourteenth-floor nightclub, was where, said the writers of a popular guidebook, "the Chinese who are not admitted to the French Club or the Shanghai Club invite their European friends and vice versa." It was full of Chinese playboys who "play tennis and speak English with each other and go to Paris once in a while and take their favorite wives out." Of the Chinese-owned nightclubs, one of the most popular was the Vienna Garden, where one was likely to, as John Pal put it, "bump buttocks" with Edda Ciano, Mussolini's daughter (whose husband, Count Ciano, was Shanghai's Italian consul general), or with such visiting Hollywood celebrities as Anna May Wong and Douglas Fairbanks. The Vienna Garden was Tu Yueh-sen's favorite nightclub. At one point, the cabaret's most outstanding hostess was a tall, willowy beauty who wore only European-style evening gowns instead of the *chi-pao*, and who was always surrounded by at least two "fat, well-built Chinese, with perceptible bulges under their long gowns." These were gangsters sent by Tu Yueh-sen to protect the dancer, who was then his favorite among his many "girlfriends."

A "grim doggedness," in Emily Hahn's words, characterized the frenetic social agendas that Shanghailanders pursued. "Everybody was on the move for no particular reason. There were international parties, and plain British parties, and plain American parties, and there were beginning to be a lot of parties with Chinese people," she said of the early 1930s. "The diplomats among the Chinese went to a lot of parties, and so did the rich young businessmen and their beautiful wives. Foreign ladies and Chinese ladies invited each other to luncheon." These Chinese, almost all of them Western-educated, if not the products of foreign universities, were known as Shanghai's "smart set." At one dinner party given at the home of a prominent Chinese banker, another American, Edna Booker, was dazzled by the dress of the Chinese women. "We of the European world wore trailing French creations which bared our backs. But the women of the Orient wore clinging, seductive gowns of shimmering flowered silks, of gold and silver brocades, enhanced by diamonds, jade and pearls." One "stunning girl" wore a "very Parisian . . . form-fitting black metallic gown on which gold flowers glowed. Long gold earrings dangled from her ears while a spray of gold leaves sat as a coronet on her sleek hair. Even her fingernails were tipped with gold polish."

The most energetic of the foreign hostesses was Bernardine Soltz-Fritz, the Hungarian-born wife of a British stockbroker, who sought to "shake up the old bran pie" by inviting to her parties members of the Chinese literati along with opera stars and musicians. These Sunday-evening parties, the closest thing Shanghai had to a salon, did indeed attract a mixed crowd. "There were Chinese painters in the Western style—one had exhibited at the Royal Academy; representatives of Western firms who welcomed an escape from business; the first German Jews aware of the trend at home; journalists and professors," remembered Harold Acton. Over the hostess's elaborate table leaned "some giggly Chinese flappers who had blown in late from a mah-jong party and were soon to blow out again," alongside a German baroness or a Chicago millionaire. The critic Lin Yu-tang, along with his wife—"one of those self-assured matriarchs who rule every Chinese roost"—attended Soltz-Fritz's parties, as did Morris "Two Gun" Cohen, Sun Yat-sen's former bodyguard and sometime gunrunner, whenever he was in town. Almost sure to put in an appearance would be Emily Hahn, her pet gibbon ("Mr. Mills") perched on her shoulder dressed in a gray felt suit. Not the least of the extravagant personalities present was the hostess herself, whose flamboyant personality was accentuated by her fondness for turbans and bright-colored clothing. In her determination to "grasp the Chinese soul," Soltz-Fritz also formed a club of foreign and Chinese women to put on productions of Chinese plays and sponsor lectures.

It was Soltz-Fritz who took Harold Acton to Chinese parties of "unforgettable sumptuousness." One of these was an affair at the home of Li Hung-chang's son, Li Ching-mai, a garden party to which "Lord Li," as the viceroy's son called himself, had invited some five hundred foreign and Chinese guests. Li was one of the wealthiest landowners in Shanghai, "and he looked it," remarked Acton. "He never went out but in an armored car with Cossack guards, and Cossack guards patrolled his extensive domain." As his guests entered his garden, the host, resplendently dressed in a satin robe, "stood like a burly policeman to welcome every one of them, telling them all to keep to the right and see the garden before it got dark." Electric lights lit the grounds, which contained a summerhouse and pagoda, rockeries, a lotus pool, and pathways behind trees. "A band which might have been military was playing extracts from Gilbert and Sullivan on the central lawn, where a crowd had congregated before a towering buffet." Foreign diplomats were found gathered there, along with "money retrievers" like one businessman, a large Dutchman, who appeared with his wife, a former chorine, an "extravagant, ultra-vivacious blonde" who "glittered with diamonds and cocaine." She was, said Acton, "a publicity agent" for her husband's wealth, "and in consequence one of the more popular hostesses in Shanghai."

But the gay and giddy life had its price. "Perhaps in no other city does so much human energy go into the search for amusement as among the foreign population in Shanghai," lamented newspaperman George Sokolsky. "Ladies go to their amusements with even greater avidity. Work at home can always be done by boys and amahs and club life becomes the center of one's aims and ambitions. Dinner parties at clubs and hotels, night after night of dancing and jazz, turn the sweet girl who comes here to marry a man out East into a tired matron while still in her thirties: blasé, wearied and uninterested in the finer things of life." Worse still was the corrosive effect of the "foreign exchange" upon the younger Chinese, Sokolsky complained. "It would seem that every foreign vice and extravagance has its votaries among the younger Chinese in Shanghai who, meeting largely with the wilder elements of the foreign population, copy their lust for pleasure as though it were the hallmark of modernity."

A small circle of foreigners lived outside the world of clubs and cabarets, shunning the hedonistic preoccupations of their fellow Europeans for other pursuits. These Westerners, left-leaning to radical in their politics and sympathetic to Chinese nationalism, protested Nanking's repression of civil liberties while actively aiding those who sought to undermine Chiang Kai-shek's government. In marked contrast to most of their foreign counterparts, they closely allied themselves with Chinese nationalistic causes and were dedicated to advancing the ideals that liberal and left-wing Chinese had borrowed from the West. Among this group of nonconformists were writers and journalists like the radical Agnes Smedley and her Trotskyite friend Frank Glass, along with idiosyncratic individuals like George Hatem, an American doctor who had come to China to aid the Communist cause, and Rewi Alley, a New Zealander who inspected factories for the Municipal Council. Unlike the missionaries, who were the only other members of the foreign community to take up Chinese causes, these agitators for justice and liberty in China were in no way puritanical. Smedley, a staunch feminist and fiery champion of the world's downtrodden, had already passed through Colorado mining towns, bohemian Greenwich Village, and Berlin, where she had entered into a disastrous "revolutionary marriage" with a leading Bengali nationalist before arriving in Shanghai as the *Frankfurter Zeitung*'s China correspondent in 1930.

The tough-minded and outspoken American woman had a galvanizing effect on the leading Chinese intellectuals in Shanghai. Mao Tun, an underground Communist and the most talented Chinese novelist of his day, likened Smedley to a "comet shooting loftily and leisurely across the sky." Because she was, as Smedley herself noted, not only a foreigner but also "no longer young, not beautiful and a woman who earned her own living and associated with men as an equal," she gathered around her the male literary luminaries of Peking and Shanghai. Uncompromising in her views, she took pleasure in pointing out the contradictions in the views of the "patricians," as she called the sons of privilege who introduced her to the restaurants, teahouses, and theaters of Shanghai and Peking. After a dinner party at one of the finest restaurants in Peking where one of her hosts complacently declared himself and his ricksha coolie to be "old friends" and disclaimed the existence of classes in China, a drunken Smedley bawled out loudly to her companions as they left the restaurant in rickshas: "Get out and pull your ricksha coolie home! Let's all get out and pull our ricksha coolies home! Let's prove there are no classes in China!"

While a vigorous advocate of "free love"—that is, she believed that women should "love when, where and how they liked"—Smedley nonetheless took her scholar friends to task for their preference for youth over maturity and vacuity over intelligence in their romantic ideals. With her friend the celebrated poet Hsu Chi-mo, Smedley went to teahouses, theaters, and restaurants and asked him to point out the women he considered most beautiful. When the Oxford-educated Hsu, who had already abandoned his first wife and taken up with a younger woman, confessed to her that "he could love no woman over twenty who was not beautiful, did not have a willowy waist, or weighed more than a hundred pounds," the forty-year-old Smedley retorted, "You choose empty, baby-faced women." At the same time, the American journalist disdained marriage, maintaining that relations between men and women should be unconstrained by anything as "bourgeois" as marriage or monogamy. Consequently, Smedley conducted numerous open affairs while in China; the poet Hsu was one of her many lovers.

This unfettered attitude toward love and sex was to have embarrassing consequences at Yenan, the Communist stronghold, in 1937. Smedley's exuberant promotion of social dancing among the Communist cadres coincided with the arrival of attractive, educated women from Shanghai at the Communist base and enraged the wives of the Long March veterans. Ostracized by these wives, the American was finally forced to leave Yenan after her interpreter, a pretty Shanghai actress and poet, was discovered by Mao Tse-tung's second wife, He Zhizhen, in a midnight bedside tête-à-tête with her husband. The interpreter was banished and Mao himself divorced He Zhizhen, but Smedley's presence became even more controversial than ever at Yenan, and she voluntarily left two months after the incident.

In Shanghai, Smedley was one of the Communist movement's most trusted foreign contacts. She gave refuge to party members sought by the police, acted as a conduit for messages, and joined prominent Chinese in denouncing the Nanking regime's heavy-handed silencing of its opponents. With Madame Sun Yat-sen, she publicized the plight of intellectuals in China by arranging for her own pieces or those by Chinese writers detailing Nanking's repressive tactics and its summary execution of political prisoners to appear in American publications. She joined with a small group of prestigious Chinese activists and intellectuals to form the China League for Civil Rights, which tried, unsuccessfully, to prevent the execution of arrested Communists and also called for investigations into the disappearance of opponents of the government. The league's other sponsors included Madame Sun Yat-sen; Tsai Yuan-pei, the former president of Peking National University and head of the Academica Sinica in Nanking; Yang Chien, Tsai Yuan-pei's assistant and the Academica's general secretary; and Harold Isaacs, an adventurous and intellectually precocious Columbia graduate and son of a New York real estate magnate whom Smedley had lured away from his job as a reporter with the *China Press* to edit a left-wing journal funded by the Communists, the *China Forum*.

Madame Sun Yat-sen and Tsai Yuan-pei were able to take a stand against the Kuomintang only because of their enormous personal prestige. For others to do so was to invite speedy arrest, as the Nanking government promulgated a law early in 1931 that made it a crime punishable by death or life imprisonment for any citizen to criticize the government. Over the next six years, with the aid of a highly efficient anti-Communist apparatus consisting of spies and secret police modeled after Hitler's Brownshirt and Mussolini's Blackshirt operations, the regime aggressively hunted down and imprisoned or put to death both Communists, real and alleged, and its critics. As foreigners were protected by extraterritoriality, Smedley, Isaacs, and other Westerners who aided the revolutionary underground could not be arrested, though they were harassed and put under surveillance by both the Kuomintang and the foreign police of the International Settlement and French Concession.

In a place like Shanghai, so rife with intrigue and infighting among innumerable factions, so flush with money and power, so powerful in its effect on the whole of China, it was also only natural that a strong and covert spy operation came into existence. The Shanghai Municipal Police, for one, maintained an elite unit, the Special Branch of its Criminal Investigations Division, which tracked the comings and goings of left-leaning visitors or of any foreigner whose politics were considered suspicious. Eugene O'Neill—a "radical" in the eyes of the Special Branch—complained that "Shanghai had more snoops and gossips to the square inch" than any New England town. The Special Branch also engaged in smear campaigns against selected foreigners, spreading false information to discredit or harass them. When Smedley traveled south to Canton, for example, she found herself put under house arrest and detained for weeks by the Canton police after they received an "official document" from the Shanghai Municipal Police informing them that the journalist was a "Russian Bolshevik traveling on a false American passport." Another rumor about Smedley that constantly cropped up in the foreign press—a rumor that may or may not have originated with the Special Branch—was that while visiting Moscow, she had sung the "Internationale" drunk and stark naked in front of a congress of Chinese Communists.

Though Isaacs too came under the Criminal Investigation

Division's scrutiny, he faced a battle of a different sort: a battle to prevent the longtime American consul, Edwin Cunningham, from shutting down the *China Forum* for its incendiary articles. Many of these attacked not only Chiang Kai-shek and the Kuomintang but Shanghai's foreign power structure as well. Under pressure from Mayor Wu Te-chen, who had been pictured on the cover of one issue of the *Forum* drinking cocktails with a Japanese general above the caption "Drinking the Blood of China," Cunningham launched an all-out campaign to put Isaacs out of business, even urging the State Department to revoke the journalist's extraterritorial rights—a dangerous precedent threatening the privileges of other foreigners in China. Cunningham also tried to prevent Isaacs from registering the *China Forum* as an American company. Word of the brouhaha found its way to the *New York Times* in a feature headlined "American Warned of Trial by China—Death Penalty Possible." Once the issue became international news, Cunningham acknowledged defeat and gave up attempting to deport Isaacs entirely, while Isaacs went back to putting out the *China Forum,* albeit in abbreviated form and printed in his apartment, as no Shanghai printer would take the job. As a result of the controversy, Isaacs was so intensely detested by Cunningham and his staff that when his American fiancée, Viola Robinson, arrived from New York to marry him a few months later, the chief judge of the United States Court for China "refused to have anything to do with this obnoxious young Bolshevik," Isaacs wrote. Instead, a lower official, U.S. Commissioner Jacob Krisel, performed the ceremony, telling Isaacs's father, whom the official encountered years later, that "it would have been his duty to act in the judge's place, but particularly so in this instance of a Jewish boy who was doing so many wrong things and wanted to do this one right thing by this nice girl."

If the chief judge of the American court considered Isaacs an "obnoxious Bolshevik," it was perhaps because Shanghai was filled with Communist and Comintern agents in the early 1930s and nearly every other journalist seemed be a spy. Agents could be found behind the counters of European bookstores, teaching English at Chinese universities, or disguised as artists, YMCA employees, or businessmen. Who knew whether the German pilot for the Chinese aviation company was working for the Comintern or whether the distinguished Japanese author of books and articles on Sino-Japanese relations was not a top operative in the Japanese Communist Party? Nearly every top Communist operated in or moved through Shanghai at this time—everyone from Earl Browder, the former head of the American Communist Party, to the French trade unionist Jacques Doriot to the Indian nationalist M. N. Roy. Among them was the fabulously successful Richard Sorge, a handsome, brilliant Russian-born German national who organized the legendary Sorge spy ring in Tokyo during World War II. The ring, which penetrated to the highest levels of the Japanese government and into the German embassy as well, provided the Soviet Union with its most valuable intelligence of the war. Sorge had gained some of his most valuable recruits in Shanghai, where he had been assigned in the 1930s, operating as a German journalist. Through Agnes Smedley, with whom he had an affair (one of many), Sorge met Ozaki Hotsami, another Communist spy posing as a journalist, whose contacts with the Tokyo elite were key to the success of Sorge's spy ring. It was in Shanghai too that Sorge discovered yet another important recruit to his cause: a young German woman married to an architect, Ruth Kuczynski, who, under Sorge's influence, abandoned her husband, trained as a spy in Moscow, and went on to run another famous spy network in Oxford under the name Ursula Bureaton.

The Chinese metropolis had become "Red General Headquarters of Asia" after the Comintern Third International dispatched representatives to Shanghai to establish a Far Eastern Bureau. The bureau received and distributed funds for its operations through a network of couriers who traveled through Berlin, Moscow, and Shanghai, usually Russians holding false foreign passports. Aside from providing intelligence to Moscow, one of the Far Eastern Bureau's main functions was to coordinate the activities of the various Communist-backed revolutionary movements throughout Asia. Cosmopolitan, polyglot Shanghai was the ideal base for the Far Eastern Bureau: its agents—Indian, Malaysian, Formosan, and Korean revolutionaries, among others—blended in among the city's international population and could easily elude the notice of the foreign police.

For more than a year, a slim Vietnamese who had once made pastry at Auguste Escoffier's London establishment, Nguyen Ai-quo, later better known as Ho Chi Minh, stayed at the YMCA on Hankow Road and went about his quiet business, occasionally meeting with friends like Chou En-lai (who had known Ho in Paris) and Harold Isaacs, without attracting the notice of the foreign authorities despite the fact that the French colonial government had a price on the Vietnamese revolutionary's head. Isaacs, for one, was struck by the "humorous detachment" with which Ho regarded his situation. Indeed, Ho had long become accustomed to being the object of surveillance, having written these gently mocking words to a French inspector (with whom he later became friends) when living in Paris a decade earlier: "I am grateful for your solicitude, which does honor to an Annamite like myself. . . . Your police are excellent chaps and deserve praise, but Sherlock Holmes they are not. . . . Thus, every morning, I shall provide you with a schedule of my daily movements in order to facilitate their surveillance of me." For Ho and others like him, the Far Eastern Bureau provided funds for basic needs while in Shanghai, and it put him in touch with members of the Communist underground who arranged to have him smuggled out of the country and to Europe.

But the Comintern's Shanghai operation went far beyond

aiding the occasional revolutionary on the run. Just how well organized an operation it was was revealed in the spring of 1931 when the arrest in Singapore of Jacques Ducroux, a French Communist Party member and courier, led to the uncovering of a post office box maintained by the head of the Shanghai bureau and the unmasking of its head, a Russian national, Hilaire Noulens. Noulens, who had been running the organization for fifteen months with his wife, lived in the International Settlement under the identity of a professor of German and French. When the Shanghai Municipal Police raided his home on Szechwan Road, they found three steel boxes containing bureau archives and those of the Pan-Pacific Trade Union. The seized documents revealed a wealth of information, including the names of Chinese Communists employed by the Nanking and Shanghai governments and moles in the Shanghai Municipal Police itself. Raids were made on five homes that Noulens had rented under various names, all safe houses for Communist operatives, and their occupants were arrested. In addition, the bureau had eight different post office boxes and four telegraphic addresses, all again in different names. Its financial records showed bankbooks and deposit receipts in ten different banks, the funds totaling $500,000. Most devastating of all, the police discovered that the Comintern used two different systems of codes for its communications, and, having broken them down with the aid of the seized materials, they were able to uncover the identity of Comintern agents throughout the Far East.

Because the Noulenses refused to acknowledge being citizens of Russia but instead gave a bewildering array of names and nationalities, none of which were genuine, they were handed over to the Kuomintang authorities, who announced their intention to execute the couple. However, the raising of a Noulens defense committee by the Shanghai leftist community brought international attention to the couple's plight, and their sentences were commuted to life imprisonment. In 1937, after serving five years, they were released during the confusion of the Japanese invasion. In the meantime, the Far Eastern Bureau had been completely dismantled, the agents who had not been arrested having speedily left the country shortly after the exposure of the spy ring to avoid being caught in the dragnet.

The bureau's collapse had a barely discernible effect upon the Chinese Communists. Since the 1927 Shanghai Massacre, the Communist Party had been struggling to survive in the face of both the White Terror and a fragmentation of its ranks. Though the persecution had driven most of the Communist movement into southeastern China, where Mao Tse-tung and his Red Army guerrillas were holding out against Chiang Kai-shek's armies, the party's Central Committee remained in Shanghai. Even as the Red areas grew in strength and numbers while the Shanghai organization shrank, the party's leadership refused to shift its base to the countryside. The resulting rift saw those who espoused the Soviet-sanctioned "urban path" dominate the Central Committee in Shanghai while Mao steered his separate course in the distant hills of Kiangsi, rallying an army of 100,000 peasants and deserting Kuomintang soldiers to his cause.

In Shanghai, in the meantime, the Communists had learned to operate in deep secrecy and in constant fear of exposure. Chou En-lai, back in Shanghai as head of the party's security and military affairs, tightened its internal discipline by imposing new rules on its membership. To minimize the danger to the organization of members' names being betrayed to the police, the entire organization operated in cells, so that if a cadre was caught, he could divulge the identities of only those in his group. And once a member was arrested, everyone connected to him immediately moved to a new apartment or hideout, leaving the police to raid fully furnished but unpeopled rooms. Among the other new orders, many of them based upon the Russian secret service model, which Chou had studied during a recent trip to Moscow, were directions prohibiting discussion of politics among cadres in public, a limit of three hours for any single meeting, and restrictions on the use of the same meeting place more than three times a week.

Because an unmarried man living alone attracted attention, single male and female comrades were assigned to live together so as to appear to be husband and wife. In the early days of the Communist movement, and especially in Shanghai, where radical young men and women sought to liberate themselves from "bourgeois" moral and sexual restraints, there was nothing unusual about such an arrangement. Sometimes, important meetings might be disguised as an innocuous social gathering at a respectable family's house. For one important Central Committee meeting, for instance, the venue was a town house in the International Settlement, where the party leaders met on the third floor guarded by servants and gunmen disguised as chefs and servants while a contingent of female cadres threw mah-jongg tiles and played records of the latest Shanghai torch singer on the phonograph to throw off suspicious neighbors. The underground even ran businesses—rice shops, furniture stores, real estate agencies, drugstores—which were used as meeting places and courier drop-off points, but the managers and employees were often ignorant as to the true nature of their concerns.

The Communists and those who aided them sought to appear as much like ordinary Shanghai citizens as possible and thus make themselves invisible to the police and Kuomintang agents. Chou En-lai himself, like other top party leaders, changed his address every three months. To throw off those who might have seen the posters that still appeared with his face in certain parts of Shanghai, Chou frequently altered his appearance, gait, and voice, but even so, he never left his rented safe house until four-thirty in the morning and always returned by seven. Then too, like every other experienced Communist in the city, he knew all Shanghai's lanes and alleyways as well as the locations of all the entrances and exits of its hotels and department stores. Chou's mother-in-law, an elderly, respectable-looking woman who lived in a safe house rented by the party but registered in her name, appeared to her neighbors to be a widow who enjoyed dispensing advice on herbal medicine to the many visitors who called on her. But her real work was to serve as a party courier. Other Communists had even more complicated double lives, passing themselves off as antique dealers, barbers, or businessmen, or, most dangerous of all, infiltrating the Kuomintang government as high-level moles.

Chou had many reasons to be concerned with security breaches in the underground movement. The Shanghai Municipal Police's Special Branch as well as the French Concession's gendarmerie actively hunted down Communists, in cooperation with the Kuomintang authorities. Once a Communist was arrested by the police of either foreign area, he was turned over directly to the Kuomintang military police with none of the formalities that accompanied the extradition of even the pettiest Chinese criminal from foreign into Chinese authority. Some 326 such Communists, "real or alleged," were said to have been turned over to the Kuomintang—many to be shot or buried alive on the prison grounds of Longwha.

Such was the fate that met twenty-one men and three women who were forced out onto Longwha Prison's execution ground on the snowy evening of February 7, 1931, and forced to dig their own graves. All who died that evening had been arrested by the International Settlement police working with Kuomintang security forces at two hotels in the International Settlement and other locations during a twenty-four hour sweep on January 17 and 18. Most of the men and women were indeed Communists, but the raids on their meeting places had occurred only because they disagreed with the party leadership and had hoped to form themselves into a splinter faction. Their meetings had been betrayed to the Kuomintang by a high-level Communist cadre who wanted to speedily eliminate the threat to the party's leadership. Because five of the group of twenty-three executed activists had been writers and poets, their deaths and the Kuomintang's heavy-handed tactics received wide publicity in the foreign press, though the nineteen others killed were ignored.

The Kuomintang relied on more than the cooperation of the foreign enclaves' police in crushing the revolutionary underground. The Blueshirts, a paramilitary secret organization consisting of ten thousand graduates of the Whampoa Military Academy and allied gangsters, enforced the Kuomintang's increasingly fascist policies and silenced opponents or terrorized them into submission. Organized by Chen Li-fu—who was one of Chiang Kai-shek's closest aides and a nephew of his mentor, Chen Chi-mei—the Blueshirts operated in silence, but their influence was everywhere. Their censors banned books, movies, and plays; their spies in the universities reported on professors who taught "seditious" ideas; and their military cadres and gangster allies broke up meetings of student activists and illegally arrested, tortured, and murdered critics of the government. When liberals and leftists disappeared without a trace, they were usually thought to have been victims of the Blueshirts.

By far the most notorious case of such an abduction, because of the prominence of those involved, was that of Ting Ling, the outstanding popular female writer of the day. A feminist and political activist who had come to Shanghai as a teenager after breaking off with her family, Ting Ling had hoped to become a movie star but found her true calling as a writer when her first published effort, a short story about a disillusioned movie star, won her an immediate following. Both her subjects—the psychological problems facing emancipated women, among others—and her involvement in a romantic triangle that involved two well-known male writers, Shen Tsung-wen and Hu Yeh-ping, also brought her public attention. Hu Yeh-ping, whom Ting Ling married, was among the five writers executed by the Kuomintang in February 1931. After his death, Ting Ling embraced the Communist cause and became a leading member of Left-Wing Writers, a writers' organization that spoke out against censorship and Kuomintang repression. It wasn't long before the Blueshirts caught up with her. A car drew up in front of Ting Ling's home in the International Settlement and the writer and a male friend who was with her were tied and forced inside the car by Blueshirt agents.

It was assumed that Ting Ling had been murdered when nothing was heard from either her or her captors. The China League for Civil Rights immediately raised the call for an investigation of the writer's disappearance and began publicizing the case internationally. A few days later, the league's secretary, Yang Chien, was murdered by hired gunmen as he stepped out of a car with his young son. Two of the assailants were wounded and taken into custody. One confessed before he died but, according to newspaper reports, would not disclose the names of those who had ordered Yang Chien's murder "because this would involve the highest personalities in the Chinese government." As for Ting Ling, she had not been murdered but was under house arrest in Nanking for three years; she finally escaped in 1936 to make her way to Yenan.

Of all the weapons the Blueshirts employed to destroy the Communists, the most damaging was the way they turned captured revolutionaries into defectors. Once in the hands of the Kuomintang secret police, an arrested cadre had two choices—death or betrayal of his comrades. As inducements to defect, high pay and positions in the intelligence services or the government were promised. At the same time, a captive of the Blueshirts knew that even if he managed to escape or bribe his way out of prison, he would automatically be suspected of having been released so he could return as a double agent. "If we refuse to betray, they destroy us," said one captured Communist. "They take us where other prisoners can recognize us so that our comrades will never trust us again." Faced with this agonizing choice, dozens of former radicals became turncoats. Some of them became the Blueshirts' most efficient operatives, as they not only were able to identify Communist cadres but supplied valuable information about party procedures and, if they happened to be high-level cadres, about its inner workings.

As early as 1928, Chou En-lai had formed a covert intelligence and espionage unit reporting directly to the Central Committee to "discipline" renegade Communists and otherwise safeguard the party's security. As the operation's day-to-day head, Chou appointed his chief aide, Gu Shunzhang, a Central Committee member of working-class origins who had escaped the Shanghai Massacre in 1927 with Chou. Gu was something of a fabulous character. Nothing about him suggested Communist leanings. Handsome, suave, and possessing "the manner of a Shanghai playboy," he had performed as a magician under the stage name Li Ming at Sincere's rooftop garden and the Great World, among other popular venues. He usually acted the part of the "foreign devil," garbed in a Western suit and with a "big nose" attached to his face. Gu's skill at disguising himself came in useful for an undercover agent: he could easily pass himself off as a street vendor, a brothel pimp, or a gentleman of leisure. In addition, Gu had expert "security" skills. He knew his way around firearms, but if need be, he was also capable of killing "so efficiently with his bare hands that no trace of injury could be found on his victim," said one authority. Equally important, Gu belonged to the Green Gang, which enabled him to recruit skilled gunmen for his "Red Brigade," an assassination corps that liquidated traitors and other enemies of the party. The Red Brigade's attacks were carefully orchestrated, with the gunmen disguised as anything from beggars to film-crew cameramen and the pistols supplied and retrieved by female agents dressed as country women. Gu put his Red Brigade to work immediately. Sometimes their executions were staged in public, on busy street corners; at other times their victims were dispatched in deepest secrecy and their bodies buried. The members of the Red Brigade were kept on retainer and paid fifteen dollars a month by the Communists. "They did not know the names or the circumstances of the persons that they were going to assassinate," noted French journalist Roger Faligot. "It was not until the day afterward that they learned via the newspapers the names of their victims."

The Communists' espionage apparatus also placed spies and moles among the detective forces of the International Settlement and French Concession police forces and in the Kuomintang government. Some of the underground's most reliable informants "were badly paid, so they talked," one mole explained. Their most sensitively placed mole was Tsian Zhuang-fei, a Peking-trained medical doctor and sometime painter, actor, and filmmaker whose many talents and urbanity won him a position as the private secretary to Chen Li-fu's right hand and cousin, H. T. Hsu, the head of the Blueshirts' intelligence operation in Nanking. Tsian had first penetrated Hsu's bureau by passing a test to become an operator in its wireless radio unit, then obtained a promotion to head of the unit, where he had caught Hsu's eye. Working with Tsian was another mole, Li Kenong, a friend and fellow Communist who had also entered the wireless radio unit, then secured a position as an editor with the Kuomintang's Broadcast News service in Shanghai. While Li, all wit and smiling affability (for which he was nicknamed "the smiling Buddha"), talked up colleagues and became friendly with higher-ups in the Kuomintang administration, Tsian became closer to Hsu, even arranging accommodations for the secret service head's mistress. Only thanks to Tsian and Li did the Shanghai Communists survive the unthinkable—the treason of Gu Shunzhang.

Gu Shunzhang had been sent to Wuhan with an assignment to assassinate Chiang Kai-shek, who was there directing one of his anti-Communist campaigns in February. Gu had gone as Li Ming, the magician, taking with him a troupe of actors and jugglers, all Communists. While there, Gu was arrested by the head of the local secret service, whose notice the Communist leader had attracted by never leaving his hotel room except to go to the theater, but receiving a steady stream of suspicious visitors. When a photograph of Gu sent to Nanking came back with the news that the magician was Gu Shunzhang, the Wuhan security chief acted, arresting Gu on April 24. To his captors, Gu indicated that he was willing to discuss defection, but only with the highest Kuomintang officials, H. T. Hsu, Chen Li-fu, or even Chiang Kai-shek himself. That evening, a Friday, a cable was sent to H. T. Hsu's office in Nanking. Hsu himself had already left for a "dancing party," so the telegram was given to Tsian Zhang-fei instead. Tsian decoded the message with the aid of a codebook he had secretly copied, and after digesting its alarming contents, he sent his son-in-law on an express train to Shanghai to warn Chou En-lai, through Li Kenong, of his aide's possible defection. Chou, wasting no time, instructed all the party members in Shanghai to evacuate their safe houses at once and go into hiding.

Chou was not wrong in assuming the worst of the man he had personally chosen to head his secret service. By April 27, Gu Shunzhang had received a personal audience with Chiang Kai-shek and agreed to tell all. Not only did he give away the locations of safe houses, the hideaways for meetings of the Central Committee, and courier and supply routes, but he wrote a manual that detailed the Communist secret service's organization and procedures.

These revelations dealt the Communist movement in Shanghai and other major cities a severe but not completely crippling blow. The party's general secretary, Hsiang Chang-fa, was caught in Shanghai and executed, and in all the major cities, Communist leaders and cadres were rounded up. At the same time, all of the Central Committee members with the exception of Hsiang Chang-fa had managed to escape to the Red stronghold in Kiangsi or to Hong Kong, and the party archives had been transferred from Shanghai to Canton in time to escape seizure. Much of the Shanghai organization remained intact, thanks to the mole's quick action, but because they knew it was only a matter of time before their own cover would be revealed, Tsian and Li also left for the Red areas.

Gu's treachery did not go without incurring a terrible vengeance. As soon as Gu's defection was confirmed, Chou En-lai ordered the Red Brigade, his erstwhile aide's handpicked men, to execute all the members of Gu's family: his wife, his parents-in-law, and his brother-in-law. Only his young son was spared. From the first days of his defection, Gu knew that his family had disappeared, as a Kuomintang team sent to Shanghai to bring Gu's family to Nanking found the house deserted but all the family's belongings intact. He perhaps also suspected that they had been killed, as he realized, alas too late, that Chou could not allow such a betrayal to take place without a strong warning to others. Gu learned precisely what the nature of Chou's—or the Central Committee's—action was six months after his defection when he was shown a photograph of an arrested suspected Communist. "If there is any news about my family, this man is the one to know it!" exclaimed Gu, who recognized the man as Wang Chu-yu, a Red Brigade assassin who, like Gu, had come from Sungkiang and was one of the few men to know his family's address.

Wang was immediately brought to Nanking, where, after at first refusing to cooperate, he was persuaded to defect. An unlikely-looking assassin, Wang, a soft-spoken, unassuming, even "somewhat pedantic" man, told Gu that a Red Brigade squad had taken his family from their home to a house in the French Concession, shot them, and buried them in the garden. Only his young son, whom Wang said he could not bear to kill, was spared and sent to Sungkiang. Two days later, Gu, Wang, and a team of Kuomintang agents assembled beside a grass-covered courtyard off Gaston Road in the French Concession to exhume the bodies. Even before the digging had begun in earnest, a large crowd, including a number of journalists, had collected around the scene. After a few feet of digging and a disappointed flurry over an object that turned out to be a dog's tooth, the work coolies wanted to give up. But Wang calmly instructed them to go several feet deeper. As historian Frederic Wakeman describes the next developments:

> After another half-hour of digging, the soil abruptly changed texture and took on an ocher color. The workmen's shovels struck concrete. When they broke through the cement cover a terrible stench made some of the bystanders vomit. One of the workers groped into the cavity beneath the cement and felt a human leg. Four decapitated corpses were brought out of the ground naked. They were bound together two-by-two, the one folded into the other with neck tied to leg and vice-versa. As they matched the heads with the necks and arms, Gu Shunzhang stood by, tears running down his face, saying, "That's my wife. That's my mother-in-law. That's my father-in-law. That's my brother-in-law."

More horrors followed. Wang took the government agents and the Shanghai Municipal Police to five sites in the International Settlement where three dozen more bodies were uncovered, most of them in such a decomposed state that it was impossible to identify them. Wang himself knew only that the bodies belonged to men whose murders had been ordered by the Communist leadership.

In the wake of the publicity the press gave the grisly exhumations along with the effort of a deeply embarrassed Shanghai Municipal Police to crack down on the Communists, the remaining members of the underground in Shanghai found it increasingly difficult to operate. Moreover, around the same time that Gu defected, a separate secret service organization under Tai Li, one of Chiang Kai-shek's most trusted military aides, had emerged from the Blueshirt organization. Tai Li, whose contacts with the Green Gang were more overt than Chen Li-fu's, recruited many of Tu Yueh-sen's thugs to carry out his kidnappings and assassinations in the foreign parts of Shanghai. It was one of Tai Li's men who kidnapped Ting Ling and also murdered Yang Chien.

Shanghai's Communists, their secret service now headed by Kang Sheng, a canny Moscow-trained operative with long experience in Shanghai, fought back vigorously with a new spate of shootings of Kuomintang agents by its Red Brigade. But the ranks of the revolutionary underground were dwindling. More and more of their leaders were caught in the nets of either the Shanghai Municipal Police or the Blueshirts. The Chinese port's Communist apparatus was finally smashed in June 1934 when foreign police and Kuomintang agents jointly raided four dozen Red safe houses and seized seven radio transmitters, the party's lifeline to Moscow and the Red base in Kiangsi. With the information gained during this operation, they arrested the head of the Red Brigade and thirty-five of his assassins three months later. In Shanghai, the Communist organization was no more.

The Communists vanquished in the cities, Chiang Kai-shek turned his attention fully to his military campaigns against the Red strongholds. Between November 1930 and April 1933, Chiang had mounted four costly offensives against the Red bases. The first three had ended in defeat despite the Nationalists' overwhelming superiority in numbers and weaponry. The fourth had been a partial success, but the Communists nonetheless beat back the main attack. But by the time Chiang launched his fifth "Bandit Extermination" campaign in October 1933, he was facing growing criticism for his continued obsession with eradicating the Communists when the Japanese, a seemingly greater enemy, were nibbling away at China's northeast. Patriots were galled that, on top of their occupation of Manchuria, the Japanese had pierced the Great Wall in April 1933 to penetrate Hopei. But instead of demanding that the invaders retreat, Chiang met their demands for a demilitarized zone and returned to his war against the Communists. For his fifth campaign, launched in October 1933, he assembled an army of 700,000 troops and followed the advice of his German advisers to blockade the Red areas so as to slowly cut off their armies from supplies. The strategy forced the Communists to embark upon their legendary Long March. After fighting desperately to break out of the Nationalist cordon, they marched six thousand miles through western China to resettle a year later in Shansi province. Their numbers greatly reduced, they nonetheless set out to rebuild their organization, and a decade later they would reemerge to challenge Chiang Kai-shek yet again.

The clamor, meanwhile, for resistance to the Japanese mounted. It was strongest in the cities, particularly in Peking and Shanghai, where students and the intelligentsia, Chiang Kai-shek's *bêtes noires,* organized anti-Japanese boycotts and called for the Nationalists to abandon their campaign against the Communists to join in a United Front to fight the Japanese. While still on the Long March, Mao Tse-tung had proclaimed the Communists' desire to take the offensive against the Japanese in a coalition government with the Red Army fighting alongside the Nationalists. Chinese students, responding to Mao's declaration, defied the ban against demonstrations to turn out in huge numbers. In Shanghai, Madame Sun Yat-sen and the eminent writer Lu Hsun founded a National Salvation Association to coordinate the nationwide campaign for resistance to Japan. Apart from arresting seven leaders of the National Salvation Association, Chiang Kai-shek ignored the outcry. Instead, planning yet another campaign against the Communists, he went to Xian in Shansi province to rebuke

Chang Hsueh-liang, the heir of the Manchurian warlord Chang Tso-lin, for failing to pursue the Communists.

Much to his surprise, Chiang found himself kidnapped by Chang Hsueh-liang and his soldiers early on the morning of December 12. He was presented with the demand that he call off the attack on the Communists and join forces with all Chinese in an all-out effort against Japanese aggression. Some of his kidnappers wanted him killed. His bargaining chip was that he was the only main rallying point for Chinese loyalties in most of the country. Chou En-lai, the man upon whose head Chiang had twice placed a price, understood this and saved the life of the man who had put to death thousands of his comrades, arguing for a United Front, which fell in with Chang Hsueh-liang's proposal. In the face of this coalition, and with the belated realization of the strength of similar demands for a hard line against Japan that had already arisen in Canton and Shanghai, Chiang Kai-shek agreed to Chang Hsueh-liang and the Communists' terms and was released on Christmas Day.

THE LONELY ISLAND

The implications of the United Front were not lost upon the Japanese. Six months later, on July 7, 1937, after conducting maneuvers with a suspiciously large number of troops outside Peking, the Japanese discovered one of their privates missing and accused the Chinese of kidnapping him. Chinese soldiers found him in a brothel and returned the man to his commanders. But the Japanese were not about to have their "incident" spoiled. Thousands of Japanese troops poured into northern China, occupying Peking and Tientsin by the end of the month. The "undeclared war" against China was on.

The Yangtze valley was to be the war's next front, as Chiang Kai-shek knew he could not prevail against the Japanese in a northern offensive. He hoped that by engaging them around Shanghai, he could induce the Western powers to intervene. By August, Chinese troops were already settling around Shanghai's outskirts, a sign that they were preparing for an offensive.

Responding to the challenge, the Japanese had doubled the size of their landing parties in Shanghai and added a dozen more warships to their normal contingent. At the same time they evacuated their civilians to Japan and ousted the International Settlement police, declaring Japanese authority over all of Hongkew. In response to the Japanese navy's demand that the Chinese withdraw from their positions, Chiang sent in more troops—this time his crack 87th and 88th army divisions. By August 12, the Japanese advance fleet of twenty-six warships had moved down the Whangpu, with the gray bulk of the flagship, the cruiser *Idzumo*, moored directly in front of the International Settlement in clear view of the Cathay Hotel and Nanking Road.

Thousands of terrified Chinese, memories of the 1932 bombings still fresh in their minds, had begun fleeing the districts north of the Soochow Creek when sporadic firing began between both sides on the evening of August 13. By the next morning, in the middle of the worst heat of the summer, the stream of refugees had turned into a ten-mile phalanx. "How the family units stuck together!" marveled one American, Rhodes Farmer, who was caught in the swirl of desperate people heading toward the Garden Bridge, the only entrance to the International Settlement that had not been blocked off. "That ancient grandmother with the bound feet and face as old as the bark of a tree was assuredly being pushed along in the wheelbarrow by her youngest son. The smallest grandchildren—topknots nodding above their inquiring, boot-button eyes—were rocking along in baskets swinging at the ends of carrying poles slung over the gray-haired eldest son's shoulders. Two generations of sons and daughters of this family were laden with bundles of household treasures. They were on the run with everything they possessed." Once the refugees reached the Hongkew side of the bridge, a mad stampede to reach the opposite end ensued. "My feet were slipping . . . on blood and flesh," recalled Farmer. "Half a dozen times I knew

I was walking on the bodies of children or old people sucked under by the torrent, trampled flat by countless feet. A crowd of marines and *ronin* stood beside the two Japanese sentries on the far side of the bridge. One of them bayoneted an old man and pitched his body into the Creek. I saw several good-looking girls seized by the soldiers and dragged into neighboring buildings."

This, however, was just the beginning of the most horrific day in the foreign enclaves' history. Up to now, modern warfare had not touched either the International Settlement or the French Concession. Ironically, it would not be the Japanese who brought tragedy to Shanghai that day, but the Chinese. In the morning, Chinese bombers from Lungwha airfield had tried to sink the *Idzumo*, but failed to score a hit. In the late afternoon, they returned for a second attempt. One of the pilots panicked when the ship turned its antiaircraft guns toward him and prematurely released two bombs. One landed in front of the Cathay Hotel, another went through the roof of the Palace Hotel next door. Because of the large number of refugees in the area, the numbers of dead and wounded were staggering—729 people were killed, and another 861 wounded.

A grisly sight awaited those who had been inside when they made their way out onto the street. Mangled bodies and severed arms and legs lay everywhere. There was a decapitated policeman on the street corner, his arms held up as if he were still directing traffic. Blue coolie clothing was everywhere turning red. Burning cars, their occupants still inside, littered Nanking Road as well. Directly outside the entrance to the Palace Hotel lay the body of a young professor from Princeton University. Hoping that he could be saved, two people tried to drag him into the hotel through its revolving doors, but the blood drained out of his body as they smashed through the broken glass in the door to the lobby. Ambulances were late in coming to the scene, because, incredibly, another bomber had accidentally released two more bombs at the intersection of Avenue Edouard VII and Thibet Road, where many refugees had gathered to receive free rice and tea being distributed by the New World amusement center. The second pair of bombs killed 1,011 Chinese and foreigners and injured 570. All told, it was the worst civilian carnage in a single day anywhere in the world up to that moment.

Over the next two months, bitter fighting took place in and around Shanghai, especially in Chapei. Reinforcements from Tokyo had brought the total Japanese force to upward of 200,000 troops with complete land, naval, and air forces. Every advantage was on the Japanese side. Nonetheless, the Chinese troops distinguished themselves by their bravery. Chiang Kai-shek had told his officers to order their troops to attack "without regard for casualties and to defend their positions to the last man." His troops, some of them just youngsters, did just that. Hundreds laid down their lives every day on the front lines of battle, proving, as the Nineteenth Route Army had done in 1932, the sublime bravery of the Chinese soldier. An entire unit of six hundred officers and men perished at one outpost after holding out against their attackers for a week.

Refugees continued to pour into the foreign settlements by the hundreds of thousands as the battle for Shanghai raged and the Japanese advance forced even more Chinese to evacuate their homes in Chapei, Pootung, and the surrounding areas. To accommodate this unprecedented influx of homeless people, foreign and Chinese authorities worked together to find temporary shelters for them in any space with a roof over it. Warehouses, offices, stores, and even movie theaters were emptied out and made available to the refugees, while still others simply slept on the streets and in parks and alleyways. "For endless miles, the city's sidewalks became the bedroom of a million refugees," said Farmer.

Death was now impossible to ignore, as an ever larger crop of corpses greeted each day. Many of these were babies. Some had been left on the street, wrapped in straw matting or rags, a small foot protruding to warn of the bundle's sad contents; others had been stuffed into garbage cans, some while still alive. The Chinese Benevolent Association picked up hundreds of these small corpses every morning in the black vans it sent out on its "baby patrol." These corpses, their "thin, yellow faces, with open mouths," mute testimony to the senselessness of events, were brought to the association's compound, where they were "piled up like stacks of firewood," the American writer Mark Gayn recalled. Afterward they were taken to an open lot "where they were cremated by the score in huge bon-fires" or "stuffed into hastily built coffins and then buried at a makeshift cemetery within the city limits—a layer of coffins, a thin layer of dirt, a layer of coffins, and more dirt." Fearing outbreaks of disease, municipal leaders corralled scores of ref-ugees into large camps, where they were inoculated and fed meager rations of rice gruel. Some refugees tried to leave the city entirely—about 350,000 of them left Shanghai on steamers bound for their native villages in the hinterland. At the same time, intellectuals, actors and actresses, and patriots young and old were making their way to unoccupied China, either to Chungking, where the Nationalists had reestablished their cap-ital, or to Yenan, to join the Communists.

Foreigners, too, at least the ones who saw the writing on the wall, were departing. Following advisories from their con-sulates, some five thousand British and Americans boarded evacuation ships in the weeks following the August 14 bomb-ings. "Over the tragic weekend, our business had been de-stroyed and there was nothing for most of us to do," Carl Crow sadly noted. The threat of Japanese occupation of the port had seen Shanghai's silver shipped out to Hong Kong and its trade diverted to safer ports. Factory owners were pulling up stakes and relocating their equipment further inland. Many well-to-do Chinese, too, were removing themselves—and their wealth—to Hong Kong. While Chiang's troops were struggling to hold the line of fighting at the Soochow Creek, the Japanese took advantage of the Chinese army's naval and air weakness to stage an amphibious landing of three and a half divisions at Hangchow Bay on November 5. Unopposed, they moved quickly toward Shanghai, and five days later they were closing in on the Chinese army's rear and flank. Unable to hold Chapei any longer, Chiang's forces—now down to 100,000, a third of their original number—withdrew from Shanghai toward Soochow, leaving Chapei burning for the second time in five years. Retreating Chinese troops had started the fires to put a barrier between themselves and the Japanese bluejackets; when the Japanese finally took possession of the district, they would find nothing but charred ruins.

In the meantime, the rest of the Japanese forces drove toward Nanking. They would enter the Nationalist capital on December 12 to find that Chiang Kai-shek and his government had departed for Hankow. In vengeance, the soldiers of the Empire of the Sun embarked upon an orgy of violence the like of which was unparalleled in modern warfare. During the six weeks of the infamous "Rape of Nanking," Japanese soldiers raped and murdered up to 300,000 civilians with unspeakable savagery and cruelty.

Shanghai, however, was spared a similar outbreak of barbarism. The port's trade had been destroyed, and most of its industry as well, but the Japanese were in control only of the Chinese municipality following their routing of the Chinese army. Ultimately, they sought to bring the International Settlement under their authority, and they were quietly biding their time until the opportunity came. That this was their intention could not be mistaken from the "victory parade" they staged down Nanking Road on December 3. The Municipal Council would have liked not to see such a demonstration take place, but its Japanese members were renewing their demands for another Japanese seat, and, as participants in the International Settlement's government, the Japanese were within their rights in holding such a demonstration. On the appointed day, six thousand Nipponese soldiers and *ronin* marched down the thoroughfare in a far from orderly formation. Small paper flags in hand, they "pushed to the forefront through throngs of sullen, silent Chinese," said one observer. Sikh policemen stood on every rooftop and even on balconies above the marchers, but despite their vigilance, the inevitable happened. As the marchers rounded the bend of Nanking Road near the Sun Sun department store, a single grenade exploded in the street, killing four Japanese soldiers.

Surrounded on all sides by the Japanese, Shanghai's foreign enclaves were now the "lonely island." The International Settlement and French Concession had become an oasis in a sea of conflict whose neutrality the Japanese grudgingly respected, at least for the time being. With the battle for Shanghai over, a semblance of normal life returned to the International Settlement and French Concession. The Palace Hotel put new plate glass in its front windows and reopened its tearoom for business. Businessmen felt free to play tennis outdoors at the Race Club again, and the crowds were flocking to the Grand Theater to see Luise Rainer in *The Good Earth.* Now, however, Japanese sentries stood at the Hongkew side of the Garden Bridge and required all Chinese coming or going into the section to bow to them, and if their bows were deemed insufficiently deferential, they were kicked or beaten—or even thrown into the river. Even the trams that ran down the middle of the bridge were required to stop, and their Chinese occupants compelled to bow. To foreigners, the guards still said "please," but their Chinese chauffeurs had to step out and make their obeisance to the Land of the Rising Sun.

Foreign Shanghai's cabarets and bars were as crowded as ever, but the gaiety and insouciance of the old Shanghai were gone. Shanghailanders were now "living each day as if it were the last." As for the Chinese, they were packing the amusement centers as never before. "Notwithstanding bad business conditions," remarked Norwood Allman, an American lawyer, "the Great World and other amusement resorts seem to thrive as hitherto maybe on the theory that man wants amusement most when he has big worries."

A pointed reminder that China was not the only trouble spot in the world came in 1938 with the arrival of the first of what would be twenty thousand European Jews fleeing Hitler's persecution. They had come all the way to Shanghai because it was probably the only place in the world that did not require visas and had not, like almost every other port, shut its doors to them. First came Germans and Austrians, and later Poles. Almost all of them came through Genoa, on the Italian Lloyd Triestino liners, which brought them to the Chinese port after a monthlong voyage that took them through such ports as Port Said, Aden, Bombay, Ceylon, Singapore, Manila, and Hong Kong, but did not allow them to disembark until they reached Shanghai. When they set foot on the Hongkew passenger jetty, some of the men in heavy woolen suits, the only clothes they had, few were prepared to begin life in an Oriental metropolis. Most were seriously short of funds, as the Nazis had allowed them to leave for Shanghai only on the condition that they carry out no more than twenty reichsmarks in cash and one suitcase. Moreover, they were required to buy their own transportation, and the Italian liners on which they traveled charged more than double the usual rates. As a result, the newcomers arrived in desperate financial straits.

The city's wealthy Sephardic Jews came to the rescue by organizing relief committees, which arranged with the Japanese for the newcomers to be permitted to move into the bombed-out tenements in Hongkew and makeshift dormitories and barracks in former missionary quarters in the same area. Victor Sassoon himself, the leader of the relief effort, gave over all of Embankment House's unrented apartments and offices to the refugees and saw to it that all of the Jewish children had milk every day. He and other Jewish philanthropists like Ellis

Hayim and Horace Kadoorie paid for soup kitchens and even schools and a hospital for the refugees. While the few refugees with money or connections moved into apartments and houses in the International Settlement or French Concession, the majority of the Jews remained in Hongkew. A family that was able to rent one of the small lane apartments on Chusan and Ward roads was considered fortunate. Families without means and many single men slept in unheated dormitories and barracks that crowded occupants into rows and rows of wooden bunks.

All the same, most of the refugees began to find their feet. Those who spoke English had a chance of finding work with a foreign firm, and there were numerous doctors, lawyers, and engineers among the new arrivals who speedily put up their shingles. Some academics found work with the Chinese universities. Loans from Victor Sassoon and from international Jewish organizations enabled a large number of refugees to open up businesses ranging from margarine factories to watch repair shops to household goods stores. Suddenly too, Shanghai had European restaurants like the Café Louis on Bubbling Well Road, whose German proprietors made their own cakes and chocolates, and the elegant and expensive Fialker restaurant on Avenue Joffre, whose Viennese cuisine rivaled the best in Vienna. Shanghai even got an authentic German-style cabaret in the extremely popular Black Cat on Roi Albert Avenue, which featured comedic acts every bit as biting and cynical as those in Berlin.

Locating their businesses in Hongkew, the refugees attempted to replicate their European milieu with butcher shops, beauty salons, inexpensive cafés and coffeehouses, and pastry shops full of mouth-watering displays of Sacher torte and strudel. The newest Hollywood films could be seen at the newly opened Broadway Cinema on Wayside Road, and afterward patrons could go upstairs to the Roof Garden restaurant. As the refugees included a large number of intellectuals, musicians, and artists as well, the Hongkew community soon had its own newspapers, a radio program, an orchestra, and regular theatrical performances. Not everyone, however, could or would make the adjustment to Shanghai. The climate and the overcrowding in Hongkew and the prevalence of disease took a toll. Many men, particularly those who had held high positions in Europe, committed suicide. Still, for all the privation and discomfort, Shanghai's new arrivals counted themselves fortunate. One by one, the world's ports had closed their doors to stateless Jews without visas. Shanghai was the last sanctuary—at least, for the time being.

The battle for Shanghai had barely ended before the city was engulfed in another, far more insidious conflict. This was a campaign of terrorism waged by the Japanese Kempei Tei, its Gestapo, against Chinese patriots. On one side were the Kempei Tei's secret service agents and the gangsters working with the puppet regime of the quisling Wang Ching-wei, the former Kuomintang official, and on the other was an underground Chinese resistance aided by secret agents and Tu Yueh-sen's gangsters working for Tai Li. The Japanese-initiated terror got under way in February 1938 with the decapitation of a prominent Chinese editor, Tsai Diao-tu, and the appearance of his head on a lamppost in a Frenchtown police station with a piece of cloth tied to it that read, " 'Look! Look! The result of anti-Japanese elements." Over the next few months, six more Chinese opponents of the Japanese met the same fate, their severed heads appearing in the same gruesome fashion elsewhere in the city. At the same time, journalists, businessmen, and the inspector in charge of investigating Tsai's death all began receiving severed fingers, decayed hands, and bullets in the mail.

Tu Yueh-sen's "Resistance guerrillas" struck back by attempting to murder a Chinese businessman on close terms with the Japanese by firing at him outside the Cathay Hotel. The assassin managed only to wound the businessman before his White Russian bodyguard began firing back. Other efforts were more successful, notably the murder of the veteran Kuomintang statesman Tang Shao-yi. Tang, almost eighty, was rumored to be on the verge of accepting a high position with the puppet government. One afternoon, a caller came to Tang's house in the French Concession bearing a present for his daughter, who was soon to be married. Inside the package was an ax, which the well-wisher, an agent for the Nationalist Resistance, used to hatchet the politician to death in his garden.

Other assassinations, of "traitors" to the Nationalist cause on one hand and foes of the Japanese and their puppet regime on the other, were conducted in a more mundane fashion. Sam Ginsbourg, a businessman looking out his third-floor window in the Sassoon Building one day, witnessed the following scene:

> A man in a long cotton gown was racing down the narrow street behind the building, heading toward the Bund. Now and then he would look back at a bunch of men with pistols drawn who were pursuing him and appeared to be gaining on him. I could not see the man or his pursuers very clearly, but the armed men looked like the hundred other thugs one could meet any day in the streets. They accompany high officials or rich businessmen. Grabbing people and pushing their way around, they are stocky and tough and wear the invariable short coats, caps low on their brows. The man racing in front might have been a young student or worker. He was no more than twenty yards from the Bund, where he would have had more chance of escaping, when pistols spoke. Two shots, then two again. The man threw up his hands and slumped down to the ground. One of the thugs came up, poked at him with his foot, and then to make sure, emptied a barrel into his still quivering body.

Even though blood covered the dead man's body, pedestrians ignored him, for such sights had become all too familiar.

The terrorist organization of the puppet regime and the underground Resistance were both brutal, but the former was infinitely more ruthless and feared. At its head were two former Red Squad members, Ding Mocun and Li Shiqun, who had defected to the Kuomintang to join Tai Li's secret police before again switching loyalties to join the puppet government. In their days as Communist operatives in Shanghai, Ding and Li had been known for their ostentatious ways. They "habitually wore expensive suits, spent their time in restaurants, gambling dens, and brothels, and socialized with gangsters and cabaret girls." They ran Wang Ching-wei's secret services unit from a villa at 76 Jessfield Road, which became known to all Shanghainese simply as "Number 76." Behind the residence's high walls, innocent businessmen and foes of the puppet regime alike were tortured and threatened with execution unless they agreed to join the puppet government or hand over their personal fortunes to their captors. As Number 76's day-to-day overseer they hired a particularly brutal and efficient Green Gang leader, Wu Su-pao. The stocky, dark-complexioned Wu had worked as a groom at the racecourse before graduating to a job as a chauffeur to Sterling Fessenden, the Municipal Council's chairman. Beginning by selling tires from the municipal garage, Wu managed to rise in the Green Gang as one of its more successful racketeers.

By the time Wu was recruited as Number 76's "chief jailer," his stature among the criminal fraternity was such that they had nicknamed him "Tiny Tu." Tiny Tu, a man who got results, personally wielded against his scores of victims the leather whips and electrical prods with which Number 76 was well stocked. Men who refused to capitulate—or whom Wu no longer had any use for—were taken to a corner of the compound and shot. Prisoners who needed coaxing were placed in cells where they could see the daily executions, and in the evenings Wu enjoyed taking one or two select victims out for a walk by the open graves. Number 76 was also the headquarters of a striking force of over three hundred terrorists—Kuomintang traitors, former members of the Shanghai Municipal Police, and underworld thugs.

Besides political assassinations and shakedowns of potential contributors to the puppet regime, Number 76 also took charge of the campaign of intimidation against the press. Given a choice of death or working with the collaborators, many newspaper publishers departed for Chungking or closed their operations. Of the few anti-Japanese newspapers remaining, most operated under American or British ownership to avoid seizure by the puppet Chinese government. Foreign ownership, however, was no hindrance to Wang Ching-wei's henchmen, who continued to murder journalists and lob grenades into the windows of newspaper offices. Between 1939 and 1941, seven foreign-owned newspapers were bombed, each at least three or four times. At the *Hua Mei Wan Pao*, a Chinese daily, for example, several newsboys and office coolies were killed by a bomb hurled onto its premises. The *Shen Pao* lost a printer when six hand grenades were tossed into its window, and the *Shanghai Evening Post and Mercury* had a bomb explode on the front steps of its building. The most brazen attack took place outside the printing plant of the *China Press* when six gunmen were thwarted from entering the plant by a guard who slammed a heavy gate in their face and called for policemen. A pitched battle ensued on the street that left two dead and several wounded.

To protect themselves, newspapers turned their premises into virtual armed camps. They installed burglar alarms in their offices, put sandbags and wire mesh around their buildings, and had guards posted outside around the clock. The *Shen Pao*'s American "owner," a lawyer, Norwood Allman, had his Chinese clerical and editorial staff live inside the *Shen Pao*'s building on Hankow and Shantung roads. "Outside reporters were to phone in their stories from secretly designated places, and no one, except myself and chit coolies [coolies requiring signatures on deliveries], was to enter or leave the building," related Allman. The system worked as far as it went, but it could not protect the Chinese editorial writer who, "tiring of the monotony of his imprisonment in the *Shen Pao* building, went outside in search of a little recreation. As he was sipping tea and eating watermelon seeds, assassins who had followed him there shot and killed him."

Yet another means of intimidating the press was the publication in July 1940 of a "blacklist" by the Wang Ching-wei regime; this list named eighty-seven Chinese and seven foreign journalists whom it wanted deported from Shanghai. The Shanghai Municipal Police immediately provided each of the foreigners on the list with two bodyguards, but this did not prevent the puppet assassins from making attempts on their lives. John B. Powell, whose name topped the list, had a grenade thrown at him on the street when his bodyguard was only a few feet behind him. Fortunately, the grenade was faulty and failed to explode.

At the same time as it was terrorizing businessmen and journalists, the puppet government had embarked upon a separate campaign to demoralize the Chinese by encouraging vice to flourish on a large scale in an area of the western suburbs bounded by Yuyuen, Jessfield, and Great Western and known locally as the Badlands. (Though foreigners had settled in this area, the Municipal Council had authority over only the roads themselves while the Japanese actually controlled the district.) The American Country Club, the plush campus of St. John's College, and Jessfield Park were in the "extra-Settlement." But so too were Number 76 and, not far from it, Wang Ching-wei's own fortresslike villa on Yuyuen Road. The villa, a den of iniquity, housed more than a hundred brothels, opium dens, gambling dives, and drug-dispensing stations, all of them run by the Japanese, aided by their *ronin* and the lowest of Chinese gangsters. The sudden availability of all the vices which the International Settlement had outlawed and the Nanking government had similarly tried to stamp out kept the Badlands establishments packed with Chinese (as well as Russian and European refugees) eager to escape their cares. From the various businesses in this "Shanghai Supervised Amusement Department," the puppet regime received substantial license fees as well as tax revenues that began "at the rate of $150 per day for medium-sized institutions, with prices running up to $500 a day from the more elaborate 'palaces.' "

Bearing such names as Peach Blossom Palace and the Good Friend, many of these vice establishments were located inside villas which their foreign occupants had been forced to abandon by the Japanese. All of their former elegance was gone, as the Japanese jammed their central rooms with roulette wheels, fan-tan tables, and other gambling apparatus. The other rooms were partitioned into curtained cubicles for smoking opium. Other places, flimsy, hastily constructed houses, sold "red pills"—a deadly mixture of opium, heroin, and arsenic favored by ricksha coolies for an instant boost of energy—and other manufactured drugs. Neon lights garishly illuminated the bigger places, and the alleyways leading to their entrances were plastered with advertisements. The biggest was the Hollywood, a rambling, many-winged gambling and opium resort located on property owned by the quisling Wang Ching-wei not far from his home. Some ten thousand customers, arriving by rickshas, taxis, and private cars, daily passed through the gargantuan establishment, which boasted eight hundred employees. "Down a long narrow passageway, far back from the foreign-policed road, we entered a low building whose maze of rooms, covering something like a city block, seemed to stretch on and on," said one foreigner who visited the Hollywood. "A silvery haze hung over all, a haze which rose from the pipes of the smokers of opium.

The air was cloying, heavy, drugged." Crowds milled around the gambling tables, and "guards with drawn guns paced back and forth, ever on the alert."

For Chinese patriots, the Badlands was all too powerful a sign of Japan's determination to undermine the Chinese will. Shoot-outs, murders, kidnappings, and bombings engineered by the Resistance occurred daily in the puppet regime's "land of evil."

If Shanghai had not yet reached its nadir, it was close to it.

THE UGLY DAUGHTER REPENTS

By 1939, the lonely island found itself not so lonely any-more. Events on the other side of the world that had been a distant rumble were gradually catching up with Shang-hai. The outbreak of World War II was followed in 1940 by the sailing of Shanghai's British troops for Singapore and other strategic points, along with the departure of a large contingent of Britishers for Australia for training to join the war effort. Now only American and Japanese soldiers patrolled the Inter-national Settlement's waters. In July too, with France's defeat by Germany, the French Concession came under the control of the Vichy government. With each departing ship, more for-eigners were leaving. Since the 1937 hostilities, the American government had insisted upon the evacuation of American women from China, so very few remained. At the same time, the bigger American firms had cut down their staffs and, in many cases, transferred their head offices to Hong Kong or

Manila. On the other hand, many British families chose to remain in Shanghai despite the issuance of periodic warnings from their consulate. Many of the British women "should have taken advantage of the opportunities to leave with their children," remarked one Englishman, but stayed because they "preferred the easy life of the Orient with numerous servants and chose to remain hoping that nothing serious would happen to them."

The event that many of Shanghai's Westerners thought they would never live to see occurred on December 8, 1941. That morning, shortly after four o'clock Shanghai time, Shanghailanders living near the Bund woke to the sound of a half-dozen explosions. Thinking the noise came from firecrackers set off by people celebrating an unknown Chinese holiday, some went back to sleep. But when the blasts continued, they called their friends with penthouse views or went up to their roofs. What they saw was the British gunboat *Petrel* on fire from stem to stern and Japanese bluejackets, bayonets and guns in hand, massing on the Bund and moving their lines into the business area. Simultaneously, Pearl Harbor was being bombed, they soon learned from their wireless sets. The *Petrel,* as they also were quickly to discover, had been fired upon by Japanese warships and gunners on both sides of the river after its captain had refused to surrender to a Japanese party that had come aboard. When flames engulfed the ship, its officers and crew jumped into the river, to be picked up by Chinese sampans and later arrested by the Japanese. Nearby was the American gunboat *Wake,* which had been occupied by Japanese. Its commander and most of its crew were in Shanghai enjoying shore leave when the Japanese drew up alongside, and they took the vessel from the sailors aboard without a fight.

At the same time as the crews of the *Petrel* and *Wake* were being imprisoned, diplomats of the Allied countries were being rounded up and put under house arrest at Cathay Mansions in the French Concession. Key members of the municipality's administration staff were summoned to an early-morning meeting at the Shanghai Municipal Building and told by Japanese civil authorities that the International Settlement was now under Japanese control and instructed to continue their functions as before. Meanwhile, sentries were posted in front of the British, American, Belgian, and Dutch consulates and also at banks, cable offices, newspapers, and all the big foreign companies. Notices slapped in front of all Allied business concerns declared the properties under the control of the Japanese, and all employees were forbidden to enter without Japanese permission. The Shanghai Club, the former bastion of the British in Shanghai, was taken over as a club for Japanese naval officers, while the American Club became their naval headquarters. Before the end of the day, the bronze lions outside the Hong Kong and Shanghai Bank had been removed from their stands and the Union Jack, which had previously flown high above the bank, had been replaced by the Empire of the Sun's red-and-white flag.

With their seizure of the International Settlement, the Japanese succeeded in doing what countless generations of Chinese revolutionaries had not—ending British domination of Shanghai and bringing the entire city under one administration, albeit a Japanese one. A year and a half later, both Britain and the United States would renounce their rights in China by signing treaties with Chungking that terminated their extraterritorial privileges. France too would surrender the French Concession, its Vichy-controlled government taking the action at the urging of Germany, Japan's ally. By August 1943, Wang Ching-wei's puppet regime took over the administration of the new unified Shanghai. Almost exactly 101 years after the signing of the Treaty of Nanking in 1842, Shanghai had ceased to be a treaty port.

For most of the eight thousand citizens of Allied countries still living in the former foreign enclaves after the bombing of Pearl Harbor, life changed very quickly. From the top of

Shanghai's heap, they had plunged close to the bottom. They were forced to register with the Japanese police at their "Enemy Aliens Office" in Hamilton House by December 13, many of them standing in long lines in the cold for hours—and as they did so, their pictures were snapped by Japanese photographers, who seemed to take delight in the foreigners' discomfort. Once registered, the Allied nationals were given four-inch bright red armbands stamped with "B" for Britishers, "A" for Americans, and "N" for Netherlanders, along with individual registration numbers. On pain of imprisonment, they were required to wear the armbands at all times when they were out in public. Next, these "Number One Enemy Aliens" were forbidden to go into hotels, nightclubs, movie theaters, restaurants, bars, and similar places of amusement. Foreigners might have minded these restrictions were it not for the fact that, at the same time, the Japanese had frozen their bank accounts, allowing them to withdraw only two thousand Chinese dollars a month and opening their banks for only two hours each day. Again, foreigners stood in long lines in the streets. On the other hand, Indians and other nonwhites who held British citizenship and Filipinos, who were theoretically protected by the American government, were exempt from having to wear armbands, as the Japanese wanted to bring all Asians into their "Asian Co-Prosperity Sphere."

By forcing Westerners to live on two thousand Chinese dollars a month, the Japanese sought to bring their living standard down to that of a lower-class Chinese family, (But, in fact, most Shanghai families survived on much less than that amount each month.) Soon enough, most foreigners found themselves giving up the amenities they had previously been accustomed to. They let their servants go, shivered in the winter because they couldn't afford wood or coal for heating, and began eating simple meals of rice, fish, and cabbage—the same diet that their former servants had always subsisted on. As the Japanese had also confiscated their cars, foreigners were reduced to riding bicycles or taking the overcrowded trams and buses; even a ricksha ride was beyond their ever-diminishing means. "The bottom seemed to have fallen out of our world," sadly declared one Englishman, Arch Carey, who spent many of his days aiding indigent countrymen who sought aid at the British Residents' Association, which pooled funds contributed by other Britishers and relief groups.

In the meantime, the Japanese were taking over all foreign businesses that could be of use to their economy and liquidating and seizing the assets of all the rest. The bank accounts of all business concerns were drained as well. Any metal or machinery deemed useful to the Japanese war effort was also removed and transferred to Japan. At the British-owned Ewo mills, gaping holes in the walls of the buildings testified to the eagerness of foraging parties to load the factory's valuable machinery onto Japanese cargo ships. But the Japanese did not stop at machinery; they took out boilers and radiator pipes. Increasingly, the Japanese were requisitioning apartments in the better buildings in Shanghai for the use of their officers and other Japanese arriving in Shanghai. In an already overcrowded city, more and more foreign families were making do with less space to accommodate friends who had nowhere else to go. In the case of the taller buildings, the Japanese ordered the tenants out of the first two floors and filled the empty offices and apartments with ammunition and provisions. They did so believing that in the event of an air attack, pilots would have to bomb through several layers of floors in order to destroy the stored supplies.

As they had demonstrated in other parts of occupied China, most particularly in Nanking, the Japanese were no strangers to cruelty. In Shanghai, the scene of the most sustained forms of torture was Bridge House, an eight-story white apartment building just one block past the Garden Bridge on the Hongkew side, whose apartments had been converted into dozens of cells and torture chambers. Its very mention was guaranteed to send a chill down the spine of the most stalwart foreigners and Chinese. Bridge House was where the spy-obsessed Kempei Tei sought to elicit confessions of espionage activities from journalists, businessmen, and ordinary civilians; where it punished its enemies; and where relatives of Chinese patriots were brought to elicit information as to their activities and whereabouts. No one was immune to seizure by the Kempei Tei, who acted as a law unto themselves.

Once arrested, a prisoner was issued a cotton gown and trousers and put into a windowless cell with as many as thirty other prisoners. Men and women, foreigners and Chinese, were indiscriminately crowded into a space so confined that everyone had to sit with knees drawn up on the filthy concrete floors. Rats and disease-infested lice were everywhere, and no one was allowed to bathe or shower, so diseases from dysentery to typhus to leprosy ran rampant. A single irregularly emptied bucket in a corner served as the communal toilet. Whenever a woman needed to use the "toilet," the men formed a circle around her facing outward to give her some measure of privacy. The single meal, served at midday, consisted of a nearly inedible rice gruel supplemented by stale bread and weak tea.

Occasionally a friend or relative would prevail upon a guard to bring food in to a prisoner, but the jailer would usually push food packages through the grill of the cell in such a way that "thermos flasks filled with hot soup or coffee, more often than not, broke before the eyes of the hopeful recipient," and solid foods were unwrapped beforehand and allowed to fall on the filthy floor. From their cells, the prisoners could hear the shrieks of men and women being tortured in the floors above them.

At any time of day or night, men and women could be taken out of their communal cells and brought upstairs for interrogation and by torture. When the questioning began, they had to remove all their clothing and kneel before their captors. When their answers failed to satisfy their interrogators, the victims were beaten on the back and legs with four-foot bamboo sticks until blood flowed. Then other techniques from the Kempei Tei's vast repertoire of torture techniques were applied. Sometimes bamboo slivers or metal spikes were forced under a victim's nails. Water torture was a favorite. While lashed to a bench with a towel wrapped in a circle around nose and mouth, a victim might have filthy water poured down his nose and mouth, or the water might be poured into the victim's nostrils through bamboo pipes. To prevent the prisoner from losing consciousness, a second interrogator jumped up and down on his stomach. Every so often the victim was taken off the bench and hung by his heels from the ceiling so that the water could drain out of him. There were myriad other forms of torture. Sometimes prisoners were beaten with heavy rubber truncheons or iron pipes or kicked with hobnailed boots. Some men had the skin burned off the private parts of their bodies with cigarettes or electrical devices. Some prisoners died as a result of this abuse. Others were let go after weeks or months of torture and warned to say nothing about their experiences at Bridge House on pain of rearrest.

Prisoners were often released from Bridge House when they were on the brink of death. Among foreigners, the most famous of these cases was that of Joe Farren, the Austrian-born owner of a popular nightclub, Farren's on Great Western Road. By bribing Chinese authorities, Farren was able to run both a cabaret on the first floor of his establishment and a luxurious gambling casino on the second. But Farren's was located on the edge of the Badlands, and the Japanese wanted a share of his business. When Farren not only refused to negotiate but treated the Japanese with contempt, he was thrown into Bridge House and tortured so excruciatingly that he tried to commit suicide but was too weak to do so. Later, the secret police called Farren's wife to tell her to come to get her husband, whom they were releasing. When Mrs. Farren arrived in a cab, a guard threw Farren's slumped-over body into the cab.

He was either dead or dying, as when the cab reached Shanghai General Hospital, he was pronounced dead. Yet another celebrated prisoner of Bridge House was John B. Powell, the editor of the *China Press,* who was at the top of the Japanese authorities' blacklist of foreign journalists in Shanghai. Within two weeks of their takeover of the International Settlement, the Japanese had taken Powell to Bridge House, where he developed beriberi and his feet swelled and turned black from an infection. Only when the flesh began to peel off his toes was an American doctor called and the editor transferred to a hospital. Down to seventy-five pounds from his previous 160 pounds, Powell was such a skeleton that the sisters at the hospital jokingly called him "Gandhi." Aboard a repatriation ship that left Shanghai at the beginning of 1943, Powell had to have both feet amputated, and he died two years later, after writing his memoirs.

Powell went back to the United States on one of only two repatriation ships that left Shanghai before the end of the war. One, the *Kamakura Maru,* left in August 1942 carrying British diplomatic staff and civilians to England. The second, the *Gripsholm,* brought American and Canadian nationals out of China at the beginning of 1943. The repatriation was part of an exchange of Japanese prisoners for Allied nationals. Not everyone who wanted to leave Shanghai was able to go, particularly among the British, as there were only two hundred berths available for British citizens from Shanghai on the *Kamakura Maru,* which also carried evacuated Britons from the interior ports. Unavoidably, "jealousy and ill will" was felt by those not scheduled for repatriation toward those who made the list, including those who could have left earlier but didn't because they could not give up the "easy life in the Orient with servants, good living and about the best night life in the world."

The resentment of those left behind certainly had good cause, as the Japanese soon began relocating the city's eight thousand "enemy nationals" to concentration camps, where they would remain for the duration of the war. The relocation of the Allied foreigners to the camps was part of a general tightening of the Japanese grip over the Western colony. In February, the Japanese ordered all Jewish refugees who had arrived in Shanghai after 1937 to move to a one-square-mile area of Hongkew by May 18. Most of the stateless Jews already lived in Hongkew, but those who lived in other parts of Shanghai had to leave their more comfortable houses and apartments for an already overcrowded district. Many of the refugees feared that the Japanese, because of their alliance with Germany, would take measures to exterminate them—as it was rumored was occurring in Europe. (Immigration of further Jewish refugees had been severely restricted once the Japanese controlled all of Shanghai.) Indeed, Heinrich Himmler, head of the Gestapo, had begun pressuring Japan to implement the Nazi "final solution" almost as soon as it invaded China. When Tokyo balked, Himmler sent one of his most ruthless officers, Josef Meisinger, a colonel dubbed the "Butcher of Warsaw" for having ordered the executions of 100,000 Jews in Warsaw in 1939, to Tokyo to further pursue the question. At a meeting at the Japanese consulate in Shanghai in July 1942, Meisinger forcefully proposed the annihilation of all the Jews in Shanghai who had fled the Nazi "fatherland" by rounding them up when they were gathered at the city's various synagogues on Rosh Hashanah, the Jewish New Year, and exterminated quickly thereafter. (The methods Meisinger proposed ranged from loading his victims onto boats without food or water to die at sea, to putting them to work at salt mines upriver, to placing them in a concentration camp on a nearby island where they would be used for medical experimentation.) But Himmler's emissary's efforts went for naught. The Japanese high command turned a deaf ear to his urgings.

Though confined to Hongkew, Jews were at least able to obtain day passes that permitted them to leave Hongkew for work or other approved reasons. But for the Allied nationals whom the Japanese began interning in January, there would be much less freedom—and an even more drastic change of circumstances.

On certain days throughout January and February, anyone walking between the Anglican Holy Trinity Cathedral on Kiangse Road and the tenders on the Bund just before the Soochow Creek would witness the astonishing sight of several hundred white men, women, and children bent under luggage and bedding like proverbial beasts of burden as they made their way from the cathedral toward the boats that would take them to their new homes—in the case of unattached men, to the dilapidated warehouses of the British American Tobacco Company across the river at Pootung Point; and in the case of couples and families, to a former American missionary compound at Yangchow, twenty miles upriver. The internees were allowed to bring into their camp as much as they could carry—hence the Westerners bent over their loads, many of them having designed clever devices with hooks and straps that gave them "the appearance of an old time 'one-man-band, but less humorous," remarked Arch Carey. After the first batches of Allied nationals had been sent to Pootung and Yangchow and the Japanese had succeeded in further lowering the prestige of the white man in China, the remaining Allied nationals were assembled over the next four months at the Columbia Country Club, far from curious eyes. From there they went to camps at Chapei, in the Yu Yuen Road and Great Western Road areas, and at Lunghwa, near the airport, in the bombed-out ruins of a Chinese college. (The Lungwha camp was notable in that it was presided over by a commandant who had been repatriated to Japan after internment at the Savoy Hotel in London, "where he had been well treated," and, as a result, he "did his best to reciprocate.") The Japanese had deliberately chosen run-down and overgrown sites for the internees and did nothing to prepare the facilities for occupation in advance of the foreigners' arrival. Nevertheless, the internees began organizing committees to manage camp life and counted themselves lucky to receive a regular supply of food, no matter how small.

Gaiety and laughter had long disappeared from Shanghai. Yet its cabarets and restaurants still throve—now with Japanese and German and Italian officers as their clientele. As always, there were plenty of Chinese, Japanese, Korean, and Eurasian hostesses to go around, and almost every day, a car belonging to Chen Kung Pao, the puppet mayor of Shanghai, could be seen parked in the driveway of Haig Court, a luxury apartment building, where Chen kept one of his concubines. (His license plate bore the number 1.) Ordinary Chinese women, however, no longer flaunted their attractiveness and put away their flowered *chi-pao* dresses in favor of drab blue clothes to avoid drawing attention to themselves. With the shortage of gasoline—most cars now ran on charcoal with a samovar-like contraption replacing their fuel tanks—even the most sheltered girls were riding bicycles or walking between home and school. They feared, and with good reason, being raped or molested by Japanese soldiers. "Many Japanese soldiers stride about arrogantly on Avenue Joffre, speed by in military vehicles transporting arms and supplies, and occasionally trot along on horseback glancing down at pedestrians who carefully avoid their gaze, hoping to escape attention and possible trouble," said one young Russian woman of the atmosphere of fear and anxiety that pervaded the city.

Living conditions drastically deteriorated as well. The streets, even in the once immaculate French Concession, were full of stinking garbage, and corpses that would previously have been picked up in the early morning now lay on the roadsides for far longer. Beggars, more numerous and insistent than before, infested the whole city, including the downtown business district, where they lay on the streets displaying their deformities and picking at lice in their clothing. Some were professional beggars, but many more were poor Chinese at the end of their rope who had no other choice. The most desperate carried pails in which they collected discarded food from rubbish cans and other foraging places. Anyone carrying any kind of food risked having it snatched by the street urchins who lurked outside shops waiting for just such an opportunity. The cost of living had risen as well. Prices had gone up for everything, and rice and other staples such as sugar, flour, and wheat were being rationed, while hoarding for the black market emptied the shopkeepers' shelves of everything but the most minimal items. As the Japanese had seized all the rice entering Shanghai for themselves, diverting much of it to Japan, rice was now beyond the means of even middle-class Chinese. On the other hand, throughout the occupation, ample stocks of liquor, gourmet delicacies, and other luxury goods were easily obtainable on the black market.

Despite rigid censorship of all news from the outside, news of the progress of the war effort filtered into Shanghai through shortwave radios (which the Japanese had declared illegal but had been lax in confiscating) and the comings and goings of Chinese underground agents traveling between Shanghai and "Free China." That Japan was losing ground was evident from the increasing nervousness of its soldiers and the sifting of younger men to other parts of the war front and their replacement by older or disabled men. The first American aircraft appeared over Shanghai in July 1944, and by November, major air raids had begun. The Japanese had fewer aircraft to challenge the American bombers and instead ordered residents to dig trenches in their streets, sandbagged more buildings, and imposed a sundown-to-sunrise curfew. Taking advantage of the weakened Japanese authority, increasing numbers of Resistance agents were entering Shanghai and murdering collaborators on the streets in broad daylight.

By July 1945, the droning of American B-29s could be heard almost every day, along with shrieking air raid sirens. A month earlier the Americans had opened an air base at Okinawa, which they had taken over, and from there they could stage frequent air raids on Shanghai. The B-29s, a bomber far superior to anything the Japanese had, usually dropped bombs on areas outside the city, where Japanese airfields and warehouses were located. They avoided civilian areas, but once, on July 17, while staging a raid on an airplane repair factory that the Japanese maintained near Hongkew, the American bombers missed their target, releasing explosives that killed 231 civilians and wounded another 500 in Hongkew. Despite the loss of life, the city's population welcomed the appearance of the Americans. When an even bigger squadron of American planes, 250 bombers from the U.S. Fifth Air Force, flew over Shanghai on July 22 on their way to a military site outside the city, onlookers broke out in cheers.

Even with all these signs that the war was edging to a close, it came as a shock when the people of Shanghai heard over the radio and through loudspeakers on the racecourse on August 16 the somewhat high-pitched voice of the "Sacred Crane," Emperor Hirohito himself, announcing in a broadcast in Japan the previous day his country's unconditional surrender following the explosion in Japan of a "new and most cruel bomb" and urging his subjects to "bear the unbearable." Shanghai had first heard the news of an imminent surrender on August 11, but the next day the newspapers had printed a proclamation from the Japanese war minister, Koreichi Anami, vowing that the soldiers of the Rising Sun would fight till the end, even if meant "chewing grass, eating dirt and sleeping in the fields." Anami and his supporters plotted to kill the emperor's advisers and persuade him to change his mind, but they failed to muster enough support for a coup. The broadcast of the Sacred Crane's voice put an end to all doubt. Shanghai's citizens donned their best clothes, rushed out into the streets to dance and celebrate, and ripped the blackout curtains from their windows for the first time in three years so that they could turn on the lights in their windows. Jubilantly, the city's population put up bamboo victory banners and exploded what seemed like thousands of firecrackers.

Yet even as one war was ending, another was beginning anew. Rivalry started immediately between the Nationalists and Communists to take possession of the areas occupied by the defeated Japanese. The Communist forces, situated not far from the vital eastern cities, could have easily taken the surrender of Nanking and Shanghai, but Chiang Kai-shek asked the United States to airlift his troops into Shanghai and other parts of the former enemy territory, thwarting Communist moves into the metropolitan areas, though they were still able to expand their territory from 117 to 175 counties. At the same time, Chiang prevailed upon the Japanese military command in Shanghai to continue administering Shanghai until his forces and American marines arrived. As a result, though the Japanese high command had disappeared from the city, fifteen thousand Japanese soldiers continued to patrol the streets. Absurd as it was, this situation was accepted, as the soldiers of the puppet regime had disappeared. On the other hand, the wharves at Hongkew were crowded with ships being loaded with the goods their officials had confiscated from the Chinese, and their military and civil authorities themselves were slipping out of Shanghai. Trucks laden with more booty drove toward the Kiangwan airfield, while at Bridge House the Kempei Tei were engaged for days in burning evidence that could be used against them. In the courtyard, several bonfires went on at one time. After emptying the building of its arms and equipment, the Kempei Tei removed all their insignia and boarded trucks in plain khaki uniforms.

The arrival of the first American ships, the U.S. Seventh Fleet, which entered the Yangtze estuary in mid-September, was greeted with frenzied excitement by huge crowds that had gathered along the waterfront. When the vessels came into view, a deafening cheer broke out, and the Americans' flagship, the *Rocky Mount*, signified the dawning of a new order by weighing anchor at the Number One buoy, previously reserved for the British flagship. Soon the fleet was joined by units of the U.S. Army Air Corps airlifted into Shanghai from Kwangsi. Over the next year, tens of thousands of Yankees would filter through Shanghai as the city became the central processing point for American soldiers returning to the United States from the Pacific arena. Their presence transformed the city. As thrilled to be off their boats and out of the jungle as the Shanghainese were to see them, the Americans replaced the grimness of the occupation with boisterousness and exuberance. The GIs were everywhere, cheerfully dispensing chocolates and gum to street urchins (who followed them around chanting "no mama, no papa, no whiskey soda"), dancing at the cabarets with a dozen dance tickets sticking out of their pockets, eagerly buying up presents for the folks back home from shopkeepers who had raised their prices to three times their prewar level, and otherwise flooding the city with American greenbacks. Astonishing the normally unflappable Shanghainese with their antics, the crazy Yanks even pulled rickshas through the streets—putting the mystified driver in the passenger's seat. "These GIs from Nebraska and Arkansas cavorted in the streets, having the time of their lives," recalled the Shanghai-born actress Tsai Chin. "Ya hooo! . . . Ya hoooo! they shouted, whooping it up with an uncouth vivacity that astounded the populace." Not the least of those benefiting from the presence of the free-spending Yanks were Shanghai's prostitutes, who were happy to be back in business big-time. Russian prostitutes were popular, but so were the Chinese, Eurasian, and Korean girls, some of whom had even bleached their hair to "wow their new overseas clientele with an image of the li'l girl next door," said Chin.

Along with the GIs and jeeps came a plethora of American goods, chiefly UNRRA (United Nations Relief and Rehabilitation Administration) and U.S. Army surplus items that Nationalist officials, led by the "Four Families," had diverted to

Shanghai's thriving black market. Between V-J Day and the end of 1948, the United States had authorized three billion dollars' worth of aid to China, much of it in material goods. But only a trickle of the food, clothing, medicines, and other supplies sent by American and international relief agencies found its way to the intended recipients, as the bulk of it was publicly auctioned or otherwise diverted into the hands of black marketers to be sold at "scandalous prices," Carey pointed out, at the hundreds of makeshift stalls that congested the city's streets, the dealers "not even bothering to remove the Red Cross and other relief organization wrappings." T. V. Soong had a large hand in creating this situation by insisting that all relief goods from UNRRA entering China be surrendered to a government-run Chinese National Relief and Rehabilitation Administration (CNRRA) rather than being accompanied by an UNRRA representative to their final destination, as was the usual procedure. As a result, Soong and his venal confederates took charge of the goods from the moment they arrived in Shanghai, storing them in their already groaning warehouses until they could be disposed of to the highest bidder. Even blood plasma donated by the American Red Cross wound up on the shelves of Shanghai's drugstores selling for twenty-five dollars a pint. Before the misappropriation of relief supplies, the same Kuomintang higher-ups, in particular the Soongs, Kungs, and Chiangs, had been siphoning off large amounts of American Lend-Lease into their pockets. All these abuses, taken together, amounted to what one American diplomat called "one of the biggest carpetbagging operations in history."

The rapacity of the Kuomintang officialdom extended to the seizure of the assets of "traitors" to the Chinese government or those individuals whose wealth made them attractive targets for such a charge. After the Nationalists returned to Nanking, anyone in the former Japanese-occupied areas who had survived the war with his property intact or who had prospered stood a strong chance of being accused of collaborating with the puppet government, thrown into prison, and having all his assets seized. This was the same tactic Chiang Kai-shek had used so successfully almost two decades before when he arrested bankers and businessmen for supposed Communist activities in order to bankroll his new government with their confiscated wealth. The government committees appointed by Nanking to oversee the "reconversion" of businesses taken by the Japanese to their rightful owners provided another means of personal enrichment. Enterprises that should have been returned to their proprietors were instead transferred into the ownership of private individuals or closed down, their workers thrown into unemployment and their equipment sold for scrap. In Shanghai, where the pickings were richest, more than two hundred concerns from broadcasting stations to shipping companies were appropriated in this fashion, with no compensation given to the original owners. Government monopolies now ran almost every major area of enterprise in Shanghai, driving out all those who had neither connections to the Four Families nor enough money to bribe their officials for licenses to do business.

This milking of the well-to-do in the areas previously under Japanese control reflected the general arrogance with which the Nationalists regarded those who had lived under puppet rule. "While those who had gone to Chungking with the government were considered loyal citizens, all those who had remained behind were suspect," complained one Shanghainese. Instead of treating the people of Shanghai, Nanking, Peking, and the other occupied territories as compatriots who had suffered during the war, Nationalist officials regarded them as unpatriotic citizens and subject to certain punishments. Lawyers, for example, who had practiced their profession in Shanghai during the occupation were disbarred, and students who had graduated between 1942 and 1945 were required to take special courses in Kuomintang ideology. On the other hand, though a number of prominent collaborators were tried and executed—among them Shanghai's puppet mayor, Chen Kung-Pao—the Nanking government was notoriously lax in punishing most of the actual traitors. Instead, most either were given light sentences or escaped punishment entirely. A not insignificant number were offered positions in the resurrected Nanking government. (Wang Ching-wei died of natural causes just before V-J Day, conveniently escaping public humiliation.)

The rot had set in. Those who had welcomed the Nationalists with elation at the end of the war now regarded the government with disgust. Behind their claims of patriotism, Nanking's officials revealed themselves to be not only selfish and hypocritical but incapable of managing the country's economy. Inflation had begun its mad spiral even before the war ended when the Nationalists started the practice of issuing paper notes to cover their lack of gold reserves. In 1944, notes for 189 billion Chinese dollars were put into circulation. By the end of 1946 that figure had increased to more than 4.5 trillion Chinese dollars. The inflation would escalate to even more astonishing heights until the notes were literally worth less than the paper they were printed on, a fact that was driven home in 1948 when a paper mill in Kwangtung was reported to have "bought up eight hundred cases of notes ranging from hundred-dollar to two-thousand-dollar bills which it used as raw material in the manufacture of paper." Sometime in 1948, the conversion rate for an American dollar to a Chinese dollar would have passed the one million mark, and by early 1949 it reached the incredible figure of six million. By then, Chinese were going shopping with bundles of paper money tied with string, and a large bag of money barely bought a packet of butter.

With the Chinese dollar losing its value by the day, if not by the hour, workers rushed to spend their money as soon as they were paid. The hyperinflation saw stalls erected almost at the doorsteps of banks so that ordinary citizens could buy provisions as soon as they had their money in hand before prices rose. The rush of people to the rice shops and markets to spend their money as fast as they could gave daily life a frenzied, hectic quality that went far beyond the busyness of a big city. Some employees demanded that their employers pay them in rice or clothing, or anything that had more staying power than paper money, while bartering became a way of life for others.

To the eyes of outsiders, the Shanghainese appeared more prosperous than ever. The restaurants and cinemas were full of Chinese families, the shopwindows were full of merchandise, and the average person on the street was far better and more smartly dressed than before. Watches, fountain pens, and other manufactured goods were owned by many people "of modest means who would hardly have known how to use them a decade ago," said one American. Straw sandals, once ubiquitous, had virtually disappeared, replaced by leather shoes. Even ricksha coolies wore suits and could be seen "sitting at stalls on the sidewalks enjoying Maxwell House coffee with cream and sugar, plus Spam, foreign bread and American butter."

But it was all illusion. If the ordinary people looked more prosperous, it was only because they had no choice but to spend their money on consumer goods. The only ones who could actually afford to go on a spending spree were the truly wealthy, who were relieving themselves of their paper money by buying up gold, silver, jade, and anything else precious that could be easily packed away. The working class, for once, did better than under ordinary circumstances chiefly because, fearful of a wave of strikes and labor unrest, the government had set these workers' wages at a high level and tied them to a monthly commodity price index. The real victims of the inflation, on the other hand, were white-collar and salaried workers, who could barely afford to pay rents; many lived on the edge of starvation. Civil servants in the big cities like Shanghai scraped by on the same amounts as manual laborers, which accounted for much of the corruption in the government's lower ranks, while a college professor earned approximately what a ricksha coolie made in a good month. On top of these problems, some six thousand refugees a day were entering Shanghai, filling up its refugee camps and swelling its population to an unprecedented five million, two million more than only a few years earlier.

Shanghai, it was said, was "riding high for a fall." In anticipation of complete economic collapse, many had already jumped ship. An exodus of wealthy Shanghainese had begun as early as 1946, when the Nationalists had begun prosecuting the well-to-do as traitors, and by the end of 1948 it had become a well-worn path. Despite their loss of extraterritoriality, a number of the big foreign firms had attempted to resuscitate their businesses after the war, but conditions had become so discouraging that most were folding their tents. Victor Sassoon, for one, had sold off all his Shanghai holdings by the end of 1948, relocating himself to the Bahamas to reinvest his millions in South America.

Nothing about China's racking inflation had been preordained. It existed for only one reason: Chiang Kai-shek's pursuit of civil war against the Communists and his commitment of 80 percent of his budget to his armed forces. As the remaining 20 percent was insufficient to the nation's needs, the government recklessly turned to the printing press to make up the difference. But the civil war, which had begun in earnest in July 1946 following Chiang's refusal to share power with the Communists, was not turning out as Chiang had planned. His campaign to push the People's Liberation Army out of several of its bases had initially succeeded, but by the middle of 1948, the PLA had not only recovered these territories but achieved a stunning series of victories that put it on the verge of taking all of Manchuria and menaced the Nationalists' hold on the cities north of the Yangtze. During this time too, the Communist armies had grown to 2,800,000 soldiers, as against Chiang's 3,650,000 troops, through the flocking to their cause of enthusiastic peasants as well as defectors from the Nationalist armies, who had brought with them large amounts of equipment and arms. Increasingly, it seemed that the Communists were winning the loyalty of the Chinese people.

Bleak as the Nationalists' military prospects were, an even greater cause for alarm in the summer of 1948 was the runaway inflation, which threatened to bring down Chiang's government even before the Communist armies could. In Shanghai, shopkeepers were increasing prices several times a day and even closing their shops in the middle of the afternoon so that they could reopen to sell their rice, paraffin, coal, or cloth at the next day's invariably higher price. This practice and the general economic chaos precipitated riots in Shanghai. Angry Chinese crowds stormed rice shops, restaurants, and grocery stores; the police at first attempted to arrest the rioters but were soon looking the other way. "Why should I arrest them? I may be among them tomorrow," one told a foreign reporter.

On August 19, in a last desperate measure to restore economic stability, Chiang played what the Chinese newspapers would later call his "last trump card." He announced the replacement of the old currency by a "gold yuan," which would be convertible from the old Chinese dollar at the rate of three million to one and pegged at one gold yuan to four American dollars. Under penalty of death, all Chinese holding gold, silver, or foreign or Chinese currency were required to surrender their wealth to the Central Bank in exchange for the new gold yuan. To coerce the reluctant citizenry into complying with this draconian measure, Chiang Kai-shek appointed his Russian-educated son, Chiang Ching-kuo, commissioner of the program, sending him to Shanghai, where the pickings were richest. Approaching his assignment with vigor and severity, Chiang organized a large force of spies and police, who used Soviet-style methods to terrorize the public into compliance. He declared his intention to search private homes for all currency and valuables that had not been turned over to the authorities. Then he sent trucks into wealthy neighborhoods to announce through loudspeakers that the trucks contained special instruments capable of detecting the presence of hidden gold, silver, and other valuables, even those buried underground. These and other similarly heavy-handed tactics succeeded in frightening scores of law-abiding citizens into handing over their life savings for fear of arrest. Wages and prices were also frozen, and shopkeepers were forced to sell their goods at the artificial prices. To curb the black market, Chiang Ching-kuo had his secret police comb the waterfront in search of warehouses with stores of hoarded goods. Numerous culprits were arrested and a few of them, among them several prominent businessmen, publicly executed as a warning to others.

But the gold yuan slipped after a month, becoming as worthless as its predecessor. As ineptly handled as everything else the Nationalists did, the attempt at reform failed, because the government had done nothing to increase its revenues or decrease its spending. Moreover, the "reform at pistol point" had antagonized the business community in Shanghai and brought about food shortages and the ruin of many shopkeepers and merchants. Worst of all, Chiang Kai-shek had irreparably alienated the last of his supporters, the urban middle class, who had surrendered their life savings in hopes of resuscitating the economy. Instead, they had lost everything; they'd been robbed and "shaken down" by their government. Bitterly, the Shanghainese "whispered that the sole purpose of the transaction was to confiscate the people's wealth for the benefit of the Four Great Families."

Ironically, Chiang Ching-kuo himself was not close to the Chiangs or Kungs and looked upon them, as he did all of Shanghai's rich Westernized Chinese, as decadent. It was because he dared to hold the members of the Four Families to the same laws that applied to all Chinese, in fact, that Chiang Ching-kuo would suffer the worst humiliation of his brief tenure as Shanghai's economic czar. Among the warehouses where Chiang's agents discovered black market goods was one belonging to a company owned by the Kung family. The police not only confiscated the warehouse's purloined goods but prepared to arrest the company's general manager, the Kungs' eldest son, David. Upon hearing of her stepson's plans, an angry Madame Chiang Kai-shek flew to Shanghai to slap Ching-kuo in the face for his effrontery. Suffering grave "loss of face," Ching-kuo, who presumably received no backing from his father, soon resigned his position. Before he left, he apologized for "having deepened the sufferings of the people." Madame Chiang's nephew, David Kung, for his part, soon departed for the United States, where the Soongs and Kungs had been systematically transferring their takings for safe custody. (Even in the days of the Sino-Japanese War, "a plane dispatched from Chungking for Washington, D.C., with 'important secret documents' had to ditch in the river when it caught on fire," recalled the American general George Marshall. "When salvaged, what it proved to have was U.S currency which the Soong family was sending to the U.S.") No one knew exactly how much Chiang's wife and in-laws had in their overseas bank accounts, but it was thought to be in the billions.

Its "last card" played, the Nanking government's collapse was inevitable. Militarily too, the downhill slide had begun. In September, Tsinan fell to the PLA, followed in November by Mukden, whose capture was an even more crushing defeat, as the Communists had wiped out Chiang Kai-shek's 400,000-man northeastern army—an army the Generalissimo had stubbornly insisted on keeping in Manchuria despite the pleading of his American advisers to withdraw to China proper. With Mukden's capture, the Communists held all of Manchuria. Then came the defection of one important general after another to the Red Army; these defectors took entire divisions with them. In mid-December, after an eighteen-month battle, came the penultimate blow, the loss of Hsuchow, called the "key to Nanking" because it stood at the intersection of the Tientsin-Pukow and Lung-Hai railways halfway between Tientsin and the Yangtze. The way to Nanking was open. But before taking it, the Communists returned north to invest first Tientsin, then Peking. The Nationalist forces holding the imperial capital surrendered peacefully to General Lin Piao's army on January 31. By the end of January, the Communists were masters of all of China north of the Yangtze.

Ten days earlier, Chiang Kai-shek had "resigned" from office. This resignation, like those before, was only nominal, as he continued to mastermind events from behind the scenes as the Kuomintang's leader. His successor, Li Tsung-jen, had hoped to negotiate a peace settlement with the Communists but could make no progress, because Chiang not only issued secret counterorders sabotaging all of Li's actions but had shifted much of the government's remaining equipment and military troops to Taiwan. Since the fall of Hsuchow, Chiang had been readying the island as his stronghold, shipping not only the most precious of the imperial treasures there but also all of the government's gold reserves. This last bold move, the "greatest robbery of all," had taken place in the dead of night in February after Nationalist troops cordoned off the Bund to allow the 500,000 ounces of gold bullion residing in the Bank of China's vaults to be put aboard a waiting freighter manned by handpicked Nationalist officers who knew the "swiftest route to Taiwan." From the fifth-floor window of a nearby office building, George Vine, a British newspaperman who was working late, watched the entire operation in astonishment. "I could hardly believe what I saw," he recalled. "Below was a file of coolies padding out of the bank. I could even make out their hats or the sweat rags on their foreheads, and their uniforms of indigo tunic and short baggy trousers." As they descended the bank's steps—chanting, as Shanghai's coolies were wont to, the familiar "heigh-ho" of the dockyards—the coolies could be seen balancing wrapped parcels of gold bullion on either end of their bamboo poles. All the gold in China, Vine mused, "was being carried away in the traditional manner—by coolies."

The secret removal of the gold reserves left Li Tsung-jen with no funds to use as a bargaining chip in the discussions with the Communists or, in the worse eventuality, to finance a military resistance to the Red armies once they returned to the field. Then, when Li asked for contingents of Nationalist troops from Taiwan, he was told—on orders from Chiang Kai-shek—that none could be spared. Among those who refused to obey Li Tsung-jen was Tang En-po, a general widely regarded as corrupt and incompetent, whom Chiang Kai-shek had personally put in charge of the lower Kiangsu area. Li had ordered Tang to lift the martial law he had imposed on Shanghai and free up a portion of the 200,000-man force under his control so that it could be deployed elsewhere. But Tang followed only Chiang Kai-shek's commands, and in April, after a visit by Chiang himself just before departing for Taiwan, Tang announced his intention to defend Shanghai "like a second Stalingrad."

Chiang Kai-shek's henchmen made Shanghai's last weeks under Nationalist rule a nightmare of disorder and brutality. Martial law was clamped down on the city and businesses from offices to cabarets were forced to close as the authorities requisitioned their premises as billets for Tang En-po's troops, and many families found themselves the reluctant hosts of officers and their entourages. A military proclamation decreed that the soldiers were to be allowed to ride free on all buses and trolleys and admitted to all movie theaters without paying. In the meantime, these "protectors of the people" lost no opportunity to rob and loot. They broke into both shops and private homes, forcing owners of the more expensive shops to board up their windows and storefronts, "leaving only small apertures for occasional customers." But worst of all was the wave of political terror unleashed upon the city as Tang Eng-po began rounding up suspected Communists, black marketers, and other scapegoats for the Nationalists' ills and staging public executions at street corners and other public places without the benefit of a trial. Most of these victims were students or young men. "One spectacle I witnessed, which I am not likely to forget," said one American, "was the street execution of half a dozen captive students. Bound and kneeling, they had their brains blown out by Chiang's warriors before a great crowd of people in Yangtzepoo, while shouting gendarmes beat back the crowd with long bamboo whips, their customary weapon." The executions took place almost daily, the usual sites being busy street corners such as one on Foochow Road near the police station, where another American witnessed nine students being shot in the back of their heads and "their bodies removed virtually under the windows of the American Club next door."

When the Nationalists failed to accept the settlement agreement the Communists had presented them with—one of the chief points being the surrender of the "war criminal" Chiang Kai-shek—Mao Tse-tung's armies swept across the Yangtze River in mid-April. Nanking surrendered without a fight on April 24, as did the intervening cities and towns along the way to Shanghai. As they had done in previous crises, Shanghai's bankers and businessmen came to the fore, brokering a deal with the Communists to provide them with funds and medicines in exchange for a peaceful entrance. Tang En-po, who had vowed to defend Shanghai to the last, accepted a bribe of bullion and foreign currency and boarded an evacuation plane for Canton on the afternoon of May 24. On his heels would go most of his forces, retreating in the direction of Woosung. A Chinese reporter watching the Nationalist forces retreating in the direction of Woosung applauded their disciplined departure, deeming it "the most effective operation of the entire war."

Sporadic gunfire around Hungjiao to the city's southwest and around Woosung had alerted the city to the arrival of the

Communist forces a few days earlier, though not a single one of General Chen Yi's soldiers had yet been spotted. On the evening of the twenty-fourth, however, the guns suddenly fell silent and an eerie calm fell over the suburbs. Beginning around midnight, the peasant soldiers of Mao's new order entered, carefully but resolutely, the great Chinese metropolis. They came in through Frenchtown, marching two abreast up Avenue Edouard VII, some leading horses and mules, and keeping close to the walls of the buildings. When the city woke the next day, it found itself under new management. A few pockets of Nationalist soldiers were holding out across the Soochow Creek and in other parts of the city, but by midafternoon they had laid down their arms and exchanged their uniforms for black gowns—much delighting the local beggars, who donned the discarded clothing.

As the first day of Red Shanghai began, it was hard to say who was more curious about whom—the Shanghainese about their peasant "conquerors," who carried their emergency rations of crushed locust still strapped on their backs, refusing so much as a cup of tea from anyone, or the new arrivals, who gazed upon China's most cosmopolitan city with a mixture of embarrassment and fascination. What did they make of the towering hotels and the movie palaces, of the nightly parade of streetwalkers and their shrill amahs, of the department stores bursting with goods, or of the legions of starving and homeless who lay in wait for unsuspecting wharf coolies, snatching handfuls of rice or sticks of wood or pieces of coal whenever they could? Looking over their sneakered and green-cotton-clad army of liberation, more than a few Shanghainese must have been struck by the gap between these earnest representatives of the new China and jaded, apathetic Shanghai.

Yet adaptability was the byword of the denizens of the city of mudflats. Hence the popularity of a ditty whose lyrics spoke to Shanghai's cynical heart:

Me no worry
Me no care
Me going to marry a millionaire
And if he die
Me no cry
Me going to get another guy.

BIBLIOGRAPHY

1: THE UGLY DAUGHTER RISES

Alcock, Rutherford. *The Capital of the Tycoon: A Narrative of a Three Years' Residence in Japan*. New York: Greenwood Press, 1969.

Beeching, Jack. *The Chinese Opium Wars*. New York: Harcourt Brace Jovanovich, 1975.

Booth, Martin. *Opium: A History*. New York: St. Martin's Press, 1998.

Chang, Hsin-pao. *Commissioner Lin and the Opium War*. Cambridge, Mass.: Harvard University Press, 1964.

Chen Kung-lu. *Chung-kuo chin-tai shih*. Shanghai: Commercial Press, 1935.

Collis, Maurice. *Foreign Mud*. London: Faber & Faber, 1946.

Fairbank, John King. *Trade and Diplomacy on the China Coast*. Cambridge, Mass.: Harvard University Press, 1953.

Fay, Peter Ward. *The Opium War, 1840–1842*. New York: Norton, 1976.

Finch, Percy. *Shanghai and Beyond*. New York: Scribner's, 1953.

Fortune, Robert. *A Residence Among the Chinese*. London: John Murray, 1857.

Hibbert, Christopher. *The Dragon Wakes: China and the West, 1793–1911.* London: Penguin Books, 1984.

Hussey, Harry. *My Pleasures and Palaces.* New York: Doubleday, 1968.

Johnson, Linda Cooke. *Shanghai: From Market Town to Treaty Port, 1074–1858.* Palo Alto, Calif.: Stanford University Press, 1995.

Maclellan, J. W. *The Story of Shanghai.* Shanghai: North China Herald Office, 1889.

MacPherson, Kerrie L. *A Wilderness of Marshes: The Origins of Public Health in Shanghai, 1843–1893.* Hong Kong: Oxford University Press, 1987.

Matheson, James. *The Present Position and Prospects of the British Trade with China.* London, 1836.

Mayers, William, N. B. Dennys, and Charles King. *The Treaty Ports of China and Japan.* London, 1867.

Pan Ling. *In Search of Old Shanghai.* Hong Kong: Joint Publishing Company, 1982.

Pelissier, Roger. *The Awakening of China, 1793–1949.* Ed. and trans. Martin Keiffer. London: Secker & Warburg, 1963.

Shanghai Almanac for 1854, and Miscellany.

Wakeman, Frederick. *The Fall of Imperial China.* New York: Free Press, 1977.

Waley, Arthur. *The Opium War Through Chinese Eyes.* Palo Alto, Calif.: Stanford University Press, 1958.

Webster's Third New International Dictionary. Springfield, Mass.: G. C. Merriam Co., 1976.

2: GOLD IN THE YANGTZE MUD

Ball, J. Dyer. *Things Chinese.* Singapore: Graham Brash, 1989.

Bodley, Ronald Victor Courtenay. *Indiscreet Travels East.* London: Jarrolds, 1934.

Bruner, Katherine F., John K. Fairbank, and Richard Smith, eds. *Entering China's Service: Robert Hart's Journals, 1854–1863.* Cambridge, Mass.: Harvard University Press, 1986.

Burke, James. *My Father in China.* New York: Farrar & Rinehart, 1942.

Carr, Caleb. *The Devil Soldier.* New York: Atlantic Monthly Press, 1993.

Cooke, George Wingrove. *China: Being "The Times" Special Correspondent from China in the Years 1857 and 1858*. Wilmington, Del.: Scholarly Resources, 1972.

Crisswell, Colin N. *The Taipans: Hong Kong's Merchant Princes*. Hong Kong: Oxford University Press, 1991.

Croll, Elisabeth. *Feminism and Socialism in China*. New York: Schocken, 1980.

Crow, Carl. *Foreign Devils in the Flowery Kingdom*. New York: Harper, 1940.

Darwent, Charles Ewart. *Shanghai: A Handbook for Travellers and Residents*. Shanghai: Kelly & Walsh, 1920.

Drage, Charles. *Servants of the Dragon Throne, Being the Lives of Edward and Cecil Bowra*. London: Peter Dawney, 1966.

Dyce, Charles M. *The Model Settlement: Personal Reminiscences of Thirty Years' Residence in the Model Settlement*. London: Chapman & Hall, 1906.

Evans, Hilary. *The Oldest Profession: An Illustrated History of Prostitution*. Newton Abbot, England: David Charles, 1979.

Fewsmith, Joseph. *Party, State and Local Elites in Republican China: Merchant Organizations and Politics in Shanghai, 1890–1930*. Honolulu: University of Hawaii Press, 1985.

Gamewell, Mary Ninde. *The Gateway to China: Pictures of Shanghai*. New York: Fleming Revell, 1916.

Goodman, Bryna. *Native Place, City and Nation: Regional Networks and Identities in Shanghai, 1853–1937*. Berkeley: University of California Press, 1995.

Gronewald, Sue. *Beautiful Merchandise: Prostitution in China, 1860–1936*. New York: Harrington Park Press, 1985.

Hauser, Ernest O. *Shanghai: A City for Sale*. New York: Harcourt, Brace, 1945.

Hershatter, Gail. *Dangerous Pleasures: Prostitution and Modernity in the Twentieth Century*. Seattle: University of Washington Press, 1997.

Hinsch, Bret. *Passions of the Cut Sleeve: The Male Homosexual Tradition in China*. Berkeley: University of California Press, 1990.

Hsiung, S. I. *The Life of Chiang Kai-shek*. London: P. Davies, 1948.

Jackson, Stanley. *The Sassoons*. London: William Heinemann, 1968.

Keimach, Joseph W., ed. *Shanghai Commercial and Shopping Pocket Guide*. Shanghai: Kwang Hsueh Publishing House, 1936.

Lane-Poole, Stanley. *The Life of Sir Harry Parkes, K.C.B. . . . Sometime Her Majesty's Minister to China and Japan, 1894*. Vol. 1, *Consul in China*. London: 1894.

Little, Alice H. *Intimate China: The Chinese as I Have Seen Them*. Philadelphia: J. B. Lippincott, 1899.

Macfarlane, W. *Sketches in the Foreign Settlements and Native City of Shanghai*. Shanghai, 1881.

Medhurst, Walter. *The Foreigner in Far Cathay*. New York: Scribner, Armstrong, 1873.

Miller, G. E. *Shanghai: The Paradise of Adventurers*. New York, Orsay Press, 1937.

Miller, J. M. *China: Ancient and Modern*. Chicago: J. M. Miller, 1900.

Parker, E. H. *China: Past and Present*. New York: Dutton, 1903.

Pott, F. L. Hawks. *A Short History of Shanghai*. Shanghai: Kelly & Walsh Ltd., 1928.

Sharman, Lyon. *Sun Yat-sen: His Life and Its Meaning*. New York: John Day, 1934.

Spence, Jonathan D. *The Gate of Heavenly Peace*. New York: Norton, 1981.

————. *In Search of Modern China*. New York: Norton, 1990.

Townsend, Ralph. *Ways That Are Dark*. New York: Putnam, 1933.

Wing, Yung. *My Life in China and America*. New York: Ayer, 1979.

Wang, Y. C. "Tu Yueh-sheng (1881–1951): A Tentative Bibliography." *Journal of Asian Studies* 26 (1967).

3: CITY OF TRANSFORMATIONS

Booker, Edna Lee. *News Is My Job*. New York: Macmillan, 1940.

Cook, Christopher. *The Lion and the Dragon: British Voices from the China Coast*. London: Elm Tree Books, 1985.

Ding Ling. *Miss Sophie's Diary and Other Stories*. Peking: Panda Books, 1985.

Elvin, Mark. "The Administration of Chinese Shanghai, 1905–14." In Mark Elvin and G. William Skinner, eds., *The Chinese City Between Two Worlds*. Palo Alto, Calif.: Stanford University Press, 1974.

Gasstner, Michael. *Chinese Intellectuals and the Revolution of 1911*. Seattle: University of Washington Press, 1969.

Jones, Susan Mann. "The Ningpo Pang and Financial Power in Shanghai." In Mark Elvin and G. William Skinner, eds., *The Chinese City Between Two Worlds*. Palo Alto, Calif.: Stanford University Press, 1974.

Kennedy, Thomas L. *Testimony of a Confucian Woman: The Autobiography of Mrs. Nie Zen Jifen, 1852–1942*. Athens: University of Georgia, 1993.

Kuhn, Irene Corbally. "Shanghai: The Vintage Years." *Gourmet*, January 1986, pp. 54, 115–17.

Lee, James Hsioung. *A Half-Century of Memories*. Hong Kong: South China Photo-Process Printing Co., n.d.

Mao Tun. *Midnight*. Beijing: Foreign Languages Press, 1979.

Pal, John. *Shanghai Saga*. London: Jarrolds, 1963.

Pan, Lynn. *Sons of the Yellow Emperor: A History of the Chinese Diaspora*. Boston: Little, Brown, 1990.

Rankin, Mary. *Early Chinese Revolutionaries: Radical Intellectuals in Shanghai and Chekiang, 1902–1911*. Cambridge, Mass.: Harvard University Press, 1971.

Rodzinski, Witold. *The Walled Kingdom*. New York: Free Press, 1984.

Schuman, Julian. *China: An Uncensored Look*. Sag Harbor, N.Y.: Second Chance Press, 1983.

Wakeman, Frederick, and Yeh Wen-hsin, eds. *Shanghai Sojourners*. Berkeley: University of California Press, 1992.

Wang, Y. C. *Chinese Intellectuals and the West, 1872–1949*. Chapel Hill: University of North Carolina Press, 1966.

Wright, Mary. *China in Revolution: The First Decade, 1900–1913*. New Haven, Conn.: Yale University Press, 1968.

Zhang, Yingjin. *The City in Modern Chinese Literature and Film*. Palo Alto, Calif.: Stanford University Press, 1996.

4: CAPITALISTS, WARLORDS, AND THIEVES

Akimova, Vera Vladimirovna Vishnayakova. *Two Years in Revolutionary China: 1925–27*. Cambridge, Mass.: East Asian Research Center, Harvard University, 1971.

All About Shanghai and Environs: A Standard Guidebook. Hong Kong: Oxford University Press, 1983.

Bergère, Marie Claire. *L'Age d'or de la bourgeoisie chinoise, 1911–1937.* Paris: Flammarion, 1986.

Bergreen, Laurence. *Capone: The Man and the Era.* New York: Touchstone, 1994.

Bland, J. O. P. "Shanghai Revisited," *National Review* (London), Vol. 6, 1920, pp. 520–535.

Ch'en, Chiej-ju. *Chiang Kai-shek's Secret Past: The Memoir of His Second Wife, Ch'en Chieh-ju.* Ed. Lloyd E. Eastman. Boulder, Colo.: Westview Press, 1993.

Clifford, Nicholas R. *Spoilt Children of Empire.* Hanover, N.H.: University of New England Press, 1991.

Clark, Elmer T. *The Chiangs of China.* New York: Abingdon Press, 1943.

Clark, Paul. *Chinese Cinema: Culture and Politics Since 1949.* New York: Cambridge University Press, 1987.

Fontenoy, Jean. *The Secret Shanghai.* New York: Grey-Hill Press, 1939.

Hahn, Emily. *The Soong Sisters.* New York: Doubleday, 1941.

Honig, Emily. *Sisters and Strangers: Women in the Shanghai Cotton Mills, 1919–49.* Palo Alto, Calif.: Stanford University Press, 1986.

Hsiung, Hsi-i. *The Life of Chiang Kai-shek.* London: P. Davies. 1948.

Isaacs, Norman. *Straw Sandals.* Cambridge, Mass.: MIT Press, 1974.

Karns, Maurine. *Shanghai: Highlights, Low Lights, Tail Lights.* Shanghai: The Tridon Press, 1936.

Klingaman, William K. *1929: The Year of the Great Crash.* New York: Harper & Row, 1989.

Koo, Mme. Wellington, with Isabella Taves. *No Feast Lasts Forever.* New York: Quadrangle, 1975.

Kuhn, Irene. *Assigned to Adventure.* New York: Lippincott, 1938.

Leyda, Jay. *Dianying: An Account of Films and the Film Audience of China.* Cambridge, Mass.: MIT Press, 1972.

Link, Perry. *Mandarin Ducks and Butterflies: Popular Fiction in Early Twentieth-Century Chinese Cities.* Berkeley: University of California Press, 1981.

Malraux, André. *Man's Fate.* New York: Random House, 1968.

Martin, Brian. *The Shanghai Green Gang: Politics and Organized Crime, 1919–1937.* Berkeley: University of California Press, 1996.

Pan Ling. *Gangsters in Paradise.* Hong Kong: Heinemann Asia, 1984.

Peters, Ernest William. *Shanghai Policeman.* London: Rich & Cowan, 1937.

Seagrave, Sterling. *The Soong Dynasty.* New York: Harper & Row, 1985.

Smedley, Agnes. *Battle Hymn of China.* London: Pandora Press, 1984.

Snow, Helen. *Women in Modern China.* The Hague: Mouton Press, 1957.

Spunt, George. *A Place in Time.* New York: Putnam, 1968.

Sues, Ilona Ralf. *Shark's Fins and Millet.* Boston: Little, Brown, 1944.

Wakeman, Frederick. *Policing Shanghai, 1927–1937.* Berkeley: University of California Press, 1997.

Wang, Y. C. "Tu Yueh-sheng (1887–1951). A Tentative Political Biography." *Journal of Asian Studies* 26 (May 1967): 433–55.

Windsor, Wallis Warfield. *The Heart Has Its Reasons.* New York: McKay, 1956.

5: THE SHANGHAI MASSACRE

Bianco, Lucien. *Origins of the Chinese Revolution.* Palo Alto, Calif.: Stanford University Press, 1967.

Candlin, Enid Saunders. *The Breach in the Wall.* New York: Macmillan, 1973.

Chapman, H. Owen. *The Chinese Revolution of 1926–1927.* London: Constable, 1928.

Chow, Rey. *Woman and Chinese Modernity: The Politics of Reading Between West and East.* Minneapolis: University of Minnesota Press, 1990.

Coble, Parks M. *The Shanghai Capitalists and the Nationalist Government, 1927–37.* Cambridge, Mass.: Harvard University Press, 1980.

Conn, Peter. *Pearl S. Buck: A Cultural Biography.* New York: Cambridge University Press, 1996.

Crow, Carl. *Four Hundred Million Customers.* New York: Harper, 1937.

Crozier, Brian. *Chiang Kai-shek: The Man Who Loved China.* New York: Scribners, 1966.

Hahn, Emily. *China to Me: A Partial Autobiography.* Philadelphia: Blakiston, 1944.

Hinder, Eleanor M. *Life and Labour in Shanghai.* New York: Institute of
Pacific Relations, 1944.

————. *Social and Industrial Problems of Shanghai with Special Reference to
the Administrative and Regulatory Work of the Shanghai Municipal
Council.* New York: Institute of Pacific Relations, 1942.

Holcome, Arthur N. *The Spirit of the Chinese Revolution.* New York:
Knopf, 1930.

Isaacs, Norman. *The Tragedy of the Chinese Revolution.* Palo Alto, Calif.:
Stanford University Press, 1951.

Johnstone, William. *The Shanghai Problem.* Palo Alto, Calif.: Stanford
University Press, 1937.

Lee, Leo Ou-fan. *The Romantic Generation of Modern Chinese Writers.*
Cambridge, Mass.: Harvard University Press, 1973.

Lu Xun. *Diary of a Madman and Other Stories.* Trans. William A. Lyell.
Honolulu: University of Hawaii Press, 1990.

Morwood, William. *Duel for the Middle Kingdom.* New York: Everest
House, 1980.

Pilnyak, Boris. *Chinese Story and Other Tales.* Tulsa: University of
Oklahoma Press, 1988.

Ransome, Arthur. *The Chinese Puzzle.* London: Allen & Unwin, 1927.

Sheean, Vincent. *Personal History.* Secaucus, N.J.: The Citadel Press,
1969.

Snow, Edgar. *Journey to the Beginning.* New York: Random House,
1972.

Terrill, Ross. *The White-Boned Demon: A Biography of Madame Mao Ze-
dong.* New York: Morrow, 1984.

Wilson, Dick. *Chou: The Story of Chou En-lai, 1887–1976.* London:
Hutchinson, 1984.

6: ENTER THE DWARF BANDITS

Abend, Hallett. *My China Years, 1926–1941.* London: Bodley Head,
1944.

Astor, Brooke. *Patchwork Child.* New York: Random House, 1993.

Belden, Jack. *China Shakes the World.* New York: Monthly Review Press,
1949.

Cuthbertson, Ken. *Nobody Said Not to Go: The Life, Loves and Adventures
of Emily Hahn.* Boston: Faber & Faber, 1998.

Gayn, Marc J. *Journey from the East: An Autobiography*. New York: Knopf, 1944.

Ginsbourg, Sam. *My First Sixty Years in China*. Beijing: New World Press, 1982.

Gunther, John. *Inside Asia*. New York: Harper, 1942.

Hamilton, John Maxwell. *Edgar Snow: A Biography*. Bloomington: Indiana University Press, 1988.

Isaacs, Norman. *Re-encounters in China*. Armonk, N.Y.: M. L. Sharpe, 1985.

Karnow, Stanley. *Paris in the Fifties*. New York: Times Books, 1998.

Koo, Mme. Wellington, with Isabella Taves. *No Feast Lasts Forever*. New York: Quadrangle, 1975.

MacKinnon, Janice R., and Stephen R. MacKinnon. *Agnes Smedley: The Life and Times of an American Radical*. Berkeley: University of California Press, 1988.

Powell, John B. *My Twenty-five Years in China*. New York: Macmillan, 1945.

Rand, Peter. *China Hands*. New York: Simon & Schuster, 1995.

Sargeant, Harriet. *Shanghai: Collision Point of Cultures, 1928–1939*. New York: Crown, 1990.

Snow, Edgar. *Far Eastern Front*. New York: Random House, 1933.

Snow, Helen. *My China Years: A Memoir*. New York: Morrow, 1984.

von Sternberg, Josef. *Fun in a Chinese Laundry*. New York: Collier, 1965.

Thomson, John. *Through China with a Camera*. London: Westminster, A. Constable & Co., 1898.

7: THE LONELY ISLAND

Allman, Norwood. *Shanghai Lawyer*. New York: Whittlesey House, 1943.

Byron, John, and Robert Pack. *The Claws of the Dragon: Kang Shen—The Evil Genius Behind Mao and His Legacy of Terror in People's China*. New York: Simon & Schuster, 1992.

Carey, Arch. *The War Years in Shanghai, 1941–45*. New York, 1967.

Davidson-Houston, James. *Yellow Creek: The Story of Shanghai*. London: Putnam, 1962.

Edgerton, Robert B. *Warriors of the Rising Sun: A History of the Japanese Military*. New York: Norton, 1997.

Faligot, Roger, and Remi Kauffer. *The Chinese Secret Service: Kang Sheng and the Shadow Government in Red China.* New York: Morrow, 1987.

Farmer, Rhodes. *Shanghai Harvest: A Diary of Three Years in the China War.* London: Museum Press, 1945.

Fischel, Wesley. *The End of Extraterritoriality in China.* Berkeley: University of California Press, 1952.

Fu Poshek. *Passivity, Resistance and Collaboration: Intellectual Choices in Occupied Shanghai, 1937–1945.* Palo Alto, Calif.: Stanford University Press, 1993.

Harries, Meirion, and Susie Harries. *Soldiers of the Sun: The Rise and Fall of the Imperial Japanese Army.* New York: Random House, 1991.

Heppner, Ernest G. *Shanghai Refuge: A Memoir of the World War II Jewish Ghetto.* Lincoln: University of Nebraska Press, 1993.

Kranzler, David. *Japanese, Nazis and Jews.* New York: Yeshiva University Press, 1976.

Ross, James R. *Escape to Shanghai: A Jewish Community in China.* New York: Free Press, 1994.

Tuchman, Barbara. *Stilwell and the American Experience in China.* New York: Macmillan, 1971.

Wakeman, Frederick. *Shanghai Badlands: Wartime Terrorism and Urban Crime, 1937–1941.* New York: Cambridge University Press, 1996.

White, Theodore H., and Annalee Jacoby. *Thunder Out of China.* New York: William Sloane Associates, 1946.

8: THE UGLY DAUGHTER REPENTS

Barber, Noel. *The Fall of Shanghai.* New York: Coward, McCann, 1979.

Barnet, Robert. *Economic Shanghai: Hostage to Politics, 1937–41.* New York: Institute of Pacific Relations, 1941.

Barnett, A. Doak. *China on the Eve of the Communist Takeover.* London: Thames & Hudson, 1963.

Beal, John R. *Marshall in China.* Garden City, N.Y.: Doubleday, 1970.

Cartier-Bresson, Henri. *China.* New York: Bantam, 1964.

Chou Shun-hsin. *The Chinese Inflation, 1937–1949.* New York: Columbia University Press, 1963.

Krasno, Rena. *Strangers Always.* Berkeley: Pacific View Press, 1992.

Leys, Simon. *Chinese Shadows.* New York: Viking Press, 1977.

Loh, Pichon. *The Kuomintang Debacle of 1949: Conquest or Collapse?* Boston: Little, Brown, 1965.

Pan, Lynn. *Tracing It Home: A Chinese Family's Journey from Shanghai.* New York: Kodansha International, 1993.

Pepper, Suzanne. *Civil War in China: The Political Struggle, 1945–1949.* Berkeley: University of California Press, 1978.

Rossi, Paolo. *The Communist Conquest of Shanghai.* Alexandria, Va.: Twin Circle Publishing Co., 1970.

Tsai Chin. *Daughter of Shanghai.* London: Chatto & Windus, 1988.

INDEX

Chapei, 95, 124, 159, 160, 183
  cabarets in, 132–33
  in Japanese invasion, 254, 256
  in Shanghai Incident, 214–17
Chekiang, 65, 87, 90, 181
Chen Chieh-ju, 170–71, 191
Chen Chi-mei, 86, 87, 90–92, 171
  assassination of, 92, 170
  background of, 85
  Chiang Kai-shek's relationship with, 90–91, 92, 182, 186
Chen Kung Pao, 277, 284
Chen Li-fu, 241, 244, 245, 248
Chen Tu-hsiu, 157, 158, 185
Chen Yi, 293
Cheng Ju-cheng, 90, 91
Cheng Kuan-ying, 69
Cheong-sam, see chi-pao
Chi Shi-yuan, 122–23, 124
Chiang, Madame, *see* Soong Mei-ling
Chiang Ching, 147–48
Chiang Ching-kuo, 287–89
Chiang Kai-shek, 75, 90–93, 108, 170–73, 177–86, 188–93, 210–14, 230, 234, 248–52, 254
  assassination attempt on, 244–45
  businessmen backers of, 180–81, 185, 186
  Chen Chi-mei's relationship with, 90–91, 182, 186
  Japan policy of, 211–14, 249–52
  marriages of, 106–8, 170–71, 190–92
  postwar activities of, 280, 286–92
  resignations of, 186, 190, 290
  in slaughter of Communists, 106, 182–86, 217
  Soong Ching-ling's criticism of, 106, 186, 191–93
  in Taiwan, 290, 291
  Tsai Ting-kai and, 214, 216
Chicago, Ill., Shanghai compared with, 16, 45, 75, 113
Chicago Crime Commission, 118
Chien Lung emperor, 5
children, in factories, 160–62
Chin, Tsai, 281
China:
  blows to white prestige in, 130–35
  Boxer Rebellion in, 78–79, 80, 165, 167, 175
  British blockade of, 9
  Communist revolution in, 158–59, 289–93
  country vs. city in, 75
  Japan's invasion of (1937), 212, 217, 238, 251–57
  Japan's war with (1894–95), 71–72, 80, 158
  nationalism in, 78–79, 156–59, 165–75, 213–16, 249–56

near bankruptcy of, 8, 79
1911 revolution in, 84–89, 104, 124, 146, 149, 156, 182
in Opium War, 2, 4, 23
puppet regime in, 260, 262–66, 269, 277, 280, 282–84
Taiping Rebellion in, 13–18, 21, 64, 65, 66
Treaty of Nanking and, 3–4, 269
Western credo in, 15
China Forum, 232, 234
China League for Civil Rights, 232, 242
China Merchants Steam Navigation Company, 67–68, 69
China Press, 177, 232, 263, 274
China Repository, 32
China Weekly Review, 176–78
Chinese, written, reform of, 157
Chinese Benevolent Association, 255
Chinese City Council, 84, 86, 87
Chinese Maritime Customs Service, 200–201
Chinese National Relief and Rehabilitation Administration (CNRRA), 282
Ching dynasty, 7–8, 14, 23, 63, 70
  after Boxer Rebellion, 79
  Li Hung-chang's power base in, 17–18
  revolutionary politics vs., 79–82, 84–93, 104, 105
  Taiping Rebellion against, 13–18, 21, 64, 65, 66
chi-pao (cheong-sam), 141–42, 143, 146, 277
Chiu Chin, 146
Chou En-lai, 169, 173, 179–80, 185, 236, 238–40, 243
  Gu Shunzhang and, 243, 245, 246
  Japan policy of, 250
Chou Hsuan, 145, 146
Christianity, 14, 48, 103, 104
  see also missionaries; *specific sects*
Chungking, 166, 255
Chung Wai Bank, 189
Church of England, 28–29
Ciano, Count, 227
Ciano, Edda, 227
Ciro's, 222
citizenship certificates, sale of, 128
civil service examinations, 79
Civil War, U.S., 22
climate, 11, 12, 30, 260
clothes, 227
  of Chinese students, 150–51
  see also chi-pao
Cohen, Morris ("Two Gun"), 228
Comintern (Communist International), 158, 165, 169, 172, 235–38
Commercial Press, 80, 159, 183

Hu Tu, 12
Hu Yeh-ping, 241–42

Ibsen, Henrik, 147
Idzumo (Japanese cruiser), 252, 253
indentures, 61, 63
India, 5, 6, 81, 115
industrialization, 66–67, 71–72, 94–95,
    112, 158
    Japanese and, 211–12
    working conditions and, 159–62
inflation, 284–88
International Arms Embargo Agreement
    (1919), 128
International Settlement, 59, 78, 94, 126–
    27, 137, 159, 180, 181, 233, 259,
    265
    antidrug initiatives of, 119, 120–21
    antiforeigners' sentiment in, 166
    Art Deco in, 217–18, 219
    brothels in, 44
    Chinese area compared with, 88–89
    Chinese-owned publications in, 80–81
    Communist activities in, 237, 239,
        240, 244
    crime in, 113, 129–30
    depression in, 63–64
    edifices of Bund in, 195–201
    foreign preservation efforts in, 174,
        175, 183, 184
    Japanese in, 211, 212, 252
    Japanese invasion and, 252, 253, 256–
        57
    Japanese seizure of, 269
    Mixed Court of, 48, 81, 181
    municipal code of, 18, 21
    Municipal Council of, *see* Shanghai
        Municipal Council
    opium and, 52, 61
    rioting in, 83–84
    Shanghai uprising and, 86, 87
    Sikh policemen of, 163–64
Isaacs, Harold, 107, 232, 233–34, 236
Israel, Al, 138
Ito, Hirobumi, 71

Jackson, Sidney, 56, 60
Jackson, Sir Victor, 220
Japan, 79, 113, 156–60, 191, 211–17, 249–
    57, 260–80
    China invaded by (1937), 212, 217,
        238, 251–57
    China's war with (1894–95), 71–72,
        80, 158
    Chinese revolutionaries in, 85, 89–90,
        91, 104, 105–6
    demonstrations against, 165, 166
    General Labor Union negotiations
        with, 168

Manchuria occupied by, 212–13, 249
modernization in, 70
piracy of, 12–13, 211
Russia's war with (1905), 82, 152,
    158
in Shanghai Incident, 213–17
surrender of, 279
terrorist campaign of, 260, 262–64,
    272–73, 280
Versailles Treaty and, 156
in World War II, 200, 235, 268–80
Jardine, Matheson and Company, 6–9, 27,
    54–55, 94, 100, 159, 198
    Tong King-sing and, 67, 68
Jardine, William (Iron-Headed Old Rat), 6–
    9, 54, 55
Jejeebhoy, Sir Jamsetjee, 57
Jesuits, 29
Jewish Country Club, 222–23
Jews, 197, 198, 205, 218–23
    in China trade, 55–60
    in Hongkew, 258–60, 275–76
journalists, blacklisting of, 264, 274
Julian, Courtney C., 127–28
Jung Te-sheng, 100
Jung Tsing-ching, 100, 187
junk trade, 12, 13

Kadoorie, Horace, 259
Kaiping Coal Mines, 69
Kamakura Maru (repatriation ship),
    274
Kang Sheng, 248
Kang Yu-wei, 79–80
Kempei Tei, 260, 262–63, 272–73, 280
Kiangnan Arsenal, 66–67, 86–87, 117
Kiangnan Dock and Engineering Works,
    95
Kiangse Road, prostitution on, 135–36
Kiangsi, 210, 246, 248
Kiangsu province, 65, 76, 87
    Taipings in, 14, 15, 17, 65
Kiangwan International Race Club, 99,
    108
kidnappings, 46, 85–86, 114, 116–17, 129,
    187, 248
    of Chiang Kai-shek, 250
    Japanese invasion and, 251
Kiukiang, 174, 210
Korea, 71
Krisel, Jacob, 234
Kuczynski, Ruth (Ursula Bureaton),
    235
Kung, David, 289
Kung, H. H., 105, 107–8
Kuo family, 101
Kuo Hsuan (Phillip), 101
Kuo Hsun (William Gockson), 101
Kuo Le (James), 101

Shanghai (*continued*)
  as leading port, 11–12, 18, 209
  May Thirtieth Movement in, 165–66, 167
  modernization efforts in, 66–72, 77–80
  moral laxity in, 1, 28–32, 61, 73–75
  Nationalist support in, 174–75, 180–86
  native investment in, 64–68
  origin of name, 2
  Sino-Japanese War and, 71–72
  skyline of, 24, 195
  slaughter of Communists in, 106, 182–84
  street names in, 22
  style of, 98
  Taiping Rebellion and, 13–18, 64
  traditions abandoned in, 73–75
  underworld of, 93, 109–15, 117–27, 182–83, 187–89
  Versaille protests in, 156
  after World War II, 281–89
  in World War II, 268–81
  see also specific topics
Shanghai, Chinese, 58–59, 126–27
  characteristics of Shanghainese, 76–78
  growth of, 75–76, 95
  history of, 12–13
  industrial districts of, 95
  International Settlement compared with, 88–89
  Japanese control of, 256, 257
  looting in, 124
  municipal council for, 84
  queue cutting in, 88
  revolt in (1911), 86–91
  rich in, 98–109
  Small Swords' capture of, 14
  sting of foreign domination in, 78
  walls of, 10, 13, 88
  warlords' control of, 117–20, 122–26
Shanghai, European, 10–15
  growth of, 12, 14–16, 18, 20, 21
  tenement building in, 14–15
  see also American Settlement; British Settlement; French Concession; International Settlement
"shanghai," in English usage, 2–3
Shanghai Club, 24–25, 165, 176, 197, 201, 226, 269
Shanghai Cotton Cloth Mill, 69
Shanghai Customs House, 200–201
Shanghai Evening Post and Mercury, 263
Shanghai Express (film), 117, 206
Shanghai Incident, 213–17
Shanghai Massacre, 182–86, 243
Shanghai Mercury, 31–32
"Shanghai mind," 175–76

Shanghai Municipal Council, 18, 25, 52, 81, 138, 165, 167, 168, 175, 183, 264
  antidrug initiatives of, 119
  Chinese representation on, 83–84, 100, 109, 181–82, 210
  effects of depression on, 64
  Japanese representation on, 211, 212, 256
  prostitutes and, 47–48, 49, 50
Shanghai Municipal Police, 130, 131, 211, 237, 247, 248, 264
  Special Branch of Criminal Investigations Division of, 233–34, 240
Shanghai Power Company, 95, 168
Shanghai Provisional Court, 181
Shanghai Race Club, 99–100, 204, 257
Shanghai Steam Navigation Company, 65, 67
Shanghai Stock and Commodities Exchange, 170
Shanghai '37 (Baum), 127
Shanghai Times, 191
Shanghai University, 164
Shanghai Volunteer Corps, 131, 174, 225
Shansi Bankers Guild, 209
Shansi province, 249–50
Shantung bandits, 116
shanty towns, 155
Sheean, Vincent, 164, 176
Shen Man-yun, 87
Shen Pao, 88, 263–64
Shen Tsung-wen, 241
Sheng Kung Pao, 36
Sheng Shing-shan, 113
Shimonoseki, Treaty of (1895), 71, 211
Shiozawa, Koichi, 214, 215, 217
shoes, high-heeled, 142, 146
shu-yu ("storytellers"), 41
silk factories, 159, 161
Simpson, Bertrand Lennox, 126
Simpson, Wallis Warfield, 97–98
Sincere Company Department Store, 187, 243
sing-song girls, 42–43, 74, 91, 143–44
Sino-Japanese War (1894–95), 71–72, 80, 158
slavery:
  of Chinese laborers, 61–63
  white, 134
slums, 155
Small Swords, 14, 24
Smedley, Agnes, 230–33, 235
Snow, Edgar, 106, 107, 113, 133, 177, 178, 224
Snow, Helen, 225
Society for Common Purpose, 152
Society for the Suppression of the Opium Trade, 55

Tu Yueh-sen (*continued*)
  as Huang Jin-rang's protégé, 93, 111,
    114–15
  in opium trade, 115, 118–23, 126, 188–
    89
  Resistance guerrillas of, 260–62
T'zu-hsi, dowager empress of China, 69–
    71, 78–79, 201

unequal treaties, 4, 156
  protests against, 165–68, 211
United Front, 249–50, 251
United Nations Relief and Rehabilitation
    Administration (UNRRA), 281–82
United States, 11–12, 115, 216–17
  Shanghai's boycott of goods from, 82,
    83
  World War II and, 267–70, 274, 278–82
    xenophobia in, 82
  see also American Settlement
Urabe, Mr., 212

Van Kah Der, 90
venereal disease, 49–51
Versailles, Treaty of (1919), 156
Victoria, Queen of England, 60
Vienna Garden, 227
villas, 36, 99, 109, 264–66
Vine, George, 290–91
virgins, 46–47, 200
von Sternberg, Josef, 117, 206–7

Wake (U.S. gunboat), 268
Wakeman, Frederic, 247
Wang Ching-wei, 172, 173, 260, 262–65,
    269, 284
Wang Chu-yu, 246–47
Wang Shou-hua, 185
Wanghsien, 166
Ward, Frederick Townsend, 17
warlords, 115–20, 122–26, 129, 157, 159,
    168–69, 210, 212
  Northern Expedition against, 173,
    178, 179
  opium trade controlled by, 115, 117–
    20, 122–26
  Sun Yat-sen's relations with, 171, 172
Warnings to the Prosperous Age (Cheng Kuan-
    ying), 69

weapons, 179–80, 183
  manufacture of, 66–67
  trade in, 17, 128–29
Weihaiwei, battle of, (1895), 71
Wesleyan College, 105
Whampoa Military Academy, 169–70, 172,
    241
Whangpu River, 10–13, 18, 47, 252
Wheel, the, 130
wheelbarrow coolies, 162–63
White Russians, 130–35, 137–40, 197, 208,
    224, 225, 281
  as army recruits, 123
  divorce and, 139–40
  statelessness of, 131, 139
white slavery, 134
Wifley, Lebbeus Redman, 137
Wing On, 97, 174
women, Chinese, *see* females, Chinese
Wong, H. S. (Newsreel), 216
Woosung, 23, 86, 102, 292
working class, 95, 155–56, 285
  Shanghai takeover by, 179–80
  wages of, 155, 159, 160
  working conditions of, 159–64
World War I, 94, 100, 128, 155, 177, 211,
    221
World War II, 200, 215, 235, 267–82
Wu Pei-fu, 116
Wu Su-pao (Tiny Tu), 262–63
Wu Te-chen, 213–14, 234
Wuchang revolt, 84, 85, 86, 87
Wuhan, 173, 185, 186, 244–45

xenophobia, 82

Yalu River, battle of (1894), 71
Yang Chien, 232, 242, 248
Yangtze River, 12, 22, 23, 54, 200, 280–81,
    290, 292
Yangtzepoo, *see* Hongkew
yao-kao, 8
Yenan, 231–32, 242, 255
Yu Hsia-ching, 82–83, 84, 87, 181
Yu Ta-fu, 152–53
Yuan Shi-kai, 89–92, 104, 117
  death of, 115–16
Yung Wing, 66–67
Yunnan province, 84